Leadership and Ambiguity

THE AMERICAN COLLEGE PRESIDENT

Michael D. Cohen

James G. March

SECOND EDITION

Harvard Business School Press
Boston, Massachusetts

Harvard Business School Press, Boston 02163

Printed in the United States of America

90 89 88 87 86   5 4 3 2 1

Library of Congress Cataloging-in-Publication Data

Cohen, Michael D.
  Leadership and Ambiguity

  Bibliography: p.
  Includes index.
  1. College presidents — United States. 2. Universities
and colleges — United States — Administration. I. March,
James G. II. Carnegie Commission on Higher Education.
III. Title.
LB2341.C56 1986   378' .111   85-27268
ISBN 0-87584-174-0
ISBN 0-87584-131-7 (pbk.)

Contents

8 *Presidential Tenure,* 153

The measurement of tenure ▪ Departure rates and the career surface ▪ Modes of departure from the college presidency ▪ Presidential tenure and the presidency ▪ Conclusion

9 *Leadership in an Organized Anarchy,* 195

The ambiguities of anarchy ▪ Leader response to anarchy ▪ The elementary tactics of administrative action ▪ The technology of foolishness

List of Figures

List of Tables

Preface to the Second Edition

This book examines some general ideas about leadership and ambiguity in the context of the American college president. Although those ideas are built on specific research findings, much of the attention the first edition of the book has received has been stimulated neither by the specific studies on which it is based, nor by the specific predictions it makes, but rather by the metaphors it develops to describe leadership in organizations. We defined the book as an interpretive essay, and it has been treated as one.

Leadership and Ambiguity was originally published in 1974. If we were writing the book now, we would undoubtedly say some things differently and say some different things. Despite this, the present edition leaves the original text untouched. We think the book comes close enough to what we would say now to discourage tinkering with it. In a modest effort to reflect changes, both in the world and in our understanding of it, however, we have added a few short commentaries. In addition to this preface, these include brief empirical addenda to the chapters on presidential activities (Appendix E), and presidential careers (Appendix F), and an essay on administrative leadership (Appendix G).

Since the research for the book was completed, several thousand college presidents have been appointed to their posts, replacing several thousand who have left. That turnover is reflected in the sample of colleges and universities we used for our study. In the 14 years from 1970 to 1984, 53 new presidents were appointed to office in the 41 colleges and universities in our sample. Of the 41 college presidents on whom our study was based, only 6 were still in the same presidency in April of 1985, some 15 years later. It is a new generation of presidents.

The world of colleges and universities has also changed. At the time the research was completed and the book published, the political activism and revolutionary rhetoric of the late 1960s were just ending, though it was not certain that they were, and the crises of budgets were just beginning. Now, budgetary difficulties seem to be a chronic, rather than acute, part of the routine; and the distinctive ferment of the 1960s seems as remote as the distinctive ferment of the 1930s seemed then. The problems of war, racism, and injustice remain, as do the solutions of revolution, demonstration, and disruption; but the attention of colleges and universities has mostly drifted, at least for the moment, to other problems and solutions.

The changing role of women in the United States has affected the characteristics of students, faculty, and administrators in ways that are modest relative to reasonable aspirations, but dramatic with respect to the conditions at the time the research was done. The demographics of birth cohorts and population movements, changes in the family, and the changing market for educated people have produced pressure on colleges and their curricula that have changed both. These changes, combined with public concerns about the quality of education and the internal dynamics of universities and colleges have led to an increase in the scale and visibility of training for the professions and business, and subsequently to considerable emphasis on systematic curriculum reform and to widespread reexamination of the role of liberal arts education in a modern society.

Many faculty members born between 1920 and 1930, hired during the boom years of 1950–1960, and given tenure before 1965 have, finally, moved close enough to retirement to open opportunities for appointing a new generation of colleagues and relieving the budgetary and other administrative complications of an aging faculty. Expenditures on computers and related information technolgy have increased significantly in American colleges and universities, as have the costs of energy and intercollegiate football. Although the general contentiousness of campuses and other institutions appears to have declined, lawyers, litigation, and regulation play a more important part in university administrative life. The 1980s are different from the 1970s, which were different from the years before.

It would be extraordinary if these changes did not bring important changes in the college presidency. College presidents attend to somewhat different agendas, use somewhat different staffs, and have somewhat different relations with their various constituencies than they did 14 years ago. The problems and solutions they confront are perceptibly different. It is reasonable to ask whether these changes so transform the presidency as to make a book published in 1974 hopelessly archaic. It may not be surprising that we believe they do not. Indeed, studies done since 1974 persuade us that the problems of ambiguity are endemic to top management, not only in universities but in other organizations as well.

In the book, we report four groups of empirical studies concerning the college presidency, including studies of presidential careers and tenure, of presidential time allocation, of presidential images, both those held by presidents and those held by others, and of decision processes in universities and colleges and the presidential role in them. Since the book was originally published, there have been additional studies bearing on each of these. We have added brief appendixes (done jointly with James R. Glenn, Jr.) that report more recent data on time allocation and tenure for the same sample of college and university presidencies. Research and commentary by numerous colleagues have considerably extended our understanding of university decision making. Research on the images of college presidents is less systematic, but can be found in various semi-popular reports.

Although each of these has augmented our understanding of college presidents and thereby invites reconsideration of what was said in 1974, most of the changes seem, at least to us, elaborations of our main themes rather than contradictions of them. The role of the college president and our understanding of it have changed, but the changes have occurred within a remarkably stable structure of experiences, processes, and behavior. Indeed, some of the more obvious changes are anticipated in the text. For example, presidential attention to students (as constituents) and press attention to presidents (as heroes or goats) seem to have declined somewhat; stories of presidential successes in guiding schools (particularly richer schools) to peace and progress are common; academic expectations and curricula have been renegotiated through a process largely independent of presidential activity, but consistent with the factors identified in 1974; if there are small changes in presidential tenure expectations, they appear to be in the direction and in the kinds of colleges anticipated by the 1974 analysis.

The detailed empirical description of the college president that we would make on the basis of these additional data would be (as we indicate in the addenda) slightly different from the details of the text, but the broad interpretive conclusions would not change appreciably. And it is those broad interpretive conclusions and their normative implications that have attracted the most commentary. Against a background of visions of leadership that tend to be rather more heroic, the book portrays colleges as organized anarchies and their leadership as constrained by ambiguities of objectives, technologies, and experience. The decision-making processes we identify describe a world in which both problems and solutions on the one hand, and decisions and decision processes on the other, tend to be loosely coupled. Leadership seems to be less a matter of straightforward instrumental action and hierarchical control than is anticipated by classical descriptions. In examining those decision processes and the president's role in them, we picture college presidents as generally more powerful than others in the college but as having less power than casual observers or participants frequently believe they do, or than they often expect to have on entering office. In a world that is difficult to predict and control, we commend an approach to leadership that recognizes, even encourages, ambiguity.

In the years since the book first appeared, the ideas reflected in it have received some attention from college presidents, from research students of organizations, decision making, and leadership, and from leaders of other organizations as diverse as business firms, public agencies, and military commands. That attention is happily acknowledged and endorsed by the authors, as is the interest of the Harvard Business School Press in publishing a new edition.

Our interpretation of leadership in organizations has provoked a variety of responses. Many of those responses report observations or impressions that confirm the broad framework we proposed. They elaborate the description and interpretation, provide additional detail, identify new implications and qualifications. Ambiguity, organized anarchy, garbage can processes, and loose coupling have become familiar terms. The ideas they reflect appear to have been useful to students of leadership in higher education, as well as in business firms, public institutions, and military organizations.[1]

Some readers of the book, however, express concern that we may have exaggerated the chaos of decision making and underestimated the possibilities for leadership. We believe we have not, indeed we

---

[1]For a review of these developments, see James G. March and Johan P. Olsen, "Garbage Can Models of Decision Making in Organizations," in James G. March and Roger Weissinger-Baylon, eds., *Ambiguity and Command: Organizational Perspectives on Military Decision Making* (Marshfield, Mass.: Pitman, 1986.) For discussions of how these perspectives affect more general conceptions of organizations, see Karl E. Weick, *The Social Psychology of Organizing, 2nd ed., (Reading, Mass.: Addison-Wesley, 1979); W. Richard Scott, *Organizations: Rational, Natural, and Open Systems* (Englewood Cliffs, N.J.: Prentice-Hall, 1981); and Lawrence B. Mohr, *Explaining Organizational Behavior* (San Francisco: Jossey-Bass, 1982.)

think we are substantially more conservative in that respect than many others are; but we can use the commentary as an excuse for recording here a few observations about what we do, and do not, say in the book.

First, we do not say and do not believe that university decision processes are chaotic in the sense of exhibiting total disorder. On the contrary, the discussions of organized anarchy and garbage can models of decision making emphasize the existence of considerable order. What makes the processes seem disorderly and confusing is not the absence of order but the fact that the order that we observe is different from that assumed in conventional theories of choice. For example, garbage can models of choice describe decision processes as combining problems, solutions, and decision makers primarily according to their simultaneity (within given access and decision structures). Those combinations may appear strange, even perverse, from the viewpoint of conventional instrumental linkages; but their links are orderly. The process is driven by temporal connections rather than substantive ones, but the combinations of problems and solutions that are generated are far from random.

Second, we do not say and do not believe that most choices in universities and colleges result from garbage can combinations of problems and solutions. On the contrary, we show that (under conditions of at least moderate load) one of the major features of garbage can processes is the disconnection of the content of choices from the manifest processes of decision making. Most choices are made through what is called "flight" or "oversight"; that is, by routine procedures without much connection to the collection of problems, solutions, or decision makers.

Third, we do not say and do not believe that college presidents are powerless. Although we observe that presidential power is more ambiguous and more circumscribed than many imagine, whatever can be said about the limits of presidential power can be said even more forcefully about the power of other actors. Consequently, we argue that college presidents, like other chief executives, are generally the most powerful individuals in an organization. We think there are things they can do to increase that power. Indeed, one of our friends and colleagues has criticized us for our attempt to show how willful presidents can exercise somewhat more effective power in an organized anarchy.

The assertions in the book are both more conservative and more careful than is implicit in some interpretations of it, including some by enthusiasts as well as some by critics. It would be easy to let the matter rest with such a comment, observing that there will always be a gap between the diligence of readers and the diligence authors hope for; but such a course would not be an entirely fair joining of the issues. There are important differences between our characterization of leadership and that of some others, and those differences should not be glossed over by emphasizing inaccuracies in the specifics of protesting misleading interpretations. On the whole, we believe that both observers and practitioners underestimate the complexity of leadership processes and situations and overestimate the significance of individual leaders.

We observe organizations, including colleges, to be changing continuously in response to various internal and external pressures and opportunities. Markets for labor and prestige, the demographics of the society, the changing focus of politics all influence the directions taken by universities composed of many people, each pursuing mixes of altruistic and self-interested intentions in the context of changing social and organizational roles. New ideas and practices spread through colleges and universities like measles through an elementary school. Attention shifts from one thing to another within colleges and outside them, thus changing the feasibility of coordinated action.

College presidents operate within, and are a significant part of, this mélange. For colleges to adapt smoothly to their external environments and internal necessities college presidents must do well the things that a qualified chief executive is expected to do. These include a host of complicated things often dismissed as mere administration but easily recognized as important when they are not performed well: assuring that human and physical resources are matched and available when needed, that the routines by which large bureaucracies function are working well, that bills are paid and people are not left standing in the rain, that the telephone is answered, letters are read, and lawns are cut. They also include the symbolic activities that surround leadership, presiding over the rituals of organization by which meaning is provided and the young are socialized, through which new objectives are discovered and given credence, and in terms of which history is written. Institutions organized in the way American colleges and universities are organized require presidents who do the things that presidents do. Neither the resources the university commits to its president, nor the time the president commits to the job are irrelevant to the health of the institution.

We are convinced that leadership is essential within a college, and that it properly exhibits the ambivalent relation to substantive rationality that the book details. But establishing that a particular individual is uniquely important is much more problematic. To be sure, there are some radically foolish things a president might conceivably do which could have disastrous, and causally unambiguous, consequences for the institution. Most of the time, however, the procedures by which presidents are socialized and selected assure that they will not do those catastrophic things. Within the range of behavior that a college president is willing to consider, it is extremely difficult for a president, or anyone else, to be confident that much arbitrary presidential control can be, or has been, exerted over the major course of events within a college. Although there are powerful social constructions that dispose presidents and others around them to belief in the unique importance of specific individuals, those constructions are characteristically not based on the kind of evidence that a careful person requires to unravel the causation of historical events.

To those of our friends who argue that we threaten the motivation of leaders by recognizing their limitations, we reply "not so." The ambiguities of purpose, technology, and experience undermine conventional views of leaders; they do not undermine leadership. We offered the metaphor of a sailor who confronts both reliable currents and variable winds. In such a situation, we contend, we have too often envisioned an organizational leader as being like an admiral leading an armada in pursuit of strategic objectives that are both obvious and clear. Instead, we have argued, one might more reasonably see an organizational leader as having the tactical cleverness and profound capability of mixing foolishness and consistency that we honor in Ulysses and other resourceful leaders of voyages of discovery.

We happily confess that the leaders we admire most are not those who seek the appearance of exercising high levels of prediction and control, but rather those whose enthusiasm for life and commitment to humanity allow them to sustain leadership of intelligence, power, and grace in the midst of ambiguity. Thus, we believe that effective top executives are heroic; but their heroism lies not in their ability to lead their institutions to a pre-chosen destiny, nor in their responsibility for the major successes and failures realized by their institutions, but in their willingness to try to do better in a world where neither the meaning of "better" nor the route to its realization is clear. In various ways, this book celebrates such a view of heroism in leadership.

University of Michigan   Michael D. Cohen
Stanford University   James G. March

January 1986

Preface

This book reflects three major interests: a concern for the development of organization theory; a fascination with institutions of higher learning; and a commitment to understanding modern organizational leadership. The American college and university presidency is a natural focus for such interests.

In sharpening that focus, we made two explicit decisions that narrowed the scope of our attention. First, we did not consider the role of the two-year college president, but restricted ourselves to colleges and universities offering baccalaureate or higher degrees. Second, we emphasized particularly the activities of the presidency that impinge on decision making, governance, and leadership.

We also made a style decision. The book combines empirical data with speculation to form an interpretive essay. We have tried to be judiciously attentive to data. At the same time, we have tried to present an interpretation of the presidency and of university organization that ties together a number of empirical and theoretical themes. Thus, we have tried to indicate the limitations of the data without abandoning the pleasures of inference from them.

The book depends on the contributions of a long list of friends and associates who have shared money, ideas, data, and wine. Our greatest debt is to a group of college and university presidents and their assistants who participated in our basic 42-college panel. We talked at some length with 41 of the presidents, 39 of their chief academic officers, 36 of their chief business or financial officers, 42 of their secretaries, 28 other college or university officials close to the presidents, and student leaders or editors of student publications at 31 institutions. The more concrete data gathered from this panel are reported in the book, but the major contribution of the interviews is the contextual richness of exposure to the problems, experience, and insights of the men and women in the job.

The 42 presidents were: John T. Caldwell, Vernon I. Cheadle, James E. Cheek, Harlan Cleveland, Andrew W. Cordier, Dale R. Corson, John L. Davis, Roland Dille, Glenn W. Ferguson, Ivan E. Frick, Lewis A. Froman, Lincoln Gordon, Milton J. Hassel, S. I. Hayakawa, James M. Hester, Joseph F. Kauffman, William R. Keast, William W. Kelly, Charles E. S. Kramer, Glenn E. Leggett, Malcolm A. Love, Charles K. Martin, Jr., David L. McKenna, John A. Middleton, M. Madonna Murphy, Samuel L. Myers, Lewis Nobles, J. Ralph Noonkester, Charles E. Odegaard, Raymond M. Olson, Joseph C. Palamountain, Jr., Anne G. Pannell, John M. Pfau, Wesley W. Posvar, Nathan M. Pusey, Walker H. Quarles, Jr., Charles E. Shain, Edgar F. Shannon, Phillip R. Shriver, Alan Simpson, Kenneth Slattery, and Charles Young.

We have exploited a number of other friendly presidents and ex-presidents in a less systematic way. In particular, we thank Daniel Aldrich, Norman Hackerman, Roger Heyns, Ivan Hinderaker, Clark Kerr, Richard Lyman, Grover Murray, Martin Myerson, Jack Peltason, Richard Sullivan, Fred Thieme, Donald Walker, and Meredith Wilson.

We have learned from good colleagues. We have collaborated closely with Johan P. Olsen. His ideas, and the joint results of our conversations, permeate the book. Lance Bennett and Patricia Nelson Bennett shared in our early discussions, introduced us to the literature, and undertook to do much of the early research work. Later, James R. Glenn, Jr., played a similar heroic role of research assistant, sympathetic scold, and colleague. In addition, we wish to acknowledge our gratitude for significant comments or other help from J. Victor Baldridge, Nancy Block, Michael Butler, Søren Christensen, Hilary Cohen, Michel Crozier, Richard Degerman, Harald Enderud, Daniel Gardner, Edward Gross, Denis Hayes, Gudmund Hernes, Helga Hernes, Harold Leavitt, Lewis Mayhew, John Meyer, John Miller, Lyman Porter, Kare Rommetveit, Richard Snyder, William Starbuck, Per Stava, Steinar Stjernø, David Sudnow, Eugene J. Webb, Gail Whitacre, and Harrison White.

We consistently overextended our credit with three exceptional executive secretaries. Jackie Fry managed the beginning, Carolyn Nattress the middle, and Marsha Mavis the end of the project; and we are particularly thankful for their tolerance of our affection.

The Carnegie Commission on Higher Education supported our work through a grant and through thoughtful comments on the manuscript by Verne A. Stadtman and Terry Y. Allen. The financial support by the Commission was supplemented by related grants from the Ford Foundation and the Spencer Foundation. We are grateful to the three foundations and to their human embodiments: Clark Kerr, Marshall Robinson, and H. Thomas James.

If despite this array of assistance, we have erred, we happily attribute the errors to the corruptions of irremediable stupidity, ordinary perverseness, and seductive wives.

Michael D. Cohen
James G. March
Stanford University

1973

1. Some Introductory Conclusions

This book is an essay on the American college presidency.[1] It examines the job, the people who occupy it, and the interaction between the two. It attempts a reconsideration of the assumptions of the presidency. Most of the essay elaborates the implications of some observations that we and others have made. In anticipation of that elaboration, we summarize the major observations here.

The American college presidency is a reactive job. Presidents define their role as a responsive one. They worry about the concerns of trustees, community leaders, students, faculty members, law enforcement officials. They see themselves as trying to reconcile the conflicting pressures on the college. They allocate their time by a process that is largely controlled by the desires of others. Though they are, for the most part, individuals of considerable energy, they often become tired.

The presidency is a parochial job. Presidents are normally not strangers to the institutions that choose them. Although they have typically worked in one or two other colleges, the colleges are similar in type and close in geography. Insofar as a president compares his performance with other presidents, he tends to compare it with a group of presidents who are in his own experiential "neighborhood." Insofar as he is visible through the media, he is ordinarily visible only to his local community.

Presidents are academics. Their careers are almost entirely in academic institutions; their values are those of academe. The details of their values vary considerably. The academic creed of a small, marginally surviving church-related school is not the same

---

[1] "College president" is ambiguous. We refer to the heads of colleges and universities within the United States that offer (at least) baccalaureate degrees. Thus, we use the terms "college president" and "university president" interchangeably to refer to both; and we do not consider presidents of two-year colleges.

as that of a major prestigious university, and presidents reflect that variability. Since the academic creed is not completely different from the general American organizational creed, college presidents are similar in many ways to administrative heads of other kinds of institutions. Nevertheless, they are recognizable as products of academe.

The presidency is conventional. The president comes to his job through a series of filters that are socially conservative vis-à-vis his major constituents. He sees his job in the standard terms reported in the academic and management literature. He allocates his time in response to a series of conventional expectations. He leaves and enters his job in a manner that has strong normative components. The president cannot effectively argue with conventional claims on him; nor does he really wish to do so. His actions, his activities, and his self-perceptions are constrained within social expectations that he accepts as essentially legitimate.

The presidency is important to the president. It is the peak of his career. He obtains the job as a reward for his previous record. It is the best job he has ever had or is likely to have. It is a mark of his success. His self-esteem depends on being viewed as a good president, but his reputation depends on the reputation of the school more than it does on his activities as president. Although the route to the job is clearly not random, each president's "career" tends to be a *post factum* construct. Typically, each stage of his career is a relatively discrete event produced by a vacancy.

The presidency is an illusion. Important aspects of the role seem to disappear on close examination. In particular, decision making in the university seems to result extensively from a process that decouples problems and choices and makes the president's role more commonly sporadic and symbolic than significant. Compared to the heroic expectations he and others might have, the president has modest control over the events of college life. The contributions he makes can easily be swamped by outside events or the diffuse qualities of university decision making.

In our judgment, these major features of the presidency and presidents need to be elaborated and interpreted within an understanding of the American college and university as an organization. It belongs to a class of organizations that can be called *organized anarchies*. By an organized anarchy we mean any organizational setting that exhibits the following general properties:

1   *Problematic goals* It is difficult to impute a set of goals to the organization that satisfies the standard consistency requirements of theories of choice. The organization appears to operate on a variety of inconsistent and ill-defined preferences. It can be described better as a loose collection of changing ideas than as a coherent structure. It discovers preferences through action more often than it acts on the basis of preferences.

2   *Unclear technology* Although the organization manages to survive and (where relevant) produce, it does not understand its own processes. Instead it operates on the basis of a simple set of trial-and-error procedures, the residue of learning from the accidents of past experiences, imitation, and the inventions born of necessity.

3   *Fluid participation* The participants in the organization vary among themselves in the amount of time and effort they devote to the organization; individual participants vary from one time to another. As a result, standard theories of power and choice seem to be inadequate; and the boundaries of the organization appear to be uncertain and changing.

These properties are not limited to educational institutions; but they are particularly conspicuous there. The American college or university is a prototypic organized anarchy. It does not know what it is doing. Its goals are either vague or in dispute. Its technology is familiar but not understood. Its major participants wander in and out of the organization. These factors do not make a university a bad organization or a disorganized one; but they do make it a problem to describe, understand, and lead. As a result, it is impossible for us to consider the American college presidency without making some rudimentary attempts to develop a theory of organized anarchy.

With respect to a behavioral theory of organizations, we need to investigate two major phenomena that are critical to an understanding of the kind of organizations described above. First, we need a better understanding of the processes used to make choices without the guidance of consistent, shared goals. It is clear that organizations sometimes make choices without clear goals. Decision making under ambiguity is common in complex organizations, particularly those outside the sector of private enterprise. Decisions appear often to be made without recourse either to explicit markets or to explicit bargaining (the two processes most commonly cited as procedures for decision making in the absence of consensus). Second, we need to study the process by which members of the organization are activated, by which occasional members become active ones, by which attention is directed toward, or away from, the organization. Not everyone in an organization is attending to everything all the time; and we need to understand how to predict the attention pattern within the organization.

With respect to normative theory, organized anarchies pose three major problems. First, we need to develop a normative theory of intelligent decision making in situations in which goals are unknown (i.e., under ambiguity). Can we provide some meaning for *intelligence* that does not depend on relating current action to known goals? We are convinced it is possible. We are far from certain what the theory will look like. Second, we need a normative theory of attention. Managers and others who might participate in an organization operate within the constraint of a scarce resource — the attention they can devote to the various things demanding their attention. In organizations such as those described above, in which a substantial part of the variability in behavior stems from variations in who is attending to what, decisions about the allocation of attention are primary. Third, organized anarchies require a new theory of management. Much of our present theory of management introduces mechanisms for control and coordination that assume the existence of well-defined goals and technology, as well as substantial participant involvement in the affairs of the organization. When goals and technology are hazy and participation is fluid, many of the axioms and standard procedures of management collapse.

The agenda is long. This book is short. We do not intend to resolve the dilemma posed by the discrepancy. We have tried to make the following chapters an introductory essay both on the American college presidency and on the understanding of organized anarchy. We try to report some data and draw some inferences about the American college and university president. Where the data are thin, we have tried to speculate. Where the data are thick, we have tried to attend to them. Wherever possible we have tried to relate the observations on presidents to more general observations on universities and other organizations.

Given the tenor of recent writings on the university and the mood of our time, it is tempting to proclaim some conspicuous manifesto of presidential inadequacy and to promise some magic revealed by our explorations. On the whole, however, we believe the enthusiasm for drama that enfuses our newspapers and our evening conversations assures an adequate supply of impossible crises and miraculous salvations in public and university life without our contributing more.

The world may collapse tomorrow; it may not. The university may survive another ten years; it may not. The differences are important, and the problems are serious. But the outcomes do not much depend on the college president. He is human. His capabilities are limited, and his responsibility is limited by his capabilities. We believe there are modest gains to be made by making some changes in the perception of his role. We believe presidents can be more effective and more relaxed. We do not believe in magic.

2. Prepresidential Careers

Executive careers provide persistent fascination. Individuals who live in academe have an understandable interest in the natural life history of their executive leaders. Presidents find it personally comforting—or disturbing—to fit themselves into the company of their fellow college presidents. Intrigued, annoyed, or bemused by the antics of academic organizations, nonacademics find some clues to the nature of the university from an understanding of presidential careers.

Our primary justification for looking at presidential careers, however, lies in the possible clarification of the ways in which leadership functions within an organized anarchy and of the special problems associated with leadership in colleges and universities. The American college president arrives at the presidency after previous experience that conditions his behavior as a college leader. We will try to attend to four major consequences of that experience:

1 What systematic biases in the presidency are produced by careers prior to the job and the process of recruitment? In what ways are presidential careers and recruitment unique to presidents?

2 What are the possible interpretations of the patterns of careers for presidents and what consequences do alternative interpretations have for presidents? Is there a career "line" to the presidency?

3 How might we expect presidential behavior to be influenced both by anticipation of such careers and by the experience in them?

4 What are the problems for the college and president implicit in his background?

SOCIAL CHARACTERISTICS OF COLLEGE PRESIDENTS American college presidents today and in the recent past are most commonly middle-aged, married, male, white, Protestant academics from a relatively well-educated, middle-class, professional-managerial, native-born, small-town family background.[1] They represent, in social terms, a conventional elite group for the general population of the American college and university students and faculty. There are numerous exceptions to the general pattern. The frequency of those exceptions appears to be related systematically to variations among colleges and universities in their student clientele and faculty personnel. Atypical student and faculty populations are more likely to have atypical presidents.

Age   Figure 1 shows our estimates of the average age of American college presidents from 1900 to 1970. That is, for each year we estimate the average age of presidents in office at that time. The two different estimates represent the results of our two different weighting procedures.[2] One shows the average age of presidents (i.e., weighting the president of each college or university equally). The other shows the average age of a students' president (i.e., weighting each president by the number of students in his type of institution).

We estimate the average age of presidents in office to be about 53 today. Over the past 70 years that average appears to have varied slightly. It was lower in the first 10 years of the century than it is now. In fact, the recent modest drop in the average age of presidents—sometimes attributed to the increasingly rigorous demands of the job—seems much more to reflect a simple phasing out of the increases in average age produced first by the Depression

[1] We have relied heavily on four previous studies of presidents: Bolman (1965), Demerath, Stephens and Taylor (1967), Ferrari (1970), and Ingraham (1968). In addition, with the collaboration of James R. Glenn, Jr., we have considered the characteristics of four cross-sectional slices of the presidents from our sample of 42 colleges. We have considered the set of presidents in office in 1924 (a pre-Depression year), 1939 (a late Depression year), 1954 (an early college-boom year), and 1969 (a postboom year). The data are nearly complete for all presidents. Since some schools were founded later than 1924, the sample consists of 42 presidents in 1969, 40 presidents in 1954, 38 presidents in 1939, and 36 presidents in 1924. Thus, there are 156 "presidents"—the quotation marks being required by the fact that 5 presidents are included in both the 1924 and the 1939 samples, that 5 presidents are included in both the 1939 and the 1954 samples, and that 6 presidents are included in both the 1954 and the 1969 samples. This overlap has been retained, since our primary interest was in comparing the "state of the presidency" over time; but it means the units of analysis for our grand totals are presidents in office and double count those presidents whose terms extended over two cross sections.

[2] See Appendix A, "Procedures for Estimating Various Statistics for the Universe of Presidents."

FIGURE 1 *Estimated average age of American college presidents from 1900 to 1970*

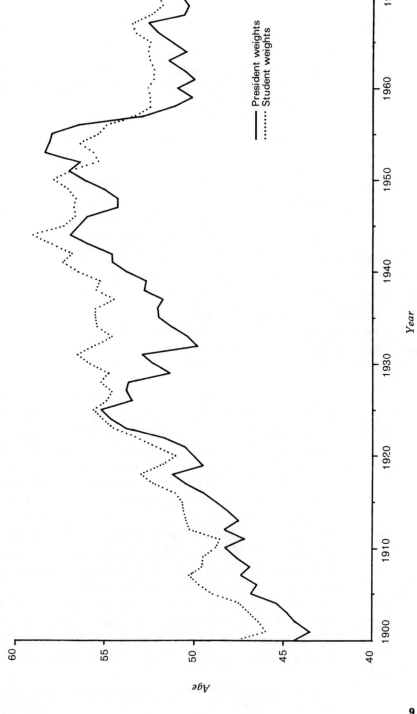

President weights
Student weights

Age

Year

and then by the Second World War. Estimates of the mean or median age of college presidents in other studies are relatively consistent despite wide variations in the sample and procedure used. Table 1 shows such estimates.

TABLE 1 *Estimates of average age of college presidents*

Year	Reference	Sample	Mean	Median
1914	Bryan (1914)	415 past and present presidents		57
1928	Kruse and Beck (1928)	25 universities		58.5
1930	Demerath et al. (1967)	52 "leading state" universities		50
1938	Warren (1938)	300 "important" presidents		52.5
1945	Adams and Donovan (1945)	60 "leading universities"		57
1946	Demerath et al. (1967)	812 "major" presidents		53
1955	Donovan (1955)	Information n.a.	56	
1960	Demerath et al. (1967)	270 presidents		55.7
1968	Ingraham (1968)	723 presidents	53	54
1969	Ferrari (1970)	760 presidents	52.9	

Similarly, the average age at which presidents begin their presidencies appears to have varied only slightly over the past 70 years. Figure 2 shows our two estimates of the *mean age at accession* to the presidency of presidents who *held* office at each year from 1900 to 1970.[3] Two recent estimates of the average age of incoming presidents by Ferrari (1970) and Bolman (1965), based on much larger current samples, are consistent with these estimates. Bolman found the average age of 116 newly chosen presidents in 1964 to be 46 years. Ferrari found the mean age of presidents selected in 1967–68 to be 45.6 years. Other estimates of the mean and median age of accession to the presidency of presidents holding office at a particular time are shown in Table 2.

Taken in total, the age data indicate that American college presidents ordinarily come to the job in their mid-forties and that at any point in time most presidents are in their fifties. There is moderate variation around those averages. Presidents who are

[3] Note that this is a different statistic from the mean age of presidents *entering* office in any one year. Estimation of mean age of presidents entering office in any one year would require a larger sample than we have over the entire time period. The apparent stability over time of the estimates shown in Figure 2 suggests that the two statistics may be fairly well correlated.

FIGURE 2 Estimated mean age at accession to the presidency from 1900 to 1970

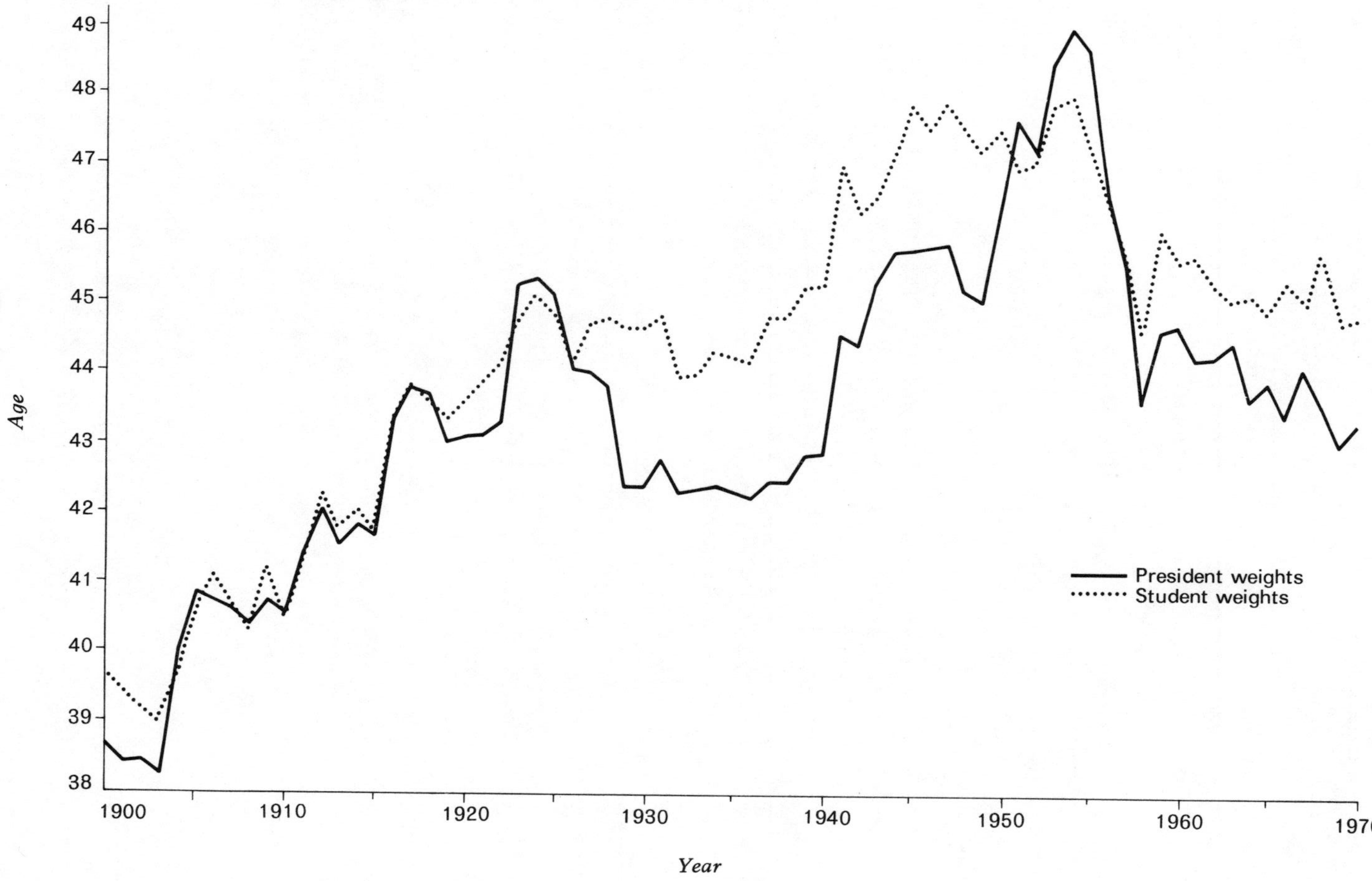

President weights
Student weights

Age

Year

TABLE 2 *Estimates of mean and median age at accession for presidents holding office at a particular time*

Year	Reference	Sample	Mean	Median
1900	Demerath et al. (1967)	34 AAU presidents		41
1920	Demerath et al. (1967)	34 AAU presidents		47.8
1929	Demerath et al. (1967)	Information n.a.		43
1942	Demerath et al. (1967)	Information n.a.		45
1945	Adams and Donovan (1945)	60 "leading universities"		46
1952	McVey and Hughes (1952)	300 presidents	45.3	45
1967	Demerath et al. (1967)	45 relatively large universities		46.5
1969	Ferrari (1970)	760 presidents	45.1	

under 40 or over 70 years of age represent about 12.3 percent of the presidents at any one time. These results seem to hold substantially for all types of schools. It appears to be true that presidents are slightly younger in small schools than in large schools, slightly younger in poor schools than in rich schools, slightly younger in church-affiliated schools than in private or public schools. These differences, however, are small.

Marital status Although there are many unmarried presidents, virtually all unmarried presidents are members of celibate orders and are presidents of Roman Catholic colleges. Bolman (1965) reported that only 2 of 116 new presidents in 1964 were unmarried. Ferrari (1971) found that less than 2 percent of the presidents (excluding Roman Catholic schools) were unmarried.

Sex Ferrari (1970) found that 11 percent of the college presidents in his sample were women. Over 90 percent of the women presidents were found in Roman Catholic women's schools. The rest were in non-Catholic women's schools. All eight of the women presidents in our own cross sections[4] were presidents of women's colleges.

Race Published data on the race of American college presidents were not available to us—perhaps because the data were scarcely problematic. As nearly as we can tell, black presidents have existed historically in small numbers. All were presidents of colleges with

---

[4] See footnote 1.

student bodies that were overwhelmingly black. The number of black colleges with black presidents has increased over time. The only conspicuous cases of black presidents currently heading schools with a majority of students who are white are Presidents James G. Bond of California State University, Sacramento, and Clifton R. Wharton, Jr., of Michigan State University.

Religion Bolman (1965) found that 110 of the 115 new presidents who responded to his questionnaire were Protestant. Two were Catholics, one Jewish, and two professed no religion. From these data and the data on marital status it is clear that Bolman's sample excludes most Roman Catholic schools. It seems safe to assume that almost all Roman Catholic schools have Roman Catholic presidents, that almost all Jewish schools have Jewish presidents, and that almost all church-related Protestant schools have Protestant presidents. In addition the data show that the presidents of non-church-related schools in the United States are overwhelmingly Protestant.

Political affiliation Data on political affiliation is sparse. Bolman (1965) found in his sample of 115 new presidents that 37 percent reported themselves as Republicans, 41 percent as Democrats, and 22 percent either as having no affiliation or as having a third-party affiliation. From the general pattern with respect to other social variables, we would expect some variation associated with the student population and thus the type of school and region of the country. Demerath et al. (1967) report that 88 percent of presidents in 110 state colleges and universities had the same political affiliation as the governor in office when they were selected. Stephens (1956) found 70 percent of his sample of presidents had the same political affiliation as that of the governor.

Academic background The most obvious point about presidential career paths is that presidents are academics. The proportion of presidents who have doctorates seems to have been increasing steadily since the beginning of the century and is now apparently about 75 to 80 percent of all new presidents and more than 90 percent of the presidents of better-known schools. Published estimates of the proportion of presidents holding doctorates (including both Ed.D. and Ph.D.) during the 1900–1950 period are hard to evaluate; but it seems reasonable to conclude that the proportion has been increasing for all schools and increasing faster in the less prestigious schools — so that the gap with respect to this attribute between schools is decreasing.[5]

The graduate degrees of presidents reflect the institutions they serve, both historically and currently. If we consider three major studies of backgrounds of current presidents, we discover very similar estimates of the distribution of graduate work. Table 3 shows the estimates made by Bolman (1965), Ferrari (1971), and Ingraham (1968). They are based on slightly different classification systems. The treatment of graduate work in religion is not clear in all cases. In addition, Ferrari includes history in the humanities; the others call it a social science. Despite these differences, the total picture is consistent. Presidents tend to come from the dominant groups within a college. This becomes even clearer when we examine the relation between type of school and type of president. Presidents with degrees in education are heavily concentrated

TABLE 3 *Three sets of* *estimates of the* *percentage* *of current* *college* *presidents* *holding* *graduate* *degrees in* *various fields*			
Fields	*Bolman*	*Ferrari*	*Ingraham*
Education	25	30	24
Humanities	27	37*	27
Social science	28*	14	24*
Other	20	20	22

* Includes history.

in those public institutions that have grown from teachers colleges into universities. Presidents with degrees in liberal arts are concentrated heavily in liberal arts institutions.[6]

A similar story emerges from an examination of historical trends in the background of presidents. On the basis of our cross sections, we have estimated the postbaccalaureate education of presidents in office in 1924, 1939, 1954, and 1969 (see Table 4). Those estimates are subject to greater sampling error than are the earlier ones as well as to some differences in classification. History has been treated as a social science, and religion as a part of humanities (the subtotal for religion is indicated in parentheses).

[5] See Demerath et al. (1967), Knode (1944), Kruse and Beck (1928), Beard (1948), Bolman (1965), Ferrari (1970), and Ingraham (1968).

[6] See Hodgkinson (1971, pp. 271–276) for additional data based on a sample that also included two-year colleges.

TABLE 4 **Estimates of** **the percentages** **of presidents** **with graduate** **work in major** **fields, by year**		

Fields (by year)	Estimated percentage (presidents)*	Estimated percentage (students' presidents)*
1924		
Education	21	39
Humanities	50	23
(Religion)	(35)	(10)
Social science	5	9
Other	23	29
1939		
Education	26	29
Humanities	29	28
(Religion)	(14)	(5)
Social science	6	13
Other	39	30
1954		
Education	20	29
Humanities	36	26
(Religion)	(20)	(6)
Social science	26	18
Other	17	27
1969		
Education	17	22
Humanities	58	33
(Religion)	(23)	(7)
Social science	17	34
Other	8	10

*See Appendix A.

The fields of humanities, education, and religion continue to be important sources for presidents, as they have been throughout the century. Social science has become an important source, particularly in larger schools, over the same period that it has grown in numbers of students and faculty. Religious training, as might be expected from the relatively large number of small church-related schools, is more likely to characterize a randomly selected president than a randomly selected student.

Not only do presidents have the standard academic degree credentials, they also have almost exclusively academic experience. Bolman (1965) asked his sample of new presidents to record their nonacademic (and nonmilitary)[7] work experience. Of those sampled, 41 percent had had no experience outside of academia; 96 percent had had less than five years' experience outside. Similar patterns have been found by Ferrari (1970), Demerath et al. (1967), Ingraham (1968), Knode (1944), Kruse and Beck (1928), McVey and Hughes (1952), and Warren (1938). Historically, the only significant alternative routes to the American college presidency have been through the ministry or through secondary school administration. Both routes have become distinctly less important in recent decades.

Thus American college presidents are *academic* administrators. They have had almost all their work experience within academic organizations. Experience specialization does not distinguish them from most other administrators. Business executives, military commanders, or medical chiefs of staff are also generally without significant experience outside their respective fields. The president is in this respect not unlike administrators of other groups of professionals.

However, the academic background of most presidents has two major effects. First, it means that they have some close attitudinal and personal ties with the academic establishment; they consider themselves part of the academic community—most typically the faculty. Second, it means that the presidency is the capstone of their careers. Despite all the jokes about it, the presidency is the highest status position that one can reach within the academic community. It is the end of a natural chain of promotion within an academic organization.

Family background   Ferrari (1971) has made a systematic study of the social backgrounds of presidents. The results of his study should be perused by anyone interested in a major focus on that subject. We will simply summarize here the main thrust of his results. He studied a large sample of current American college presidents and found that although the fathers of presidents were from all economic and occupational groups, working-class and farmer fathers tended to be underrepresented relative to their proportion of the population, while professional, executive, manager, and proprietor fathers tended to be overrepresented. Fathers who were

---

[7] The presidents in his sample were of prime military age during the Second World War. Forty-four percent had served in the armed service for a median term of three years.

clergymen or secondary school teachers appeared to be particularly overrepresented.

Although fewer than half of the presidents' fathers had any college education at all, the proportion of fathers who attended college (41 percent) and the proportion who completed college (27 percent) were both substantially above the general United States figures for the appropriate age group. Even more distinctive when compared with women of the appropriate age group in the United States was the proportion of mothers who attended college (34 percent) and completed college (16 percent).

Two-thirds of the paternal grandfathers and 85 percent of the fathers of this sample of college presidents were born in the United States. In Ferrari's sample, 1.4 percent of the fathers and 1.1 percent of the fathers-in-law were college presidents. Both results are considerably above chance expectations, even given the general social class and parental occupation groups from which presidents are drawn.

All these general results are subject to considerable variation across schools. Some of the variation is consistent with our basic observation that the attributes of presidents and the attributes of student and faculty populations tend to covary. For example, Roman Catholic schools have generally drawn their students from somewhat less affluent, somewhat less educated, and somewhat more recently immigrated families than have private universities and colleges; public universities and colleges lie somewhere between the two groups. Ferrari's results show that the distribution of backgrounds of college presidents varies similarly, though, at all levels, the average president comes from a more affluent, better educated, and longer-resident family than does the average student. Presidents of Roman Catholic schools are more than twice as likely to come from working-class backgrounds than are presidents of independent private schools. Presidents of independent private schools are about four times as likely to come from professional backgrounds as are presidents of Roman Catholic schools. Of the paternal grandfathers of presidents of independent private colleges, 81 percent were born in the United States; one-third of the paternal grandfathers of presidents of Roman Catholic schools were born in the United States.

Geography Ferrari (1970) shows that the birthplaces of current college presidents are distributed geographically in approximately the same way as the population in 1920 (the closest census date to the mean date of birth for the sample presidents). Predictably, there is some variation. Presidents of schools with relatively urban student populations (e.g., private independent colleges, Roman Catholic colleges) have relatively urban birthplaces. Presidents of schools with relatively rural student populations (e.g., public liberal arts colleges) have relatively rural birthplaces.

We can also examine the geographic mobility of presidents. As Ferrari indicates, it is almost certainly greater than that of the average American, but it is not extraordinary. We have used our cross sections to estimate the mean distance from birthplace to place of presidency for the universe of presidents and for the universe of students' presidents at four points in time.[8] The results are shown in Table 5, and they reveal some interesting features of the spatial mobility of presidents.

TABLE 5 *Estimated mean distance from place of birth to place of presidency, by size of school*

	Mean distance in miles (presidents)				Mean distance in miles (students' presidents)			
Year	Large schools	Medium schools	Small* schools	All schools	Large schools	Medium schools	Small* schools	All schools
1924	672	378	312	363	648	375	312	480
1939	462	333	177	252	483	336	177	375
1954	798	606	333	462	795	584	333	639
1969	702	501	507	519	708	492	507	585

* The two weighting schemes produce almost identical values for small schools.

The table shows two rather clear phenomena. First, there is a size effect. Larger schools consistently draw presidents a greater distance from their birthplaces than do smaller schools.[9] Second, there is an apparent Depression effect. The mean distance between

[8] This analysis excludes foreign-born presidents and presidents of the University of Hawaii who were born on the mainland.

[9] This result is confounded by the fact that a larger share of the large schools are found in the West, where one would expect — strictly from population movement and population distribution considerations — greater distance between birthplace and presidency. Of the nine Western schools in the sample, six (including Hawaii) are large schools and three are small schools. Removing the Western schools from the data reduces the estimates in the later years for both large and small schools, but still leaves an apparent size effect that is substantial.

birthplace and place of presidency declined for all size groups in 1939 and has risen subsequently in all size groups. Presidents who were in office in 1939 were apparently significantly more "local" in a geographic sense than were presidents in office in any of the three other cross-section years.

The 1939 "dip" is primarily a phenomenon of the poorer schools. Table 6 shows the estimated mean distance in miles for schools that were (in 1967) in the top 20 percent of all schools in terms of income per student compared with the mean distance for schools in the bottom 80 percent.

		Mean distance in miles (presidents)		Mean distance in miles (students' presidents)	
	Year	*Rich schools*	*Poor schools*	*Rich schools*	*Poor schools*
	1924	357	363	459	492
	1939	459	201	546	282
	1954	471	459	633	642
	1969	528	516	603	576

TABLE 6
Estimated mean distance from place of birth to place of presidency for rich and poor schools

In subsequent sections we will examine some other dimensions of mobility. With respect to simple geography, the mean distance between a president's birthplace and his current job is about equivalent to a day's drive by automobile. Presidents of small schools appear to work somewhat closer to their birthplaces than do presidents of large schools, a consistent pattern through the past 50 years. The radius of recruitment appears to decrease in times of economic stringency, particularly among poorer schools.

PATHS TO THE PRESIDENCY
Although the career path to the presidency varies from one type of school to another and has varied over the past 70 years, presidents are made, for the most part, by the logic of hierarchy. That is, most presidencies in American colleges are now occupied by individuals who entered an academic career as a college teacher, were asked at some point to assume administrative duties as a department chairman, institute director, dean, or similar position, were subsequently promoted to a higher administrative position, and then to a presidency.

The pattern is distinctly—and increasingly—promotion through the hierarchy of academic administration. Presidents either start as professors, or soon become professors. Although the ministry or secondary school teaching have been frequent first steps and Ferrari (1970) indicates that half the current college presidents began in such positions, the same data indicate that 86 percent of current presidents have had college teaching experience, with 11 years as the median number of years in teaching. In Bolman's sample (1965) of recently appointed presidents 81 percent had been full-time members of a college faculty, with 11 years as the mean number of years on the faculty.

Some presidents move directly to the presidency from the faculty without prior full-time academic administrative experience (although we suspect with a fair amount of relatively formal faculty leadership experience). Such a jump is much more common in small schools than in large ones. Sixty-nine percent of the presidents in Ferrari's study and 73 percent of those in Bolman's study reported prior full-time administrative experience. The mean number of years of experience is about 10 (10.6 in Ferrari, 8 in Bolman). The proportion of presidents with prior administrative experience is closer to 90 percent if we limit our attention to large public or independent universities.

The standard promotional hierarchy for American academic administrators is a six-rung ladder:

This hierarchy is, of course, subject to considerable variation. Recent developments in recruitment to the faculty have probably reduced considerably the frequency of "teacher" and "minister" as entry steps of future presidents. Many presidents will bypass one or more of the rungs. Some institutions, particularly smaller ones, may have fewer steps in the hierarchy.

Moreover, for most current presidents, the presidential career ladder is not a ladder within a single institution. Indeed, most cur-

rent presidents have come to their presidency from another institution. Ferrari estimates that only 33 percent of his sample of
presidents came (immediately) from another job within the same
institution. Ingraham (1968) puts the estimate at 45 percent.
McVey and Hughes (1952) cite a 1940 study that places an estimate at about 30 percent. Our own estimates based on our four
cross-sectional samples are shown in Table 7.

	Estimated percentage (presidents)	Estimated percentage (students' presidents)
TABLE 7 *Estimated percentage of current presidents who were promoted to the presidency from a job within the same institution* — *Year*		
1924	51.2	57.4
1939	42.5	45.6
1954	45.4	45.5
1969	32.1	27.0

The path to the presidency displays horizontal as well as vertical
movement. American academic administrators and faculty move
from one institution to another; and movement of academics from
institution to institution is a significant feature throughout the
career path to the presidency. Ferrari (1971) has shown that on the
average presidents were full-time teachers or administrative officers
at about three institutions, including the one of which they were
president. From the results in our sample, we would estimate that
the chief academic subordinates of current presidents are not as
likely as the president to be appointed from outside, but that chief
academic subordinates to the presidents of 40.3 percent of the
colleges and of 35.4 percent of the students in American colleges
and universities came to their jobs from outside the institution.

This movement of administrators is subject to at least three
restrictions. First, there is specialization. There is very little movement into or out of the class of church-related schools. Administrators in Roman Catholic schools are very unlikely to spend a
significant amount of time in other kinds of schools; administrators
in non-Catholic schools are very unlikely to spend a significant
amount of time within Catholic schools. The pattern is less sharp
with respect to Protestant colleges but is generally consistent.
Faculty and administrative transfers tend to be within major sub-
categories of schools.

Second, there is exceptional parochialism of administrative movement. American colleges and universities typically engage in a national search for a new president and end up choosing someone who has a relatively close present or past connection with the school. For each of our four cross sections we have determined three measures of "distance" between a president and the school in which he serves: (1) the distance in miles between the birthplace of the president and the institution, (2) the distance in miles from the school at which the president received his baccalaureate degree and the institution, (3) the distance in miles between the closest known workplace of the president and the institution. If we take the least of these for each president, we are in effect asking how "close" the president has been to the institution.[10] From these data we have estimated in Table 8 the median recruitment radius in terms of the minimum of the three measures for each of four cross sections. The presidential career path includes horizontal movement, but it apparently has a strong tendency to circle back to institutions previously visited. The American college president is distinctively a "local."

TABLE 8
Estimated median recruitment radius for presidents

Year	Estimated median minimum distance in miles
1924	0
1939	0
1954	0
1969	2

Third, there is a status order. At each stage of the career path, horizontal movement is usually not really horizontal. The richer and larger schools are generally viewed as better schools. Horizontal movement "up" the pecking order of institutions is recognized as a promotion. Movement "down" the pecking order normally requires a compensating vertical promotion. We will document this phenomenon below when we discuss presidents who transfer from one presidency to another, but the phenomenon is much more general. It is also true of movement from undergraduate to graduate education, of movement from graduate school to a faculty, of movement from faculty to an administrative position, and of movement from one administrative position to another.

[10] Since there obviously can be other ways in which presidents might be close, these estimates are subject to error in the direction of exaggerating the distance of the president from the institution.

There are some important side consequences of this pattern of movement within and between administrative hierarchies that are ordered with respect to status.

- Presidents chosen from the outside by low-status institutions will generally have less administrative experience than will presidents chosen by high-status institutions.

- The higher the status of the institution, the longer the path to its presidency, and therefore the older the president on the average.

- Presidents who move from one presidency to another will generally move to a school with a "stronger" faculty both in terms of reputation and in terms of internal authority. Thus, a president who changes institutions usually finds himself with less internal power in his new position.

On the basis of this analysis, we believe that the career path to the presidency is a fairly well-defined ladder with a relatively large number of rungs.[11] Moreover, it is like other hierarchical career paths in that the accepted sign of success is promotion. A man on the path is likely to see promotion as a validation of his achievements at his present job. Since a college is an organization in which the validation of success through objective measures is relatively difficult, academic administrators move through a series of promotions to the presidency without a clear picture of where each step is taking them. Each new job is a "report card" on the old job with all the ambiguity and all the pleasures of a high grade.

The "Peter Principle" (Peter, 1969) that each administrator will rise to his level of incompetence should not hold too firmly under these conditions. For the most part, we would expect to find as presidents men who have been successful academic administrators (e.g., provosts, deans). Some of them will also be successful presidents—perhaps many of them, if the factors involved in success are the same at the two levels. What distinguishes the presidency from other positions is the fact that it is the top. As we shall see in Chapter 8, exits are not generally "promotions." As a result, we would predict less of the promotion effect on the average quality of presidents as presidents. Even successful presidents stay in the job.

PREPRESIDEN-TIAL CAREERS AND PRESIDENTS What general inferences about the college presidency can be drawn from an understanding of presidential backgrounds and prepresidential careers? We think they are quite clear. Like most paths

[11] For an alternative view, see Riesman (1969).

to status in most stable institutions, the path to the presidency in American colleges combines selection and socialization to ensure that a person reaching a presidency will act in a predictably acceptable fashion. Presidents and colleges need to recognize the implications of the process. It is powerful and effective. It is conservative.

Future presidents move horizontally and vertically through a family of similar administrative organizations located relatively "close" to one another. They arrive in office at the end of a fairly long series of filters. At each promotion or transfer, people with the appropriate background have a slightly higher probability of moving closer to a presidency. The filtering is quite gradual. Department chairmen differ only slightly from the pool of senior faculty from which they are drawn. Deans differ only slightly from the pool of department chairmen and faculty leaders from which they are drawn.

The result of this process is the selection of presidents who are likely, insofar as one can judge from social backgrounds, to be acceptable to the main internal and external groups concerned with the college. Exceptions can occur, particularly when there is a relatively rapid shift in reference groups. But, on the whole, presidents embody the educational, racial, ethnic, sex, class, and local attributes that are recognized as appropriate. Not all presidents are the same, but they vary within limited ranges and as a function of the main groups (particularly the student and faculty clientele) with which their colleges deal.[12]

Future presidents are academics. They "work their way up through the business." They become presidents after having lived almost exclusively in academic organizations. Most enter an institution of higher education at about age 18 and except for military service spend the rest of their prepresidential life there. They move from one academic organization to another, experiencing several different levels of responsibility within the academic hierarchy. Although they move from one school to another before becoming

[12] Note that this does not mean that the president necessarily shares major attributes with his "constituents." If this were true, we would not expect to find as many male presidents of women's colleges or white presidents of black colleges as we have found historically. What has been required is that he have the attributes of a socially acceptable elite. Traditionally in American society, men have been acceptable to women as leaders of women and whites have been acceptable to blacks as leaders of blacks, but the converse has generally not been true.

president, they do not move far. As a result, presidents commonly come to the job after 20 to 35 years of socialization into the values of academe, first from the viewpoint of a student, then from the viewpoint of a faculty member, then from the viewpoint of an academic administrator. This relatively deep socialization is likely to be further reinforced by a family background of parents who are educators or whose own life history includes a fairly extended exposure to academia.

The result of the socialization is twofold. On the one hand, presidents tend to be strongly committed to conventional academic values. They may see the ambiguity of those values better than some in academia. As a result, they may seem sometimes not to defend the faith as that faith is understood by the faculty or the students or the trustees. But the commitment is real. College presidents easily recognize major normative constraints on their behavior. Quite aside from any "practical" considerations that might lead them to be unable to effect major changes in their colleges and universities, presidents do not for the most part want to make major changes. They accept the institution and support it.

At the same time, socialization produces an expectation that presidents will share the values of their subordinates and the members of important subgroups inside the college. The expectation is sometimes misguided. The socialization of presidents is different from the socialization of faculty, for example, in some important ways. But presidents and others in the college have relatively high mutual expectations of basic normative agreement. In particular, we find that presidents feel disagreement with their faculties or students to be distinctly painful. This is only partly for the obvious strategic reasons. Disagreement with students or faculty is not only a political event for many presidents; it is also a problem of identity—and a surprise.

A presidential career is an after-the-fact invention. A future president moves from one position to another, establishing with each move an apparent success at the previous position, but with little or no career planning by the organization or (in most cases) by the individual. A career is a backward-looking description of those movements. It is rarely a plan. A person is very easily deflected from completion of the full presidential "career."

Normally, when we examine the career paths of presidents we look back across the job histories of those members of the academic community who have gone all the way to the presidency. Most do not. Most faculty members do not become department chairmen. Most department chairmen do not become deans. Most deans do not become provosts. Most provosts do not become presidents. Some of these administrators stay in a particular job until they retire. Some deans, for example, have very long tenures. But characteristically they do not.[13] A great many academic administrators simply return to the faculty (or, in the case of religious schools, to the ministry). The presidential career is an easily aborted one.

It is also an incremental one. Discussions of prepresidential careers have often ignored the consequences of the extraordinary growth that higher education has undergone in recent years. Growth means vacancies. Vacancies mean promotions.[14] Promotions mean that more faculty will anticipate following administrative career paths. Unless we see a proliferation of administrative positions (a tendency that may be restrained by fiscal problems), the next few years of reduced growth are likely to produce fewer vacancies, fewer promotions, and fewer recognizable administrative careers.

Promotions are often viewed simply as rewards for success. But what is success? Given the difficulty of determining whether the work in an academic organization is being done well,[15] presidents seem to us likely to be men who can persuade themselves and others that things are going well in their particular organizational neighborhood. A principal focus of attention in recent years has been organization building (e.g., new personnel). Organization building has been a fundamental criterion employed by those who have written report cards for department chairmen, deans, and academic vice-presidents.

If we observe that organization building is much easier when resources are plentiful and that resources are often distributed in response to changing patterns of student demand for various disciplines (see Chapter 6), then we might expect that administrators in areas of rapidly growing student interest will begin to appear in the pool from which presidencies are filled some number

[13] As Ingraham (1968) has shown, the average number of years in office for subordinate academic administrators is consistently less than that for presidents. Modern commentators who have discussed (somewhat misleadingly we believe — see Chapter 8) the "short" tenures of presidents have overlooked the fact that presidents have substantially longer tenure expectations than do department chairmen, deans, or provosts.

[14] For a discussion of "vacancy chains" see White (1970).

[15] An exception might be very superior scholarship, which would be recognized by many, but very few presidents have been scholars or scientists of this caliber.

of years after the first edge of the student wave. We believe the increase in presidents with social science backgrounds to be a result of the growth of student interest in these disciplines in the years since World War II. In a similar manner the continuation of the current expansion of interest in biological and environmental sciences might be expected to produce some increase in the conspicuousness of presidential candidates with biological or environmental backgrounds a few years hence.

At the same time, it is clear that organization building is a less likely mark of success when we shift from a predominance of growth organizations to increasing concern with fiscal and student problems. Within the system of promotions we have described, the history of "success" represented in the pool of career administrators is likely to shift only gradually. Three major factors—the filtration of a series of promotions, the long socialization, and the ambiguities of success within academic organizations—make prepresidential careers strongly conservative in their impact on the college. The promotion filters produce a pool of plausible candidates for the presidency, all of whom share many key characteristics. A board of trustees that wishes to choose a president with radically different social, personal, or experiential characteristics will normally not find him represented among the group of apparently qualified candidates until selection procedures throughout the system are changed. Such changes occur, but slowly.

Socialization is likely to produce presidents with a deep commitment to academe and to development within a range of normatively accepted change. Although the norms that are defended by the presidents are likely to be somewhat different from the traditional academic values of senior faculty, they are unlikely to be consistent with far-reaching proposals for redefining the role of the university or restructuring its operation.

Finally, the success history of presidents provides them with a sense of competence in, and enthusiasm for, those things that defined success as they were establishing their reputations in lesser positions. As the perspectives about the university shift, there will frequently be a lag in a president's adaptation of his view of success to the new ideology.[16]

[16] The commitments of presidents are institutionally conservative, but not necessarily politically conservative in the usual sense of that word. In the recent contest of campus strife, the institutionally conservative posture of a college president has often made him unacceptable to many students, to many faculty, to many trustees, to many members of the community, and to adherents of a wide range of political faiths.

If a president is expected to play an active role in guiding changes in the college, these attributes of prepresidential careers can be expected to produce problems. Few presidents can hope to have their careers span a period short enough, or to have the abilities and attitudes they have developed seem inconsequential enough that they are able to avoid all strain between the pressures on them and their own sense of virtue. They have a deep involvement in the attractiveness of the institution as they have known it. They want the institution to prosper. They want to "leave their mark" in important changes associated with their tenure; they want the changes to be within the boundaries of what 20 to 35 years have taught them are good changes.

It is a classic problem and a deeply imbedded one. Although there is no question that the attributes of presidents and the pre-presidential careers of presidents can be changed, we doubt that the basic processes underlying the careers can be much affected without major modification of the nature of colleges in the United States. The conservative character of the presidency can be modified significantly only by sacrificing a structure of recruitment, selection, and socialization that is itself engrained in the traditions and values of academia.

But we ought not to pretend. A president can be an effective leader for a college or university, but he is not likely to be one if he is unable to acknowledge the obvious implications of his birth, his education, his experience, and his prior personal commitments. A university or college can be well served by a president, but it is likely often to be disappointed if it socializes a president in one way and asks him to behave in another.

3. The Metaphors of Leadership

As we have seen in Chapter 2, presidents come to the presidency in a manner that assures both variety and substantial normative homogeneity. Although there is variation among them, presidents have reasonable attitudes, reasonable backgrounds, and reasonable aspirations in terms of the student population and the major participating groups in the college or university. The process is standard social filtration.

The major consequences of that filtration for the social characteristics of college presidents were suggested in Chapter 2. We examine now some other attributes that presidents bring to their job, in particular the view they (and others around them) have of their role in the institution. These views are also reasonable and conventional. The conventionality is intellectual as well as social. Presidents share their images of their jobs with professional students of organizations and universities.

Among the many things presidents do, their role in the internal governance of their institutions is one of their more obviously important responsibilities. Whether one views that role as benign or malevolent, increasing or decreasing, wise or stupid, virtually any discussion of the presidency requires some conception of decision making and governance. Students of organizations provide a set of theories about how we might view an organization such as a university and how we might treat the president's role within the organization. Although the details of those theories are of interest primarily to specialists (Allison, 1971; Hodgkinson & Meeth, 1971; March, 1965), their general thrust is to develop and elaborate a language for describing events within organizations and for evaluating and modifying leader behavior. In this chapter we consider a set of alternative models of governance and leadership in social institutions. They are models implicit in the professional and semi-professional literature of organizations and administration.

When presidents or other participants within the university consider the possible arrangements of governing activities, they bring along an assortment of metaphors.[1] They have some ideas about the kind of organized system the university is. These metaphors, or models, are borrowed from a variety of other institutions and theories of institutions, ordinarily without much of conscious selection from the rather large set of alternative models available, but with a somewhat diffuse attention to the current dogmas of administrative theory (Foote, Caleb, Mayer, Henry & Associates, 1968; "The Invitational Seminar . . . ," 1971; Mayhew, 1971).

We have identified eight relatively distinct ways in which one might look at the governance of universities. Each of the eight has a set of implicit assumptions about the circumstances under which it operates in a "technically" efficient way—that is, the circumstances under which it renders decisions appropriately, given the distribution of power within the system. Each of the eight has a procedure for allocating formal power within the system that allows, in principle, any of them to distribute power as "equally" or "unequally" as desired. Each functions in a different way and demands a different conception of the presidential role.

The competitive market metaphor

We can describe the university and the services and opportunities it provides simply as a bundle of goods in a free market. Students, faculty, donors, and communities select from a list of alternative universities (willing to accept them) the one (or more) that comes closest to satisfying their perceived needs. Quality, price, and quantity are determined as in the usual competitive market. The distribution of wealth is the key to the distribution of power.

Internal organization is entirely arbitrary. Effective "governance" takes place through the operation of markets (e.g., labor market, student market, employer market, donor market, legislative market).

The competitive market model makes the usual free-market assumptions: (1) that there are few frictions in the relevant markets— that students, faculty, donors, and legislators have alternatives readily available to them and that they are (and feel they are) free to exercise those alternatives at minimum cost; (2) that there is sub-

[1] In this chapter we have drawn heavily on a paper written with Denis Hayes (Hayes & March, 1970). Monson (1967) suggests an alternative set of metaphors for the presidency: orchestra leader, dispensing machine, zoo keeper.

stantially perfect knowledge about the alternatives on all sides; and (3) that there is relative ease of entry for new universities.

The administrative metaphor

In the administrative model we assume that the university has a well-defined objective specified by some formal group. The distribution of access to the control group (e.g., the board of trustees) is the key power question.

The university is organized into a hierarchy of tasks and authority relations in order to achieve its objectives efficiently. Individuals within the organization agree to pursue the objectives of the university in return for various kinds of payments (e.g., salaries, prestige, degrees) provided by the university. Individuals receive their positions within the university (e.g., tenure, admission to graduate status, trusteeship) on the basis of universalistic, well-defined criteria of contribution to the objectives of the organization. Differences of opinion are resolved through analysis and persuasion (as contrasted with bargaining and politics).[2]

The administrative model assumes that the objectives of the university can be defined precisely and operationally and that the technology of the university is well defined and widely understood. It further assumes a structure of performance criteria that relate to the overall objectives of the university and that can be used to evaluate the organizational components objectively.

The collective bargaining metaphor

In the collective bargaining model we assume that there are fundamentally conflicting interests within the university. Students wish to be educated and to be certified. Faculty wish to be supported in their research and to be admired. Donors wish to enhance the prestige of the institution from which they graduated, and perhaps to influence its policies. Legislators wish to satisfy constituents. These interests are in direct conflict over some of the key activities of the university (e.g., how faculty and students allocate their time).

The conflicts are resolved by bargaining among representatives of the major interests and then enforced by formal "contracts" and social pressure. The agreements form the "constitution" within which managers of the system operate, and each interest maintains

[2] See March and Simon (1958).

its own auditors on the extent to which the agreed bargains are fulfilled by the managers. Each interest bargains by threatening to impose sanctions on the other interests, but each would prefer some compromise bargain to the alternative of imposing sanctions.

The bargaining conflict model assumes that each of the contending interests is sufficiently well defined and organized to be represented in negotiations and to be held to honoring the outcome of those negotiations. It assumes that the sets of demands can be reconciled, usually through the introduction of mutually credible information with respect to the flexibility of demands and the reality of sanctions.

The democratic metaphor

In the democratic model we picture the university as a community with an "electorate" consisting of students, faculty, alumni, citizens, parents, or some subset of those groups. The distribution of formal participation in the electorate is the underlying power question. Members of the electorate choose the president of the university by some voting procedure, after which the president seeks to manage the institution in the name of the electorate.

In order to secure votes, candidates for the presidency engage in various kinds of promises of policy actions. Each member of the electorate attempts to maximize his net return; each candidate for office seeks to maximize his likelihood of election. Candidates and the electorate engage in continuous negotiation to form coalitions and trades. Members of the electorate with consistent interests (e.g., students interested in leisure time and faculty interested in leisure time) join forces.

The democratic model assumes the rather elaborate performance of a brokerage function. That is, members of the electorate are assumed to be able to exchange extensive information about possible coalitions. Elections occur often enough and involve enough of the electorate to ensure that the campaign agreements will be enforced. Leaders are assumed to be politically ambitious—they want to remain in office. Although most presidents are not in fact elected, the model derives its relevance from the fact that many still think of themselves as having constituencies whose support must be maintained.

The consensus metaphor

In the consensus model governmental authority for the university lies in a procedure for securing apparent unanimity. This may be a daily (weekly, etc.) meeting operating under consensus–social pressure rules. Each decision is open to anyone who wishes to participate; eligibility depends only on willingness to spend the time. The distribution of ease of access to the assembly and time for attendance are the prime questions of power.

Opinions are expressed, alternatives are considered, and an effort to achieve consensus is made. Decisions thus reached are enforced on the system until changed by a subsequent decision (which could, of course, involve a different constellation of individuals). Such an "open" decision system combined with unanimity rules suggests some forms of government used in French universities during the student revolt in Paris. However, the system is much more general. It is, in fact, close to a model of some organizations (e.g., some voluntary organizations) that appear to operate under other rules.[3]

The consensus model assumes that most participants in the university are part-time participants with heavy external demands on their time. It assumes that those outside demands are generally more compelling than the inside demands; that the status certification functions of governance are important relative to the decision functions of governance; and that most decision situations in the organization are susceptible of being translated into a discussion of the current concerns of any currently active participant. It assumes rather loose requirements for consistency over time, but rather tight requirements for agreement among those active at any given moment.

The anarchy metaphor

In a university anarchy each individual in the university is seen as making autonomous decisions. Teachers decide if, when, and what to teach. Students decide if, when, and what to learn. Legislators and donors decide if, when, and what to support. Neither coordination (except the spontaneous mutual adaptation of decision) nor control are practiced. Resources are allocated by whatever process emerges but without explicit accommodation and without explicit reference to some superordinate goal. The "decisions" of the system are a consequence produced by the system but intended by no one and decisively controlled by no one.

---

[3] See Cohen, March, and Olsen (1972) and the references cited there.

The anarchy model assumes a loosely connected world, or one that can be treated as loosely connected because it is bountiful, and large resource "buffers" can be established between decisions. It assumes that the statistical properties of a large number of autonomous decisions are such that they will reliably produce jointly satisfactory states. It assumes that leaders have relatively modest status demands.

The independent judiciary metaphor

In the anarchy model we have a constituency without explicit leadership; in the independent judiciary model we assume leadership without an explicit constituency. Governmental authority in the university is bestowed by some relatively arbitrary process (e.g., birth, co-optation, revelation) on a group of current leaders. Their term is indefinite, and they are assumed to exercise their authority in the name of a hypothetical constituency reflecting the history and future of the institution.

The independent judiciary model assumes that there are substantial conflicts between the immediate self-interests of current constituencies and the long-run interests of future constituencies. It assumes that it is possible to identify or train a judge capable of perceiving the intrinsic purposes and needs of the institution. It assumes that it is possible, indeed common, to induce the members of the university to accept actions in the name of the institution that they would not necessarily have taken in their own behalf.

The plebiscitary autocracy metaphor

In this model we have a ruler chosen by some arbitrary process and a constituency consisting of everyone in the community. The exact rules for admission into the "electorate" are relatively unimportant because either the electorate overwhelmingly supports the autocrat or the autocrat abdicates. The autocrat makes all decisions on behalf of the university until such time as he may deem it appropriate to ask the community to consider his acceptability. So long as the electorate responds in such a situation by strong support, he continues in office.

The plebiscitary autocracy model assumes that the status significance of governance is small. It assumes that the decisions to be made are technically complicated relative to the amount of time and knowledge available to individual members of the constituency. It assumes that the variance in objectives among participants is relatively small—or can be made so by information and interaction. On the whole, it assumes that the making of *a* choice is usually more important than the making of any particular choice.

UNIVERSITIES AND ALTERNATIVE MODELS OF GOVERNANCE Much of the recent literature and commentary on the presidency, as well as many of the events and interpretations of events on campuses over the past 10 years, have made students of universities not only more attentive to governance but also much more prone to "political" interpretations of governance than they probably were earlier in the century. The dominant conventional description of organizations is in terms of some form of administered community democracy (Baldridge, 1971*a*, 1971*b*; Demerath et al., 1967; Kerr, 1963). This is more obvious in the research literature than it is in some management texts (where administration becomes somewhat more important), but anyone who reads the literature or talks to someone who does will know both rhetorics—the rhetoric of the bureaucratic administrator acting in the name of the board of directors and the rhetoric of the politician acting in the name of his constituents. The modern literature assumes behavior in a manner consistent with both orientations.

We would expect college presidents to accept some mix of the metaphors of administration and democracy—with a lesser touch of collective bargaining—since those metaphors are parts of the old and new traditions of interpretation provided by peer groups and the literature.

We believe that, despite their pervasiveness, the metaphors commonly used to describe decision making in organizations are partly misleading. In particular, we almost certainly overuse the administrative, collective bargaining, and democratic models of governance. For most organizations, they clearly contain some elements of truth. No one would deny the reality of either organizational politics or the board of directors. But such metaphors also have serious disabilities, both as descriptions of university reality and as prescriptions on which leaders of universities can build. We will turn to the realism issue in later chapters. Here we briefly examine the more technical problems of administration, democracy, and collective bargaining as "efficient" systems of governance.

We have indicated the assumptions underlying each of our models. That is, we have suggested some of the preconditions required for each system of governance to respond in a normatively reasonable way. A major problem with the use of administrative, collective bargaining, and democratic models of governance in universities is obvious. The areas in which the critical assumptions underlying such systems are satisfied are considerably smaller than the areas to which the metaphors are generally applied. In the case of the administrative model, the prime difficulties lie in the assumption of a well-defined goal and technology. We do not think this represents the existing situation very well, nor is it clear that it is an obviously desirable objective (see Chapters 1, 5, and 9). In the case of the democratic and collective bargaining models, the prime problems lie in the assumptions made with respect to the organization of public consent. The level of organization of faculty, students, alumni, workers, citizens, employers, etc., is essentially trivial relative to the requirements for efficiency.

We almost certainly under use the competitive market, anarchy, independent judiciary, and plebiscitary autocracy models of governance in the universities. We appear to underestimate the extent to which such models provide practical and efficient alternatives for interpreting collective choices, in large part because our professional literature ignores them also.

Consider the most obvious case—the competitive market model and student power. If we modify only a few frictions in the market, we greatly increase the individual and collective leverage of students in the universities (although not necessarily the status of student leaders). The simplest and most pervasive techniques involve strengthening the connection between individual student preferences (expressed in enrollment) and budgets. There are some obvious, immediate, practical ways to do that: (1) funnel educational subsidies through students rather than directly to institutions; (2) reduce the number of required courses; (3) make departmental budgets proportional to the number of enrollments in nonrequired courses. Indeed, these would be modifications of what is, as we will point out in Chapter 6, already an important part of the system of governance in many colleges.

The case for anarchy is in some ways less obvious but, we think, equally compelling. Anarchy as a system of governance in a university requires only two major things:

1   *The acceptance of an ideology of anarchy*   Most of the assumptions necessary for the efficiency of the anarchy model are met, so long as individual participants do not try to impose conventional bureaucratic criteria of

coordination, control, and consistency on the decisions made. Such an imposition makes little sense in the absence of known goals and technology. But every American school child is taught to be a bureaucrat, and the ideology dies hard.

2 *An effective information system for all participants regarding the current "state" of the university* To a discouraging degree, university governance and modern efforts to change it attempt to substitute administrative control for knowledge. In order to permit unobtrusive system-maintaining actions rather than brute-force interventions, anarchy requires a rather elaborate structure to provide information on the behavior of the system. To deal with the massive potential information output in a university, we probably need both a richer set of performance measures (e.g., measures of hourly student-faculty contact, waiting-line phenomena in student-faculty life, research involvement and output) and some system of public random sampling of university letters, memoranda, reports, etc.

The relevance of the independent judiciary model is obscured by two things: (1) The fact that most current university leaders are clearly not "independent." They are expected to, and do, identify primarily with the faculty in most institutions, and with the trustees in a few. (2) The contentiousness of current university governance. Governance by an "independent judiciary" presumes that many (perhaps most) issues can be made consensus issues through the acceptance by individuals of "revelation" as a legitimate means of resolving a genuine conflict of interest. It is, of course, a little hard to imagine a decrease in the contentiousness without a prior or simultaneous increase in the independence of leaders.

THE METAPHORS OF LEADERSHIP If we are right in identifying and evaluating the ways in which we think about the governance of universities, then we should also be able to identify some implications for presidential styles. It is now commonplace to observe that a president who attempts to run a political system as though it were a bureaucracy is likely to do poorly. Like so many commonplace observations, it is true. It is also true that a president who attempts to run a consensus system or an anarchy as though it were a political system will make a mess of it. Moreover, we think that this latter proposition is closer to what is likely to happen in many contemporary American universities.

The general point, of course, is that the model one has of the system of governance dictates a presidential style. The appropriateness of the style, however, is determined by the adequacy of the model.

Each of our metaphors implicitly prescribes a role for the president of a university:

Metaphor	Presidential role
Competitive market	The college president is an entrepreneur. He may establish any kind of organization he wishes within the constraints imposed by the willingness of students, faculty, donors, and legislators to take their support elsewhere.
Administration	College presidents are appointed by the trustees to pursue the objectives specified by the board and are evaluated in terms of the performance of the organization with respect to those objectives. The major tasks of the president involve controlling the operation to ensure conformity with the objectives, coordinating the several subunits toward that end, assuring consistency within the organization, and avoiding duplication of activities and waste.
Collective bargaining	The college president does two things: First, he attempts to mediate disputes between the interests in the university and help them to find mutually satisfactory agreements. In this activity, he is a facilitator of compromise or invention. Second, he supervises the implementation of the agreements, serving each of the interests to the degree specified by the bargaining outcomes.
Democracy	The college president sees himself as a hypothetical candidate for the office and offers promises of policy action in exchange for promises of support. His objective is to maintain a winning coalition of interest groups by responding to their demands for university policy.
Consensus	The presidential role involves three major activities: the management of the agendas, the public solicitation of consensus, and the implementation of agreements. The president responds to demands by placing them

Metaphor	Presidential role
	on the agenda for discussion, by inducing a discussion of them, and by implementing them if they survive the discussion.
Anarchy	The president is a catalyst. He gains his influence by understanding the operation of the system and by inventing viable solutions that accomplish his objectives rather than by choosing among conflicting alternatives. "Management" in an anarchy involves the substitution of knowledge and subtle adjustment for the explicit authoritative control of bureaucracy.
Independent judiciary	The college president is not expected to reflect or adjust to the demands of a current set of actors, consumers, constituents, owners, or employees. Rather, he is expected to capture the historic truths of the university as an institution and to reflect those truths during a brief trusteeship.
Plebiscitary autocracy	The president is a decision maker and organizer of opinion. Such consultation or assistance as he uses is simply a convenience to him and imposes no obligation to him to follow the advice. He acts on the objectives as he sees them and subsequently attempts to persuade his constituency that his rule should be continued.

When we survey the leadership roles demanded by the different models, we are struck by some important ways in which the roles associated with familiar metaphors of university governance differ from the roles associated with relatively unfamiliar metaphors. On the whole, the literature of organizations and administration provides a firmer ideological and technical base for the metaphors of administration (manager), democracy (politician), collective bargaining (mediator), and consensus (chairman) than it does for the metaphors of the competitive market (entrepreneur), anarchy (catalyst), independent judiciary (judge), or plebiscitary autocracy (philosopher-king).

What particularly distinguishes these two sets of roles are, we believe, two important things:

1   The extent to which the roles are seen as reactive to demands of others (as in the familiar metaphors) rather than as initiating ideas and structures (as in the unfamiliar metaphors).

2   The extent to which the roles are seen as requiring a relatively continuous public posture (as in the familiar metaphors) rather than a somewhat more remote posture (as in the unfamiliar metaphors).

The relationship is not perfect, and one might question the relatively arbitrary attention to organizational-administrative traditions in the literature to the exclusion of the strong entrepreneurial–competitive market traditions of the literature in microeconomics and organizational economics or the strong judicial traditions of the literature in jurisprudence. We believe that the dominant models of organizations likely to affect normatively conventional views of university leadership are those of bureaucratic administration, collective bargaining, consensus formation, and democratic politics. This is particularly true within the academic subculture from which presidents are drawn.

CONCLUSION   If college presidents accept conventional management wisdom, they will think of universities as systems of administration, collective bargaining, political democracy, consensus formation, or some combination of those metaphors. They will think of themselves as administrators, mediators, political leaders, neighborhood chairmen, or some combination of these roles. Given the processes of movement to the presidency we have described in Chapter 2, we would be surprised if presidents had substantially unconventional views of organizations and organizational leadership. As we shall see in the next chapter, they do not.

If our analysis is correct, however, these conventional views will make university leadership less effective than it might be. The technical requirements for behavior in such roles seem likely to be missing in most colleges and universities much of the time. The logic of bureaucracy is the specification of objectives and technology. The logic of democracy is the organization of consent. The logic of collective bargaining is the discipline of conflict. The realities of higher education seem to be resistant to all three logics.

4. Images of the Presidency

The scholarly interpreters of modern academic institutions view a college (for the most part) as some combination of a bureaucratic-administrative system and a system of political interest and group bargaining. In recent years the latter part of the combination has come to dominate the former. It is natural to ask what presidents and those around them think the presidency is or ought to be. These are the questions to which we now turn. What are the objectives of leadership? What are the metaphors of the actors? Does a college president see himself as a military commander or a mayor? As a clergyman or a foreman? As a mediator or a business executive? What differences are there among the images held by presidents? What do presidents think distinguishes a successful president? How do the metaphors of presidents differ from those of others around them? From those outside the academic world?

The orientation to the presidency of the president and his associates is important to understanding the problems of leadership in contemporary universities. Expectations condition not only behavior but also interpretations of events. Presidents live in an ambiguous world. The "reality" in terms of which they act, and from which they learn, is an invention that depends heavily on the models and ideologies of leadership with which they approach the sporadic, noisy information generated within their careers.

NORMATIVE IMAGES OF THE PRESIDENCY The modern college president does not suffer from lack of advice. Presidents, ex-presidents, and would-be-presidents provide a steady stream of prescriptions. Universities are filled with and surrounded by persons who believe they know how to manage a university, have access to a publisher, and have time on their hands.

Although the advice is probably overabundant and often suffers from a tendency to inflate the implications of recent events, it has the merit of encouraging presidents to think about their roles. In addition, conversational events in the life of a president naturally require him to develop a relatively conscious normative view of the presidential role. The ordinary rituals of everyday interaction require some kind of wisdom on "the present and future role of the American college president."

In our interview with the presidents and other administrators in our sample of 42 schools, we asked a number of questions that help to establish presidential images of what the presidency should be. Each respondent was asked to give the name of a current president at an institution other than his own whom he believed to have been "clearly successful." Respondents were asked what evidence could be cited for that success. Finally, each respondent was asked to summarize for us what he felt were the major aspects of a college president's job.

Normative Images— Presidential Views

Thirty-one of the presidents in the 42-college sample responded to the request that they name a clearly successful current president. The nonrespondents most commonly said that they did not know anyone who was "clearly successful." The dispersion of the answers is considerable. Twenty-three different presidents were mentioned. Only three were multiple nominees. (They were Brewster of Yale— 5 mentions, Levy of Chicago—4, and Sharpe of Drake—2.)

Table 9 displays the very strong regionalism of the nominations. Most choices were from within the geographic region of the nominator. Presidents frequently remarked that their judgment that the nominee was successful was based on reports from friends at the nominee's campus. In general, news of the quality of presidential performance travels poorly. Presidents seem to think about success

TABLE 9 Regions of nominated successful presidents

Region of. choosing president*	Region of chosen president				
	East	South	Middle-west	West	Total
East	8		2		10
South	2	6	3		11
Middle-west			5		5
West	1		2	2	5
TOTAL	11	6	12	2	31

*For definition of regions, see Appendix A, "Regions."

in local terms and do not consistently identify the members of any small group of nationally prominent individuals. They do not see themselves as belonging to a well-defined, interacting peer group with clear "culture heroes."

While no group of individuals domimated the selections, the nominated presidents did share a number of attributes that both reveal something of the origins of current notions of presidential success and further emphasize the parochialism of the reference group. Table 10 shows the relative size and wealth of the schools of choosing and chosen presidents. Presidents who were cited as successful serve in general at schools both larger and wealthier than the schools of those who cited them. "Successful" *presidents* were presidents at "successful" *schools* (relative to the school of the respondent). In addition, Table 11 indicates the types of schools of choosing and chosen presidents. The schools of cited presidents are disproportionately nonsectarian. Presidents of sectarian colleges often mentioned those from public and private colleges and universities while presidents in these latter groups had a tendency to nominate presidents of the same type school as their own. The deviations are biased toward presidents of private institutions. The nominations are thus localized by type of control as well as by region. The reference group is narrow. Where nonparochial nominations are made, they are usually made upward in *school* status,

TABLE 10
Relative size and wealth of schools of choosing and chosen presidents*

Size of chosen relative to choosing	Wealth of chosen relative to choosing		
	Greater	Lesser	Total
Larger	13	7	20
Smaller	8	3	11
TOTAL	21	10	31

*Wealth is measured in dollars per full-time student, size in full-time students.

TABLE 11
Types of schools of choosing and chosen presidents

Choosing presidents	Chosen presidents			
	Public	Private	Religious	Total
Public	5	4	0	9
Private	1	8	1	10
Religious	3	4	5	12
TOTAL	9	16	6	31

and there is an apparent tendency not to distinguish the attributes of a president from the attributes of his school.

What evidence is adduced for these judgments of success? Table 12 presents the distribution of the first three pieces of evidence mentioned by each president. The responses are coded into 10 categories defined as follows:

Fiscal	The financial status of the president's institution or his contribution to it.
Educational program	The range or quality of the educational experience offered by the institution.
Growth	The institution's physical plant, student body, or faculty have increased in size.
Quiet	The campus has not had serious disruptions or demonstrations by students, faculty, or other groups.
Quality of faculty	The institution has a good or improved faculty.
Quality of students	The institution has good or improved students.
Respect of faculty	The president has good relations with his faculty, is liked or respected by them.
Respect of students	The president has good relations with students, is liked or respected by them.
Respect of community	The president has had little conflict with the public, is liked or respected by important elements outside his own institution.
Other	All responses that could not be coded into the above nine categories.[1]

Among the defined categories, "quality of faculty" and "growth" were most frequently mentioned as evidence of success, but the dispersion is considerable. Growth was mentioned by 25.7 percent

[1] These categories were designed in advance to be used in encoding the presidents' responses. Our overestimation of the probable concreteness of the grounds for judging a fellow president successful resulted in a fairly large number of the presidential responses falling under no code but "other." "Reports from friends" is one type of evidence that occurred frequently and was coded as "other."

TABLE 12 *Evidence of success cited by 35 choosing presidents*

Criteria	Total mentions	Percentage of 83 mentions	Percentage of 35 respondents who mentioned each criterion	Estimated percentage of total mentions among all presidents
Fiscal	6	7.2	17.1	6.6
Educational program	8	9.6	22.8	10.0
Growth	9	10.8	25.7	13.7
Quiet	11	13.2	31.5	10.3
Quality of faculty	8	9.6	22.8	11.6
Quality of students	2	2.4	5.7	3.1
Respect of faculty	8	9.6	25.7	8.7
Respect of students	6	7.2	17.1	4.9
Respect of community	7	8.4	20.0	7.9
Other	18	21.7	*	23.2
TOTAL	83	99.7	†	100.0

* "Other" percentage was not calculated as it could be mentioned more than once by a single respondent.
† Does not total 100 because respondents could mention more than one.

of our responding presidents, or an estimated 32.4 percent of the universe of all presidents.[2]

It is hard to see much detailed consensus on what the presidency should be from these responses. Insofar as presidents name specific other presidents as role models, they name presidents who are close to them geographically and in terms of the type of school. They name presidents of superior schools. They see a variety of more or less conventional things as contributing to success, but they do not particularly agree on the relative importance of the items as evidence of success. The items cited seem to fall into three broad categories: constituency-oriented items (e.g., respect of faculty, quiet), institution building–entrepreneurial items (e.g., growth, quality of faculty), and functional-administrative items (e.g., fiscal, educational program). These account respectively for an estimated

[2] Table 12 provides an illustration of the stratification effects in our sample. "Quiet" was most mentioned by our 35 respondents, but its importance was reduced somewhat by the application of weights to the data. It is instructive to note that an oversampling of the large and prestigious schools, which is characteristic also of the public media, produces an overestimate of the importance of quiet as a criterion of presidential success.

41.4 percent, 37.0 percent, and 21.7 percent of the non-other responses. In terms of our earlier metaphors of leadership, these suggest a view of the president as a mixture of political leader, entrepreneur, and bureaucrat-administrator, without any clear dominance of one over the other.

We also asked each of the presidents to make a short list of the major aspects of a modern college president's job. The answers to this question were most commonly in the form of statements of what a president "should do." Thus, we have treated them as bearing on the normative images of the president. Some respondents, however, answered in terms of what a president "has to do." As a result, these responses are probably more clearly a mixture of prescription and description.

The responses were coded into one or more of the following categories:

Personal
The respondent says a president should be a certain kind of person or display some set of personal qualities (e.g., patience, scholarship).

Constituency
The respondent defines the presidency in terms of relations to various constituencies (e.g., faculty, students, alumni).

Administrative
The respondent defines the presidency in terms of various administrative duties (e.g., planning, budgeting, personnel, or curriculum).

Other
All responses that could not be coded into the above categories.

Table 13 shows the distribution of answers into the various combinations of categories.[3] (Combinations that did not occur have been deleted from the table.) Of the 41 presidents we interviewed, 21 mentioned constituency aspects of the presidency, 15 gave at least in part an administrative breakdown, 10 touched upon the personal attributes required, 4 mentioned other aspects of the presidency that could not be coded under this scheme, and 5 did not answer. Thus, 51.2 percent of all our interviewed presidents

---

[3] Presidents often combined these categories when answering. For example: "a president must have the personal qualities which will enable him to win and maintain the respect of students, faculty, and alumni." Such a response was coded as falling in both the personal and constituency categories.

TABLE 13
*Characteriza-
tions of major
aspects of the
presidency*

Aspect of the presidency	Number	Percentage of total	Percentage of all respondents mentioning the category in any combination	Estimated percentage of all presidents
Personal	5	12.2	24.4	35.7
Constituency	11	26.8	51.2	62.6
Administrative	4	9.8	36.6	51.4
Other	3	7.3	9.7	6.5
Constituency and administrative	7	17.0		
Constituency and personal	2	4.9		
Administrative and personal	2	4.9		
Administrative and other	1	2.4		
Constituency, personal, and administrative	1	2.4		
No response	5	12.2	12.2	3.4
TOTAL	41	99.7	*	*

*Total greater than 100 as respondents mentioned more than one category.

listed the major attributes of the presidency in constituency terms; but none of the alternatives strongly dominates the others. There is a preference both for a constituency breakdown (strongest in the smallest schools), and for an administrative breakdown (strongest in larger schools).

None of our measures produces wide enough agreement to serve as a basis for the construction of a single normative image of the presidency. Clearly, there are possible statements of the objectives of the presidency that would evoke higher agreement than we have found. Few presidents would disagree with the assertion that they should win the respect of students, faculty, and community; improve the quality of the faculty and educational program; display desirable personal qualities; watch the budget; and plan for the future. The literature on the presidency is filled with such assertions and they are not controversial in themselves. The literature continues to grow because these objectives are often contradictory. As soon as questions about what the objectives of the presidency should be are pressed slightly, agreement starts to break down.

In a 1966 study of 180 presidents of higher educational institutions in New York, including 59 junior college presidents, Hemphill and Wahlberg (1966, pp. 48–49) asked each of their questionnaire respondents to list what he would consider his major success in his job. The authors summarize the responses, which apparently showed fair consensus, as follows:

Most responses had to do with the organizational development of the institution. Presidents mentioned such accomplishments as developing organizational charts, administrative planning, job descriptions for subordinate administrators, and opening lines of communication. They also mentioned successes in the development of the physical plant or in the acquisition of funds for new programs, and in the strengthening of relations between the president and the students, the governing body and the faculty. Only two presidents mentioned development of the educational program as among their initial successes.

Thus, presidents in 1966 seemed to place greater weight on evidence we would classify as "fiscal" or "respect of faculty and students" than did our 1970 sample. The two data sets share an emphasis on growth. Presidential emphasis on aspects of organization building seems to reflect both learning over the prepresidential career path (see the discussion in Chapter 2) and the greater short-run tangibility of these activities. Apparently, leaders facing the complexity that we have argued is prevalent in academic life emphasize the importance of activities with short-run effects that are not difficult to measure. The fact that success in 1966 bore little relation to the question of quiet, which was heavily stressed in our 1970 data, testifies to the substantial variability of presidential conceptions of success.[4]

In general the limits on the diversity of objectives imposed by the intrinsic character of higher education appear to us to be very weak, and this view seems to be supported by the diversity of presidential responses to our questions on the subject of what the presidency should be and by apparent changes in those conceptions over time. It is striking that this situation is not matched with large variations in patterns of presidential behavior or of organizational form, but that these aspects of higher education are, it seems to us, remark-

---

[4] Although we do not have a later sample for comparison, we suspect the relatively low attention to fiscal criteria by presidents would also have begun to change in the period since our interviews.

able for their homogeneity. Presidents should perhaps be aware that interpretations of university life seem to develop and change rather more spectacularly than does the life itself.

We asked the chief academic officer, the chief business officer, and the assistant to the president at each college to name successful presidents other than their own. Their answers display some of the same general characteristics as those of the president group: Few presidents received more than one nomination and the nominations tended to be strongly regional. There were, however, some interesting differences. Tables 14, 15, and 16 show the type of college of chosen presidents by type of college of choosing academic officers, business officers, and assistants to the president, respectively. As one may see by comparing these data with those of Table 11 above, academic officers showed an even stronger tendency to "choose their own kind" than did the presidents. Assistants to the president were similar to presidents in response, including the bias toward private institutions. Business officers, however, more often chose the presidents of public colleges and universities as successful, even when the business officer's own school was of another type.

Schools of choosing academic officers	*Schools of chosen presidents*			
	Public	*Private*	*Religious*	*Total*
Public	9	2	1	12
Private	1	10	1	12
Religious	1	1	9	11
TOTAL	11	13	11	35

Schools of choosing business officers	*Schools of chosen presidents*			
	Public	*Private*	*Religious*	*Total*
Public	8	2		10
Private	3	5	2	10
Religious	3	2	5	10
TOTAL	14	9	7	30

TABLE 16
*Type of school
of chosen
presidents
and choosing
assistants to
president*

Schools of choosing assistants to the president	Schools of chosen presidents			
	Public	*Private*	*Religious*	*Total*
Public	5	4	1	10
Private	1	10		11
Religious	2	1	7	10
TOTAL	8	15	8	31

When we examine the relative wealth and size of the institutions of choosers and chosen, we find some interesting, and related, patterns. Tables 17, 18, and 19 show for each group of respondents the numbers choosing the presidents of schools wealthier or poorer, and larger or smaller than their own. When we compare those results to those from the president group (Table 10), we find that academic officers (Table 17) have some tendency to choose wealthier school presidents, but they do not do so as strongly as the president group. Assistants to the president (Table 18) exhibit no clear preferences. Finally, the choices of business officers (Table 19) are related overwhelmingly to size.

TABLE 17
*Relative size
and wealth
of schools
of chosen
presidents and
choosing
academic
officers*

Size of chosen relative to choosing	Wealth of chosen relative to choosing		
	Greater	*Lesser*	*Total*
Larger	9	8	17
Smaller	12	7	19
TOTAL	21	15	36

TABLE 18
*Relative size
and wealth
of schools
of chosen
presidents and
choosing
assistants to
the president*

Size of chosen relative to choosing	Wealth of chosen relative to choosing		
	Greater	*Lesser*	*Total*
Larger	9	8	17
Smaller	4	10	14
TOTAL	13	18	31

	Wealth of chosen relative to choosing		
Size of chosen relative to choosing	Greater	Lesser	Total
Larger	9	15	24
Smaller	4	2	6
TOTAL	13	17	30

TABLE 19
Relative wealth and size of schools of chosen presidents and choosing business officers

The same respondents were also asked to cite evidence of their nominee's success. For each group we have calculated the estimated percentage of total mentions received by each of the 10 categories of evidence, as we did for the president in column 4 of Table 12. On the basis of these calculations we were able to plot Figures 3, 4, and 5, which allow us to compare the frequency with which the groups employed the different categories of evidence of success. Criteria mentioned with nearly equal frequency are plotted as points near the 45-degree line. Criteria receiving greater relative weight from one group fall proportionately farther from the line.[5]

Figure 3 presents the data for presidents and academic vice-presidents, deans of the college, or provosts. As might be expected, chief academic officers placed considerably greater stress on the educational program as evidence of presidential success than did presidents (or, for that matter, business officers or assistants to the president). Relative to academic officers, presidents laid greater weight upon quiet and respect of the outside community.

While presidents stressed growth more than did academic officers, they stressed it less than did business officers. Figure 4 shows the greater weight business affairs placed upon fiscal and growth criteria. Relative to business officers, presidents were more concerned with educational program, quiet, and faculty quality. Finally, presidents made less use than their assistants (Figure 5) of the criteria of fiscal contributions and quiet, while giving more attention to growth, faculty quality, educational program, and faculty relations.

Similarly, we can compare the major aspects of the presidency as seen by other officers and by the president. Table 20 shows the distribution of responses by assistants to the president, chief ac-

[5] The theoretical maximum frequency, with three types of evidence for each respondent, is 33⅓ percent. In practice the maximum is slightly higher, since, on average, respondents employed about 2.4 criteria per answer.

FIGURE 3 *Comparison of estimated percentage of mentions for different categories of evidence of presidential success, by presidents and academic officers*

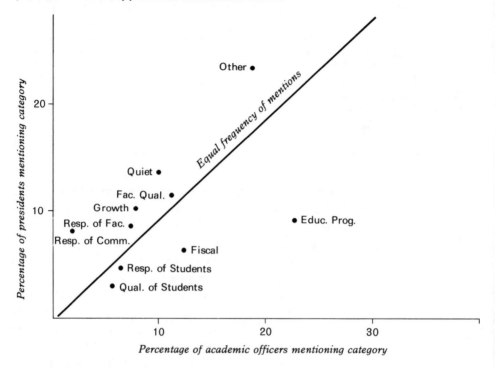

FIGURE 4 *Comparison of estimated percentage of mentions for different categories of evidence of presidential success, by presidents and business officers*

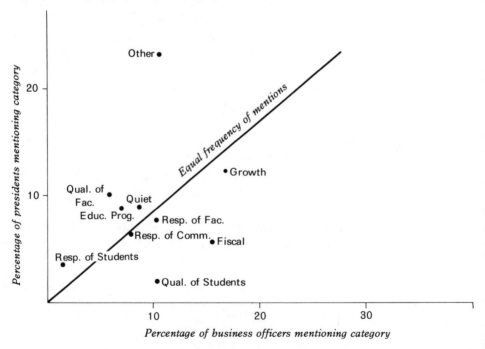

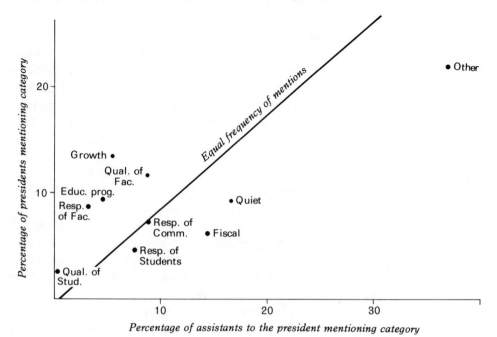

| Total respondents | | Aspect mentioned alone or in combination (excluding "other") | | | | | | Total mentions | |
| | | Personal | | Constituency | | Administrative | | | |
		Number	Per-centage	Number	Per-centage	Number	Per-centage	Number	Per-centage
Presidents	41	10	22	21	46	15	32	46	100
Academic officers	39	9	18	16	33	24	49	49	100
Business officers	35	14	31	16	36	15	33	45	100
Assistants to the president	28	11	26	16	38	15	36	42	100

53

ademic officers, and chief business officers with respect to their views of the major aspects of the college presidency. Presidents see the "political" aspects as central more often than do other respondents. Academic officers see the administrative aspects as more critical. These data are generally consistent with some other signs, which we will note below, that the chief academic officers see the presidency in more administrative terms than do other staff members.

We can summarize these comments on presidential success. College presidents themselves nominate as successful the presidents of schools which, relative to their own, are wealthier, larger, and somewhat more often private (rather than public or parochial). More than the other respondents, except for presidential assistants, they emphasized the maintenance of campus quiet as evidence of presidential success; and they tended to break down the presidency in constituency, or political, terms.

Relative to presidents, chief academic officers nominated as successful presidents individuals closer to home in terms of the type, wealth, and size of their institutions. They stressed educational program and fiscal matters more strongly and saw major aspects of the presidency more frequently along administrative-functional lines. Of all the groups, they were probably the most internal in their orientation to the presidency, less given to admiration of presidents of big or prestigious schools, the least likely to think of the presidency in response-to-pressure terms. Assistants to the president were generally similar to presidents in their choices, though their evidence of success more strongly emphasized the crisis areas of fiscal policy and campus quiet that tend to be their special concerns. Finally, business officers made consistently greater reference to the presidents of larger and public schools and relied on growth and fiscal criteria of success to a greater extent. They leaned toward what we have called an entrepreneurial view of the presidency.

Normative Images Held by Students

In the course of our visits to the 42 colleges, we also tried to collect student impressions of the presidency. At each campus in our sample we asked to have an informal meeting with the president of the student association, editor of the student paper, and members of important student committees. We were able to hold such meetings at 31 of the campuses visited. Members of the administration were not present at the meetings, which were usually held over lunch.

It should be emphasized that the student leaders whose opinions we report below have a vastly greater interest in, familiarity with, and influence upon the presidents of their schools than do most students. We are reporting, therefore, not average student opinion but something that might better be called an informal sample of effective student opinion.

To begin, we should say that images of the presidency held by these students probably had the greatest variance of any group to which we talked. Nonetheless, several important themes of the students' comments can be isolated:

- Student leaders think the presidency should be an activist, interventionist role. They do not see his role as properly limited to protecting the institution from outside forces, raising its money, and overseeing its housekeeping functions. They feel the president should intervene in its internal processes on behalf of the values *they* hold.

- A corollary of this view is a tendency to see presidents as excessively preoccupied with fund raising and the maintenance of relations with alumni and other outsiders.

- The presidents who are seen as successful are those who promote and embody the values students hold, those with whom students are able to identify to some degree.

These student leaders generally rejected all three of the familiar metaphors of leadership. They did not see the president as properly an administrator, largely because they rejected the legitimacy of a board of trustees as a controlling body. They did not see the president as properly a political leader, largely because they did not accept the legitimacy of some of the major constituency groups. They did not see the president as properly an entrepreneur, largely because the ideas of entrepreneurship and markets were quite distant from their view of educational organizations.

In one view common among these student leaders, the president was an instrument of virtue, some mixture of the independent judge and plebiscitary autocrat. The virtue of his actions legitimized his position. This moral perspective is a familiar part of student belief structure. It is also tactical. In a world in which the moral supremacy of the young is much more commonly acknowledged than is their political relevance, the practical dictates of comparative advantage encourage student leaders to accept a moralistic model of leadership; and a major instrument of co-optation is persuading them to accept a political metaphor of the university.[6]

Presidents generally viewed student conceptions of the proper role of the president as naïve or unreasonable, although often quite flattering in their perception of the importance of his position. The presidents who came closest to accepting the model of the presidency implicit in student leader arguments were not thereby assured of student support; presidents holding autocratic-moral models of leadership are not necessarily acceptable to students in political orientation.

We found a heavily symbolic mode of perceiving the presidency to be very widespread among student leaders, although there were enormous differences in the particular values currently uppermost in the minds of individuals on different campuses. At small religious colleges students often wanted the president to endorse symbolically their desire for a reduced influence of the religious community on the standards of student life. At larger schools the values that concerned them were often those made familiar by the mass media. Whatever the particular concerns of students may be, this symbolic approach to perception of the presidency leads directly to a desire to see the president take action expressing their values.

Normative Images of the Presidency —Trustees

Data from a 1968 survey by Morton A. Rauh of 5,180 trustees of public and private universities, colleges, and junior colleges[7] seem to indicate that trustees also display little consensus on what constitutes the core objectives of the presidency. Moreover, like the other groups we have examined, they tend to see his role in a mixture of political, entrepreneurial, administrative, and personal terms.

Trustees answered a series of questions on qualifications for the presidency. They were asked whether each of 10 potential attributes of a president was "absolutely essential," "important," "not

---

[6] We simply note here the obvious implication: students will become responsible members of the university as a *political* system only when they lose their clear moral supremacy. Democracy presumes moral equality.

[7] We would like to thank him for making available to us some marginal distributions from his survey responses. Readers interested in more detail on trustee opinions and characteristics should consult his *The Trusteeship of Colleges and Universities.*

important," or "undesirable." Table 21 shows the percentages responding "essential" and "important" and the total of the two percentages for the full sample and selected subsamples. (Two qualifications relevant only to religious schools have been omitted.) The data make it clear that many things are viewed as important presidential attributes, but none seem to evoke consensus as being essential. In particular, administrative experience is viewed as important by virtually all the respondents, but in no subsample are there more than 3 trustees out of 10 who will call it essential. It is the strongest performer of the set. All the others called forth even less agreement.

Trustees, as we shall see again below, are no more able to agree on a clear set of objectives for the presidency than are other groups. In this light it is more understandable that they should put relatively heavy weight on such diverse attributes as holding a Ph.D., having an unblemished personal record, or having faculty experience. These are indicators that the president is likely to hold values acceptable to trustees and to the major forces which they see him as having to reconcile. Trustees see relatively less of a president in action than do his office coworkers, and we might expect trustee evaluation of presidents to lean heavily on the values he embodies or seems to foster in his relatively public actions.

Normative Images of the Presidency — Summary Our examination of images of what the presidency *should be* indicates that there does not seem to be a clear core of objectives that presidents should pursue and, consequently, no clear set of attributes that will assure success. Neither is there a well-defined model of the presidential job. One can make numerous statements about what the presidency should be with which few will disagree. The difficulty is in finding propositions with some concrete relevance, propositions that actually exclude some possibilities and that also evoke some substantial agreement. There are many things that presidents should do or be, but none that most presidents, or most of any other group, see as taking clear priority. What priorities there are seem very likely to be unstable over time.

Among presidents and top administrative leaders in the universities, there is a tendency to define the role as some appropriate mix of political, administrative, and entrepreneurial activities, but the nature of the mix is badly specified and variable over time.

Particularly when we leave the "insiders" and turn to students,

Attributes	Total sample			Public 4-year colleges		
	a*	b†	a + b	a	b	a + b
Experience in college administration	24.7	65.6	90.3	25.0	63.0	88.0
Experience on college faculty	20.9	62.8	83.7	26.6	57.1	83.7
Holder of earned Ph.D.	15.5	48.2	63.7	21.2	48.9	70.1
Experience in high-level business management	2.6	42.7	45.3	3.3	42.4	45.7
Alumnus of the institution	0.2	4.4	4.6	1.1	3.8	4.9
Personal life free from "complications" (e.g., divorce)	13.8	56.9	70.7	14.1	55.4	69.5
Polished personal style	8.3	72.6	80.9	11.9	69.9	81.8
Contacts, the ability to raise funds	18.4	65.5	83.9	7.1	60.3	67.4
Number of trustees	5,180			184		

* a = "absolutely essential."
† b = "important."

trustees, and (presumably) faculty and members of the community, we discover greater disagreement and the addition of a relatively large "symbolic" component in the normative images of the presidency. Alumni, community leaders, students, trustees, and faculty evaluate the presidency largely in terms of the consistency of the values expressed through his more publicly visible actions with those values currently on their minds.

In the two decades following the Second World War, economic mobility, or the production of educated manpower and useful knowledge, seem to have dominated the interest in higher education of most groups. Under conditions of relatively plentiful resources, these ends were not inconsistent with each other, and all were apparently served by the strategy we have called organization building, leaving the president in the happy position of facing external norms for his role consistent with the criteria of the insiders with whom he did most of his work. More recently, when the value preoccupations of student, faculty, and community leaders have been less consistent, the situation of presidents has been less simple.

Private 4-year colleges			Public universities			Prestigious private colleges and universities		
a	b	a + b	a	b	a + b	a	b	a + b
21.6	68.0	89.6	29.7	62.7	92.4	15.3	70.0	85.3
18.9	64.2	83.1	21.7	63.6	85.3	17.3	67.6	84.9
16.3	48.7	65.0	19.6	48.4	68.0	12.0	44.9	56.9
3.2	43.5	46.7	1.9	44.2	46.1	1.1	26.4	27.5
0.1	4.1	4.2	0	2.3	2.3	0.2	10.2	10.4
15.9	56.6	72.5	5.3	59.4	64.7	7.3	47.6	54.9
8.7	72.4	81.1	8.4	76.0	84.4	4.2	67.8	72.0
23.4	66.3	89.7	7.4	64.4	71.8	16.4	68.7	85.1
	2,434			475			450	

According to his own beliefs and the beliefs of others around him the president should be an administrator, an entrepreneur, a political manager, and (in addition) should act virtuously. As we have noted, this is not necessarily a consistent set of demands. There is obviously potential for the inconsistency of specific behaviors. And there is also potential for inconsistency of styles and orientations to leadership. In particular, any model of the president as a relatively autonomous "moral leader" seems rather distant from the current conceptions held by presidents and their key staff associates of what a good president ought to be.

DESCRIPTIVE IMAGES OF THE PRESIDENCY   The distinction between normative and descriptive views of the presidency is not an easy one to maintain. Most of our presidential respondents accept their role and enjoy it. Their descriptions of the role are generally consistent with their norms for it. Other members of the organization also use terms to describe the presidency that are similar to the terms they use to describe its normative image. Only the relatively disaffected — some administrators, some student leaders, some members of the community—make sharp distinctions between the presidency as it exists and the presidency as it ought to be.

Presidents complain about the job. The dimensions of the complaints are well known. They object to both the time costs and the inconsistency of "unreasonable" demands on them. They object in various ways to the distribution of activities in which they find themselves engaged. They object to their limited career prospects; to the perceived irresponsibility of various groups within the academic community and surrounding it; to the loss of privacy; and to their lack of power.

Despite these complaints, there is substantial agreement among presidents on the major metaphorical dimensions of their jobs, and the metaphors they use are not much different from the metaphors we have discovered in describing their picture of what the role should be. They view the job primarily as a combination of the political leader and bureaucrat-entrepreneur. Although the data are not strictly comparable, agreement on what the role *is* appears to be somewhat greater than the agreement on what it *ought to be.* At the same time, there are interesting secondary differences among respondents.

Our primary data for exploring the descriptive images of the presidency come from a series of role-similarity judgments made by presidents, chief academic officers, chief business officers, assistants to the president, and presidential secretaries at schools in the 42-college sample. To provide some comparative data, the same task was also performed by two groups of business executives—one American and the other foreign.

The role-similarity judgment task is a simple (though somewhat tedious) one. The respondent is presented with a card on which is written the name of a common social role. For example, "Clergyman." Then he is given seven other cards each bearing the name of another common role. Specifically: "Bookkeeper," "Business executive," "College president," "Foreman," "Labor-management mediator," "Mayor," "Military commander." He is asked to arrange the seven roles in order of their similarity to the role of "clergyman." Then he does the same task taking each of the other roles as target (in each case ordering the seven remaining roles for similarity to the target role).

From these raw data it is possible to construct for each respon-

FIGURE 6 **A three-dimensional configuration of role similarities, by presidents**

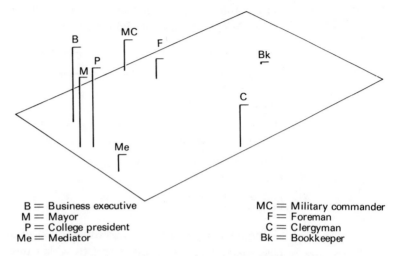

B = Business executive
M = Mayor
P = College president
Me = Mediator

MC = Military commander
F = Foreman
C = Clergyman
Bk = Bookkeeper

dent, and then for various groupings of respondents, a measure of the similarity perceived between each of the distinct 28 role pairs. Thus, we form a measure of the similarity seen between, for example, mediator and clergyman, military commander and business executive, mediator and business executive, and so on.[8]

Descriptive Images— Presidential Views A three-dimensional configuration that provides a good representation of the interrole similarities perceived by the presidents we interviewed is shown in Figure 6. This descriptive image shows the presidency in a tight similarity cluster with the roles of mayor and business executive. At some distance on one side are the roles

[8] This measure, which we will refer to as the source data, was in turn submitted to a multidimensional scaling problem. The program generated for each source data set a series of configurations of eight points, one representing each role, in spaces of various dimensionality. Each configuration has the property that the order of the distances between the various points represents as well as possible the order of perceived similarities among the roles as given by the source data. In a configuration in which this is achieved perfectly, the points representing the two most similar roles will lie closer together than any other pair of points. The next closest pair of points will correspond to the next most similar roles and so on, through the most dissimilar pair (in our case the 28th), which should lie farther apart than any other pair of points. There is, of course, no guarantee that such a representation will be possible in a small number of dimensions. A fuller discussion of the construction of our index of perceived similarity, details on multidimensional scaling, and remarks on measures of fidelity of the configurations to our source data (stress) will be found in Appendix B.

of mediator and clergyman, while foreman and military commander fall together on the other side. The role pairs involving the presidency from most to least similar were:

Role	Interpoint distances
President—mayor	0.172
President—business executive	0.345
President—mediator	1.307
President—clergyman	1.437
President—military commander	1.536
President—foreman	1.598
President—bookkeeper	2.495

The relatively small distances from president to mayor and business executive indicate the extent to which these two roles were seen as more similar to the presidency than the others. This is supported by analysis of the source data on perceived role similarity from which the multidimensional scaling configuration and interpoint distances were derived. Table 22 shows how frequently mayor and business executive were seen as most similar to the presidency in the source data from which the configuration was constructed.

The mayor role was seen as first or second most similar to the presidency by 34½ of our 39 respondents (there was a tie in the source data). This is an estimated 72 percent of the universe of

TABLE 22
Distribution of roles most similar and next most similar to that of president from the perceived similarity indices of 39 presidents, by percent

		Most similar to presidency			
		Mayor		Business executive	
Next most similar to presidency		*Actual response*	*Estimated response*	*Actual response*	*Estimated response*
Mayor				6.5	14
Business executive		11.5	19		
Other		13.5	27	1.5	7
	TOTAL	25	46	8	21

NOTE: See also Appendix A, "Procedures for Estimating Various Statistics for the Universe of Presidents."

presidents, where 28 percent would be expected by chance. Business executive was seen as first or second most similar by 21½ respondents, or an estimated 54 percent of all presidents. Presidents tended to agree on these key aspects of their descriptive images of the presidency.

The configuration of Figure 6 also clearly places the presidency near roles of higher social status and suggests an overall tendency to see it as slightly more similar to roles that could be called mediative than to those that could be called authoritative (i.e., clergyman and mediator rather than military commander or foreman).[9]

In conjunction with the agreement on the fundamental similarity between the role of college president and the roles of mayor and business executive, there was some disagreement among presidents on the "authoritativeness" of the presidency. We have divided our presidents into a *mediative* group and an *authoritative* group on the following basis: Those whose responses characterized the presidency as more similar than the median to mediator *and* less similar than the median to military commander were classed as holding a

[9] This tendency is probably even stronger in the universe of presidents than in the configuration, since in the source data on which the configuration was based, individual presidents' responses were not weighted to reflect the size of the class of schools each represented. Our examination of the data indicates few important subsample differences except (as we will show) for the inclination of smaller school presidents to view the presidency as more mediative. Thus the perceived mediativeness of the presidency is slightly masked in the configuration of Figure 6 and resulting distances.

Other		Total	
Actual response	*Estimated response*	*Actual response*	*Estimated response*
3	12	9.5	26
2	14	13.5	33
1	7	15	41
6	32	39	100

mediative view. Those characterizing the presidency as less similar than the median to mediator *and* more similar than the median to military commander were classified as holding an authoritative image of the president. Unclassified cases were allocated by a secondary criterion identical to this rule except for the substitution of clergyman for mediator and foreman for military commander. (For further details on the procedures see Appendix B.)

Table 23 shows the frequency of each type of view within our six subsample categories. It is clear that what we have identified as a somewhat more authoritative view of the presidency tends to be found most often in the larger institutions. The larger, more complex institutions tend to have presidents who see their roles as more directive. Thus, although virtually all our presidents made direct responses indicating great dissimilarity of the presidency and the roles of military commander or foreman, the source data index reveals an underlying secondary similarity in the response patterns of larger-school presidents.

	Wealth of school			
	Rich		Poor	
Size of school	Percentage	Number of presidents sampled	Percentage	Number of presidents sampled
Large	14	7	33	6
Medium	67	6	72	7
Small	80	5	72	7

TABLE 23 *Percent of mediative (rather than authoritative) views among college presidents*

The greater emphasis on mediative roles in small schools may be due in part to the small-school president's relatively smaller temporal, physical, and organizational distance from the faculty (or ministry). As the organizational pyramid beneath the presidents grows, presidents apparently come to emphasize the similarity of the presidency to more authoritative roles. We also believe that this difference among the presidents may be a function of organization and information costs. As we shall argue below, these increase more sharply with size for mediative than for authoritative presidential styles.

In Table 24 we give a collection of results that help to fill out the picture of the presidents holding more mediative images of the presidency. Presidents with a mediative view tend to have been in office longer, to hope for a subsequent job in academic administration rather than foundations or public service, to lay greater emphasis on the role of planning outside capital projects, to be more likely to describe meetings with subordinates as "advisory" and less likely to see them as making "formal" decisions, and, with reference to normative images of presidential success, to stress quiet and respect of faculty more heavily, while mentioning educational program less often. The data are too slim to examine the independent importance of these differences. Authoritative and mediative responses designate clusters of interrelated phenomena of presidential style, experience, attitude, and position.

TABLE 24 **Differences** **between** **presidents who** **view role in** **relatively** **authoritative** **terms and those** **who view role** **in relatively** **mediative terms**	*Presidential* *roles*	*Percentage of presidents* *with authoritative view** $N = 17\ddagger$	*Percentage of presidents* *with mediative view†* $N = 21\ddagger$
	Would like next job *to be public service* *or foundation*	29.4	4.8
	Would like next job *in academic adminis-* *tration*	17.6	38.1
	Say planning has *significant role out-* *side capital projects*	23.6	47.6
	Meetings with subor- *dinates are "advisory"*	29.4	47.6
	Meetings are "formal"	23.6	14.2
	Mention "quiet" as *success evidence*	17.6	28.6
	Mention "respect of *faculty" as success* *evidence*	11.8	19.0
	Mention "educational *program" as evidence* *of success*	23.5	9.6

* Average completed tenure of presidents with *authoritative* view is 5.41 years.
† Average completed tenure of presidents with *mediative* view is 7.14 years.
‡ N = number of presidents sampled.

Both the similarities and the differences in views of the presidency are important. On the one hand, it is clear that there is substantial agreement on the appropriate metaphors for describing presidents. They are politicians and executives. On the other hand, there are small but consistent differences among presidents in the extent to which they interpret those basic images in somewhat more mediative or somewhat more authoritative terms.

In Chapter 3 we outlined eight different possible metaphors (or models) for the governance of a college or university and sketched the kind of presidential leadership role that each seemed to entail. Now that we have examined some of the normative and descriptive images of the presidency held by occupants of the office, we can extract some implications from our data for five of those possible models. In particular, we can suggest a relationship between the size of a president's school and the likelihood that he will make use of a given model.

In their responses to our request for a list of the major aspects of the presidency, presidents of smaller schools had a greater tendency to view the role in constituency terms (a variant of what we called the democracy models), while larger-school presidents placed more weight on an administrative view (see Table 25). This provides some further support for our belief that the administrative model enlarges its influence at the expense of the democratic model as size of school increases.

The greater use of the growth criterion of success suggests that the model we called the competitive market, and its associated role of entrepreneur, may be more common in smaller schools. This is consistent as well with an argument we will make in Chapter 6 that in smaller schools the policy milieu within which a president must operate consists to a greater degree of markets and systems of market-like constraints, and is consistent with the data on presidential time allocation we will report in Chapter 7.

In our examination of similarity judgments we found that presidents of larger schools tend to see the presidential role as more similar to military commander or foreman and less similar to mediator or clergyman, while the opposite view prevailed in smaller

| | | Number mentioning aspect alone or | | | |
| | | Personal | | Constituency | |
Size of school	Total respondents	Number	Percentage	Number	Percentage
Large	13	2	20	3	30
Medium	14	5	33	8	54
Small	14	3	14	10	47
TOTAL	41	10	22	21	46

TABLE 25
Major aspects of the presidency as seen by presidents

institutions. We might infer from this that the model we have called collective bargaining, and consequently the presidential role of mediator, are more prevalent in smaller schools and give way as institutional size increases to a more authoritative role such as the one associated with the models we called administrative bureaucracy or plebiscitary autocracy, or to a simple recognition of the technical difficulties of collective bargaining where the groups are large and unorganized.

The three models (and associated presidential roles) that we have argued may be relatively more common in smaller schools are democracy (candidate), competitive markets (entrepreneur), and collective bargaining (mediator). All three of these models require a president who is successful in maintaining relatively high rates of contact with the members of the system being governed and reliable and fairly specific knowledge of their current preferences. In a small or homogeneous system these costs of organization and information may be moderate, but we would expect them to rise very sharply with increasing institutional size, much more sharply than the comparable costs under such models as administration or autocracy, which would seem to have a comparative advantage in larger systems.

Descriptive Images — Subordinates and Businessmen

We have used similar procedures to construct source data and generate configurations representing the perceived interrole similarities of six other groups of respondents: 34 academic vice-presidents, provosts, or deans of the college; 36 chief business officers; 29 assistants to the president; 42 presidential secretaries; 61 American businessmen participating in a summer program at the Stanford University School of Business; and 32 foreign business-

in combination		
Administrative		
Number	*Percentage*	*Total mentions*
5	50	10
2	13	15
8	39	21
15	32	46

men participating in the same program.[10]   Since our primary interest is in the differences among these groups, we will bypass displaying all the configurations and move directly to some comparisons of the interpoint distances within the respective spaces.

We may compare the interpoint distances for a particular point-pair in two different sets of responses. For example, we may compare the distance between the points representing president and business executive in the three-dimensional configuration generated from presidents' responses with the similar distance in the corresponding configuration derived from the responses of American businessmen. The procedure is possible because the distances are ratio scaled. Such an analysis shows a strong similarity of the configurations generated by presidents and businessmen, the only substantial difference between the two groups being their view of the mediator role. Presidents, relative to United States businessmen, see "mediator" as less similar to the presidency and more similar to the roles of clergyman and bookkeeper.

Figure 7 shows for each of the seven role-pairs involving the presidency the interpoint distances from the configurations based on the source data from four different groups of respondents: presidents, United States businessmen, academic officers, and business officers. The figure reveals two interesting patterns:

1   In all seven cases, whatever the difference between the perceptions of presidents and those of businessmen, the difference between presidents and campus business officers is in the same direction but larger. Proximity seems to magnify the differences in perceptions. This effect appears most clearly in the perceived similarity of the roles of president and business executive.

2   In five of the seven cases the views of the presidents fall between those of academic officers and businessmen, and therefore between academic officers and business officers.

These two regularities combine to give considerable structure to the relative views of the presidency held by the four groups.[11] In

---

[10] We wish to thank Professor H. J. Leavitt, whose patient cooperation made it possible for us to obtain the latter two data sets. Details on some differences in task administration for the business groups are in Appendix B.

[11] For any one role-pair the interpoint distances from the configurations of four groups could fall in any of 24 different orders, of which only two are consistent with the two regularities. The chance of any one such order is thus 1 in 12.

FIGURE 7 *Interpoint distances of presidency and other rules as seen by academic officers (A), presidents (P), United States businessmen (U), and business officers (B)*

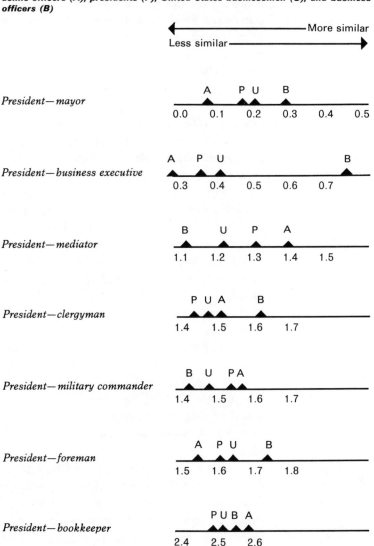

five of the seven cases we may talk about a continuum running from academic officers through presidents to businessmen and then business officers. The more "academic" the respondent, the more he sees the presidency as similar to the roles of mayor, business executive, and foreman. The less "academic" the respondent, the more the president is seen as being similar to mediator and military commander.

These intergroup differences would seem to arise from different sources than did the intragroup authoritativeness-mediativeness differences we discussed above. There we observed a size factor. Mediativeness was inversely related to distance from the lower levels of the organization. In the intergroup case, the differences observed seem to arise through comparison of the presidential role with previous experience. Judged against previous experience in the faculty, the presidency appears relatively authoritative to academic officers (nearer to business executive, mayor, and foreman, farther from mediator and clergyman). As we move through presidents, businessmen, and then business officers, we get increasingly heavier comparisons of the presidency with nonacademic experience. In the case of the business executives, the nonacademic experience is at a higher level in business (than that of the business officers) where the differences between mediator and business executive are somewhat more blurred. As a result, the college president is placed sharply away from business executive and also farther from mayor and foreman. He falls closer to mediator.

These intergroup differences are informative. In one interpretation they may even be said to reveal a slightly parochial quality in the academic view of the presidency. A more moderate interpretation comes to the conclusion that large-school presidents, who have debated the similarity of presidency to mediators (see Kerr, 1963), were likely to be a late group to notice the resemblance. The data seem to indicate that the similarity has been somewhat more widely sensed by small-school presidents and by nonpresidents.

Assistants to the president and secretaries also show strong tendencies, relative to presidents, to see the presidency as similar to the mediator role. In Figure 8 we have plotted the perceived similarity (configuration interpoint distances, with shorter distances more similar) of the presidency and the seven other roles. Each of three groups is shown relative to the perceptions of the presidents: secretaries (o), assistants to the president (+), and, for comparison, academic officers (•). The greater similarity to mediator and reduced similarity to business executive are marked. Once again it seems possible that this results from the relatively less academic experience of the groups of respondents.

The result seems also consistent with a relatively simple idea

FIGURE 8 *Interpoint distances of presidency and other roles as seen by presidents compared with academic officers, secretaries, and assistants to the president*

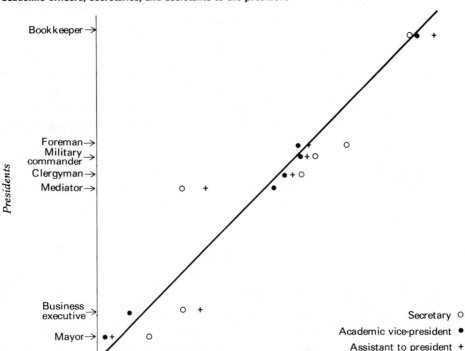

NOTE: As an example, the + in the upper right corner represents the comparison of the interpoint distances between the roles of president and bookkeeper in the configurations generated from similarity judgments by presidents and by assistants to the president. Assistants saw bookkeeper as farther from (less like) the presidency than did presidents.

of presidential behavior. Academic officers and business officers "see" different presidents. In interactions with his business officer, the president is necessarily somewhat less "business-oriented." He speaks for other dimensions and other concerns. In interactions between the president and his academic officer, the president is necessarily more "business-oriented," constraining the academic impulse with fiscal and business concerns. In this way, it is probably true that the president visible to the business officer (and to the assistant and secretary) is more a mediator than the president visible to the academic officer.

Throughout this section we have stressed the differences in perceptions of the presidency. We have been able to isolate some effects of background and position on those perceptions, and have found presidents' perceptions of their role to lie generally between those of academic and business officers.

Though these differences are useful in helping to understand the way perceptions of the presidency are shaped, we should point out that they are not large. In fact, the most striking aspect of our data on descriptive images of the presidency is not the differences but the overall similarity of the views held by the different groups. Table 26 shows a set of correlations relevant to this point. The set

TABLE 26
Correlations of descriptive images held by presidents with those of other groups

Descriptive images	Correlations
U.S. businessmen	.953
Academic officers	.942
Business officers	.912
Assistants to the president	.899
Foreign businessmen	.824
Secretaries	.814

is based on the 28 configuration interpoint distances for the president group and the 28 distances from configurations of the six other groups who did our similarity judgment task. They are generally quite high. Despite the differences among these groups, the overall level of agreement is impressive.

Descriptive Images— Students
We lack systematically comparable data on student perceptions of the presidency, but we can try to summarize the impressions gained in our interviewing, which we feel support three relevant observations:

1 Student leaders see the presidency as heavily oriented toward relations with the outside community.

2 Student leaders sometimes see the presidency as relatively independent and authoritative (i.e., able to cause things to be done).

3 Paradoxically, student leaders also see the presidency as merely an instrument of its various constituencies (faculty, donors, trustees, etc.).

The second point is, of course, the necessary condition of the normative student view that presidents should act morally and independently, but in a fashion consistent with the preferences of students. Since point 1 has often led to a belief that student opinions and preferences are not usually closely monitored by presidents, much student leader behavior seeks the redistribution of presidential attention fully as much as it is guided by specific policy considerations. In the late sixties such a redistribution seems to have occurred. Though we have little comparative data to support this judgment and president-student contact is not extraordinary (see Chapter 7), numerous presidents we interviewed said that, relative to a few years earlier, a larger share of their time was being spent in meetings and discussions with students and in attending to student concerns. Attitudes toward the change varied from regretful ("I can't get anything important done any more") to the view that the change was long overdue, but the opinion that such a change had taken place was quite widespread. From our analysis of the inherent instability of the allocation of presidential attention, however, it is problematic how deeply the concern has penetrated or how long the focus on student matters will last as other crises arise to claim attention.

As to the third point, it need not necessarily contradict the second. It could be that presidents are relatively free to act effectively in some situations and not in others, but this is not the analysis we heard in student interviews. Rather we found that students had what we might call an "everyone-else-is-an-interest-group" model of their colleges and universities. When action was consistent with their preferences, it was often viewed as independent and authoritative. When it was not, it was viewed as a response to constituency constraints.

Students are not the only ones who see everyone but themselves as an interest group. Many groups in college and university communities maintain this paradoxical perspective at least part of the time. It is related to the symbolic mode of perceiving presidential actions that we discussed above. It enables groups to see actions unfavorable to them as unfortunate necessities that need not be interpreted as personal endorsements by the president of the interests thus served, while favorable actions can still have enriched symbolic content. Though it is a bit self-righteous, this view of the world smooths organizational life, for it increases the value of winnings and reduces the bitterness of losses. To some extent it also helps to preserve the legitimacy and personal acceptance of the man in the middle. Certainly many of the student leaders with whom we talked used these dual premises to support a personal friendship with the president in parallel with a public assault.

Rauh's study (1969) of trustee opinion contained one question of interest in light of other findings on views of the presidency held by businessmen and business officers. Rauh's respondents were asked to react to the proposition that "Running a college is basically like running a business." In the total sample of trustees, 37.4 percent agreed strongly while 56.3 percent disagreed or disagreed strongly. Thus, it seems possible that trustees—some 35 to 40 percent of whom are businessmen—share the perspective on the presidency that we found among businessmen and business officers.

There are several other reasons why we might expect board members and business officers to have similar views of the presidency. One is the preoccupation of the two groups with similar questions. Rauh asked his trustee sample what decisions they were directly involved in. The most frequently mentioned were long-range planning (41 percent) and, after fund raising and choosing other trustees, physical master planning (34.2 percent). No aspect of educational program exceeded 9.4 percent. There is a clear concentration of trustee activity in areas close to the expertise of business officers. The relative closeness of business officers to boards is also borne out by our interview data on regular attendance at board meetings. We estimate that 68.8 percent of current business officers regularly attend board meetings. By comparison, only 45.8 percent of current academic officers are estimated to attend board meetings regularly. The president more often assumed the role of academic spokesman to the board.

Given their similar views of the presidency and their common interests, it is not surprising that the possibility of a special relationship between board members and business officers is a matter of frequent concern, both for presidents and for business officers. We were impressed at the number of business officers who wanted to emphasize in their interviews with us the care they took not to let their official and relatively frequent informal contact with board members undermine the president's position.

Our material on views of what the presidency is shows relatively high agreement. There are differences among presidents, particularly as a function of the size of the college. There are differences in the views held by different groups, with presidents themselves falling between academic officers and the more business-related groups: businessmen, business officers, and, perhaps, trustees.

But these differences, though informative in their directions, are not extremely large. Perhaps the most important thing to be observed about descriptive images held by the various groups we could measure (and probably trustees, as well) is that they all see the presidency as being most similar to the role of mayor and business executive, and as poised roughly midway between what we have called mediative and authoritative roles. In the frame of this consensus, there is variation both within the president group and between groups in the proximity of the presidency to the mediator role, and there is some disagreement about the nature and extent of presidential authority.

The college president sees himself and is seen by most people around him in the conventional terms of contemporary descriptions of social organization. The entrepreneur, the executive, and the politician are all familiar to the professional literature on complex organizations (although the entrepreneur is a little less conspicuous). Both the study of organizations and our culture give us experience, theory, ideology, and imagery for such roles.

IMAGES OF THE PRESIDENT IN THE PRESS

Presidents are nominally in the public eye. They symbolize an important social institution for the outside world. One complaint of colleges and universities during the late 1960s was over the level and kind of attention given to the colleges and their chief executives by the mass media. Most colleges and universities of any significant size maintain some kind of press-office function that is typically rather close to the president, both organizationally and physically. Press staff is maintained because a typical president believes that the public has an image of him and his institution and he wants that image to be as favorable as possible.

To examine the image of the presidency transmitted through the press, we undertook a systematic examination of newspaper reports of college presidents during the month of November 1969. The details of the sample and procedures are indicated in Appendix C. We considered the major local and major regional newspaper published in the area of each school in the sample and noted every article in every paper that mentioned any president of the sample schools.

The basic result of this search is a conspicuous one: Most presidents are nearly invisible. Newspapers cover a very small number of nationally conspicuous presidents fairly intensively, the presidents in their geographical region, unless they are national figures, sparsely, and all other presidents scarcely at all. Only 3 of the 41 presidents in our sample appeared in any out-of-state newspapers; only 8 appeared in newspapers from outside of their own region; only 12 appeared in anything other than their local newspaper; and 10 received no mention at all, not even in the local newspaper of the community in which the college was located. We cannot assume that November 1969 was a "typical" month. It seems likely that presidents are more visible in September and June than they are in November. We believe, however, that the hypothesis of presidential invisibility is very likely to be sustained by a more extended search of newspaper and other media coverage.

Some presidents receive considerable attention. The mean number of articles per president during the month is four; the median is only one. A handful of presidents account for much of the coverage. Figure 9 uses our standard procedures to estimate the pro-

FIGURE 9 *Proportion of presidents accounting for various proportions of newspaper coverage, November 1969*

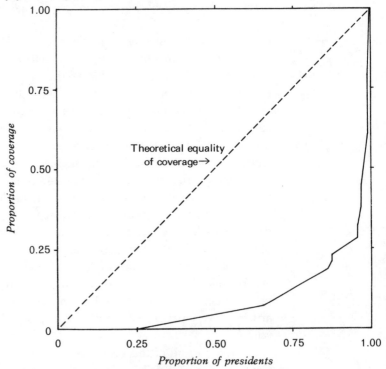

NOTE: These estimates are formed by weighting the observations in the sample according to the standard weighting scheme indicated in Appendix A, in order to make an estimate of the distribution in the universe of all American, four-year college and university presidents.

portion of presidents who account for various proportions of the coverage. If the observed proportions in Figure 9 fell on the broken line connecting the diagonally opposite corners, it would indicate that the coverage of presidents was equally distributed among presidents. The degree of deviation from that broken line is a measure of the concentration of attention from the press. As the figure indicates, we estimate that over half of the newspaper attention to college presidents involves less than 2 percent of the presidencies.

During the period we considered, public attention was overwhelmingly focused on a handful of large, poor, public institutions. Table 27 indicates the concentration. It shows the mean and median numbers of articles for presidents in our sample, classified by type of school involved. The specific schools receiving attention during the time period we considered (e.g., San Francisco State) were undoubtedly different from the specific schools that would be receiving prime attention in a different year, but the pattern of substantial invisibility for most presidents coupled with considerable attention to a few has probably characterized the coverage of presidents in recent years. As public interest in universities wanes, the effects will be more noticeable in the large, public institutions than in the great bulk of institutions that were never in the public eye anyway.

TABLE 27
Mean and median number of articles about presidents in local and regional newspapers, by size and wealth of school, November 1969

Size of schools	Relatively rich schools		Relatively poor schools	
	Mean	Median	Mean	Median
Large	3.6	2	12.7	6
Medium-sized	3.4	2	0.9	1
Small	1.5	1	1.6	1

Except for a handful of presidents, newspaper coverage is heavily ceremonial and specialized. Most presidents appear in newspapers as makers of speeches and announcements. They comment on the programs, progress, and problems of their own institutions. They appear as symbols of the institutions. Unless their schools are involved in some conspicuous controversy, they do not appear in the newspapers as individuals; nor do they often appear as general experts on social, political, or educational issues.

Although most of the reports in the press about presidents are not press releases, most of the coverage of most presidents apparently is. As nearly as we can determine, for 95 percent of the presidents (those with least visibility) about 60 percent of the newspaper articles are direct press releases from the institution. In effect, most press coverage of most presidents is written by the president's staff. For the other 5 percent of the presidents, press releases account directly for only about 25 percent of the coverage. As presidents move to the front pages of major newspapers, their direct control over the reporting declines considerably.

Though the data are not surprising, they lead to a conclusion that may be of some interest to presidents. The public image of a president, at least as derived through the media, is generally not based on any information about him. Rather it rests on inferences made from the coverage of a few highly visible men and extrapolation from conspicuous college events that receive heavy coverage. The president is rarely an important public figure; he is hardly a public figure at all—at least in the sense of penetrating the mass media.

Under these conditions it should not surprise presidents if they are unsuccessful in their efforts to shape an independent image. It seems to us that many presidents have already learned to live with a situation in which neither they nor their problems are really differentiated in the public mind from those of the conspicuous few presidents. Understandably, they wish that the conspicuous few included more comfortable, scholarly educational leaders and fewer harassed experts in confronting failure.

CONCLUSION   The images of the presidency and of university leadership that we find among presidents serve to confirm and support four major features of the recruitment filter indicated in Chapter 2. Each is, we believe, of some importance to our understanding of university leadership.

First, the presidency is *parochial.* The universe of all four-year colleges and universities in the United States is a possible object of study for investigators of American higher education, but it is not a reference group for American college presidents. Their reference groups are bounded by region of the country, by size of college, by type of college, and by wealth. Insofar as they cite explicit examples of successful colleagues, they are primarily colleagues at schools in the "neighborhood."

Second, the presidency is *honorific.* The status of a president is apparently less dependent on the quality of his tenure as president than it is on the quality of his school. Colleges make presidents, not the reverse. Few college presidents receive honorary degrees from schools of conspicuously higher status than their own.

Third, the presidency is *conventional.* The terms used to describe it are familiar constructs. They derive from shared beliefs, linked to available theories and ideologies of administration. The direct evidence available to presidents and others is interpreted in terms of the conventions. Where social interpretations change relatively rapidly (e.g., regarding the importance of research, students, quiet, etc.), so also do presidential interpretations. Where social interpretations are relatively stable (e.g., regarding the metaphors of governance), so are presidential interpretations. Presidents and those around them seem overwhelmingly to share the scholarly and tabloid interpretations of the president as a political leader-administrator-entrepreneur.

Fourth, the presidency is *heroic.* Whatever terms are used, the role is seen as an important one. The president is the man who acts, or guides, or decides, or supports, the man who is—in some sense or other—responsible for the institution. Both in their formal responses to questions and in their moods, presidents and others accept the centrality of the role in determining directions for the institution and for implementing those determinations through decision or negotiation.

A perceptive president is likely to be uncomfortable with his own characterization of the role. He is likely to feel that the metaphors of leadership fit the realities of his position rather poorly. Although we can identify processes familiar from markets, bureaucracies, and political democracies in colleges, none of those models seem to capture fully the character of higher educational institutions and their governance. However, uncertainty and discomfort do not necessarily lead to rejection of the conventional models. There is ample room for the ambiguous events of modern university life in almost any set of beliefs that might become accepted among presidents or students of the presidency. There is ample room in the presidential suite for a substantial separation of intellectual constructs from the everyday actions of presidential life. There is ample room in any man's pride for a commitment to heroic role requirements.

The images we have identified are defensible. They represent the plausible beliefs of intelligent people. They represent a reasonable version of the conventional wisdom of organization and administrative theory. If there is nothing particularly profound about them, neither is there anything profoundly wrong about them.

We believe, however, that these descriptive metaphors are somewhat misleading, that college presidents might properly question them as either uniquely accurate descriptions of modern universities or uniquely useful paradigms for leadership. In particular, we believe that they are incomplete descriptions of the processes of choice in university organization. To examine this possibility, we turn in the next two chapters to a consideration of some aspects of decision making in the university.

5. The Processes of Choice

When we look at universities as they struggle with the problems of reorganization, reform, choice, and survival, we are struck by one quite consistent theme: Decision opportunities are fundamentally ambiguous stimuli (Cohen, March, & Olsen, 1972).[1] Although organizations can often be viewed as vehicles for solving well-defined problems and as structures within which conflict is resolved through bargaining, they are also sets of procedures through which organizational participants arrive at an interpretation of what they are doing and what they have done while doing it. From this point of view, an organization is a collection of choices looking for problems, issues and feelings looking for decision situations in which they might be aired, solutions looking for issues to which they might be the answer, and decision makers looking for work.

Such a view of organizational choice focuses attention on the ways in which the meaning of choice changes over time. It calls attention to the strategic effects of timing (in the introduction of choices and problems), the time pattern of available energy, and the impact of organizational structure on these.

A key to understanding the processes within organizations is to view a choice opportunity[2] as a garbage can into which various problems and solutions are dumped by participants. The mix of garbage in a single can depends partly on the labels attached to the alternative cans; but it also depends on what garbage is being produced at the moment, on the mix of cans available, and on the speed with which garbage is collected and removed from the scene.

Although we may imagine that choice opportunities lead first to the generation of decision alternatives, then to an examination of the

[1] This chapter draws heavily on work we have done jointly with Johan Olsen.

[2] Choice opportunity may be defined as an occasion on which an organization is expected to produce a decision.

consequences of those alternatives, then to an examination of the consequences in terms of objectives, and finally to a decision, such a model is often a poor description of what actually happens. In a garbage can situation, a decision is an outcome (or an interpretation) of several relatively independent "streams" within an organization.

We will limit our attention to the interrelations among four such streams:

1 *Problems* Problems are the concern of people inside and outside the organization. They arise over issues of lifestyle; family; frustrations of work; careers; group relations within the organization; distribution of status, jobs, and money; ideology; or current crises of mankind as interpreted by the mass media or the nextdoor neighbor. All require attention. Problems are, however, distinct from choices; and they may not be resolved when choices are made.

2 *Solutions* A solution is somebody's product. A computer is not just a solution to a problem in payroll management, discovered when needed. It is an answer actively looking for a question. The creation of need is not a curiosity of the market in consumer products; it is a general phenomenon of processes of choice. Despite the dictum that you cannot find the answer until you have formulated the question well, you often do not know what the question is in organizational problem solving until you know the answer.

3 *Participants* Participants come and go. Since every entrance is an exit somewhere else, the distribution of entrances depends on the attributes of the choice being left as much as it does on the attributes of the new choice. Substantial variation in participation stems from other demands on the participants' time (rather than from features of the decision under study).

4 *Choice opportunities* These are occasions when an organization is expected to produce behavior that can be called a decision. Opportunities arise regularly, and any organization has ways of declaring an occasion for choice. Contracts must be signed; people hired, promoted, or fired; money spent; and responsibilities allocated.

Although not completely independent of each other, each of the streams can be viewed as independent and exogenous to the system. Attention will be concentrated here on examining the consequences of different rates and patterns of flows in each of the streams and different procedures for relating them.

The properties of universities as organized anarchies make the garbage can ideas particularly appropriate to an understanding of organizational choice within higher education. Although a college or university operates within the metaphor of the political system or a hierarchical bureaucracy, the actual operation of either is considerably attenuated by the ambiguity of college goals, by the lack of clarity in educational technology, and by the transient character of many participants. Insofar as a college is correctly described as an organized anarchy, a college president needs to understand the consequences of a garbage can decision process.

IMPLICATIONS OF THE IDEAS Elsewhere (Cohen, March, & Olsen, 1972) we have detailed the development of these basic ideas into a computer simulation model that has been run under conditions simulating a variety of different organizational structures. This garbage can model of choice operates under each of the hypothesized organization structures to assign problems and decision makers to choices, to determine the energy required and effective energy applied to choices, to make such choices and resolve such problems as the assignments and energies indicate are feasible.

For each run of the model we have computed five simple summary statistics to describe the process:

1 *Decision style* Within a garbage can process, decisions are made in three different ways:
   a By *oversight*. If a choice is activated when problems are attached to other choices and if there is energy available to make the new choice quickly, it will be made without any attention to existing problems and with a minimum of time and energy.
   b By *flight*. In some cases, choices are associated with problems (unsuccessfully) for some time until a choice "more attractive" to the problems comes along. The problems leave the choice, and thereby make it possible to make the decision. The decision resolves no problems (they having now attached themselves to a new choice).
   c By *resolution*. Some choices resolve problems after some period of working on them. The length of time may vary greatly (depending on the number of problems). This is the familiar case that is implicit in most discussion of choice within organizations.

Some choices involve both flight and resolution (i.e., some problems leave, the remainder are solved). We have defined these as resolution, thus slightly exaggerating the importance of that style. As a result of that convention, the three styles are mutually exclusive and exhaustive with respect to any one choice; but the same organization may use any one of them on different choices. Thus, we can describe the decision-making style of the organization by specifying the proportion of completed choices that are made in each of these three ways.

2 *Problem activity* We wish to find some measure of the degree to which problems are active within the organization. Such a measure should reflect something like the degree of conflict within the organization or the degree of articulation of problems. We have taken the number of time periods that each problem is active and attached to some choice, and added them together to obtain the total time periods for all problems.

3 *Problem latency* A problem may be active but not attached to any choice. It may be recognized and accepted by some part of the organization but may not be considered germane to any available choice. Presumably an organization with relatively high problem latency will exhibit somewhat different symptoms from one with low latency. We have measured problem latency by taking the total number of periods that each problem is active but not attached to a choice and added them together to obtain the total time periods for all problems.

4 *Decision-maker activity* To measure the degree of decision-maker activity in the system, we require some measure that reflects decision-maker energy expenditure, movement, and persistence. We have computed the total number of times that any decision maker shifts from one choice to another.

5 *Decision difficulty* We want to be able to characterize the ease with which a system makes decisions. Because of the way in which decisions can be made in the system (see the above discussion of decision style), that is not the same as the level of problem activity. We have used, as a measure, the total number of periods that each choice is active, and we added them together to obtain the total number of periods for all choices.

These summary statistics,[3] along with a more intensive look at the individual histories of the simulations, reveal eight major properties of garbage can decision processes.

First, resolution of problems is not the most common style for making decisions except under conditions where flight is severely restricted or under a few conditions of light load. In each of our cases there were 20 problems and 10 choices. Although the mean number of choices not made was only 1.0, the mean number of problems not solved was 12.3. Decision making by flight and oversight is a major feature of the process in general. The behavioral and normative implications of a decision process that appears to make choices in large part by the flight of problems or by oversight may be particularly important for university presidents to consider.

Second, the process is thoroughly and generally sensitive to variations in load. An increase in the net energy load on the system

[3] For a discussion of alternative measures, see Cohen, March, and Olsen (1972).

generally increases problem activity, decision-maker activity, decision difficulty, and the uses of flight and oversight. Problems are less likely to be solved, decision makers are likely to shift from one problem to another more frequently, choices are likely to take longer to make and to be less likely to resolve problems.

Third, decision makers and problems tend to *track* each other through choices. Both decision makers and problems tend to move together from choice to choice. As a result, decision makers may be expected to feel that they are always working on the same problems in somewhat different contexts, mostly without results. Problems, in a similar fashion, meet the same people wherever they go with the same result.

Fourth, there are some important interconnections among three key aspects of the "efficiency" of the decision processes we have specified. The first of these is problem activity—the amount of time unresolved problems are actively attached to choice situations. Problem activity is a rough measure of potential for decision conflict in the organization. It assesses the degree of involvement of problems in choices. The second aspect is problem latency—the amount of time that problems spend activated but not linked to choices. The third aspect is decision time—the persistence of choices. Presumably, a good organizational structure would keep both problem activity and problem latency low through rapid problem solution in its choices. In the garbage can process we never observe this. Some structures reduce the number of unresolved problems active in the organization but at the cost of increasing the latency period of problems and (in most cases) the time devoted to reaching decisions. Other structures decrease problem latency, but at the cost of increasing problem activity and decision time.

Fifth, the decision-making process is frequently sharply interactive. Although some phenomena associated with the garbage can are regular and flow through nearly all the cases (for example, the effect of overall load), other phenomena are much more dependent on the particular combination of structures involved. In fact, the process is one that often looks capricious to an observer. Many of the outcomes are produced by distinct consequences of the particular time phasing of choices, problems, and participant availability.

Sixth, important problems are more likely to be solved than unimportant ones. Early-arriving problems are more likely to be resolved than later ones. The system, in effect, produces a queue of problems in terms of their importance—to the strong disadvantage of late-arriving, relatively unimportant problems, particularly when load is heavy. This queue is the result of the operation of the model. It was not imposed as a direct assumption.

Seventh, important choices are much *less* likely to resolve prob-lems than are unimportant choices. Important choices are made by oversight and flight. Unimportant choices are made by resolution. The differences are substantial. Moreover, they are not connected to the entry times of the choices. We believe this property of important choices in a garbage can decision process can be naturally and directly related to the phenomenon in complex organizations of "important" choices that often appear to just "happen."

Eighth, although a large proportion of the choices are made, the choice failures that do occur are concentrated among the most important and least important choices. Choices of intermediate importance are virtually always made.

In a broad sense, these features of the decision-making process provide some clues to how organizations survive when they do not know what they are doing. Much of the process violates standard notions of how decisions ought to be made. But most of those notions are built on assumptions that cannot be met under the conditions we have specified. When objectives and technologies are unclear, organizations are charged to discover some alternative decision procedures that permit them to proceed without doing violence to the domains of participants or to their model of an organization. It is a difficult charge, to which the process we have described is a partial response.

At the same time, the details of the outcomes clearly depend on features of the organizational structure. The same garbage can process results in different behaviorial symptoms under different levels of load on the system or different designs of the structure of the organization. These differences raise the possibility of predicting variations in decision behavior in different organizations. In the next section we consider one possible application of such an approach to the domain of higher education.

GARBAGE CANS AND UNIVERSITIES Although there is great variability among colleges and universities, we think the model's major attributes have fairly general relevance to decision making in higher education. University decision making frequently does not "resolve" problems. Choices are likely to be made by flight or oversight. University decision processes appear to be sensitive to changes in load. Active decision makers and problems seem often to track one another through a series of choices without appreciable progress in solving problems. Important choices seem particularly likely not to solve problems.

What we see, both in the model and in actual observations of universities, are decisions whose interpretations continually change during the process of resolution. Problems, choices, and decision makers arrange and rearrange themselves. In the course of these arrangements the meaning of a choice can change several times—if the "meaning" of a choice is understood as the mix of problems that are discussed in the context of that choice.

Problems are often solved, but rarely by the choice to which they are first attached. A choice that might, under some circumstances, be made with little effort becomes an arena for many problems. As a result, it becomes almost impossible to make—until the problems drift off to another arena. The matching of problems, choices, and decision makers is partly controlled by content, "relevance," and competence; but it is also quite sensitive to timing, the particular combinations of current garbage cans, and the overall load on the system.

In order to consider a more specific application of the model, we have attempted to examine the events associated with one kind of adversity within organizations—the reduction of organizational slack.

Slack is the difference between the resources of the organization and the combination of demands made on it. Thus, it is sensitive to two major factors: (1) the money and other resources provided to the organization by the external environment; and (2) the consistency of the demands made on the organization by participants. It is commonly believed that organizational slack has been reduced rather substantially within American colleges and universities over the past few years. If we can establish some possible relations between changes in organizational slack and the key structural variables within the model, we should be able to show the consequences of slack reduction in a garbage can decision-making process.

Elsewhere (Cohen, March, & Olsen, 1972) we have outlined ways in which we can tie the variable in the model to some features (particularly size and wealth) of universities. With this specification, we can use the garbage can model to predict the differences we would expect to observe among several types of schools. The results with respect to our five basic outcome statistics can be found in Table 28. They suggest that under conditions of prosperity, as we have defined them, overt conflict (problem activity) will be substantially higher in poor schools than in rich ones, and decision time will be substantially longer. Large, rich schools will be characterized by a high degree of problem latency. Most decisions will resolve some problems.

Table 28 also shows the effects of adversity on our four types of schools according to the garbage can model. By examining the first stage of adversity, some possible reasons for discontent among presidents of large, rich schools can be seen. In relation to other schools they are not seriously disadvantaged. The large, rich schools have a moderate level of problem activity, a moderate level of decision by resolution. In relation to their earlier state, however, large, rich schools are certainly deprived. Problem activity and decision time have increased greatly; the proportion of decisions which resolve problems has decreased from 68 percent to 21 per-

TABLE 28   *Effects of adversity on four types of colleges and universities operating within a garbage can decision process*

Type of school/ type of situation	Outcome				
	Decision-style proportion resolution	Problem activity	Problem latency	Decision-maker activity	Decision time
Large, rich universities					
Good times	0.68	0	154	100	0
Bad times, early	0.21	210	23	58	34
Bad times, late	0.65	57	60	66	14
Large, poor universities					
Good times	0.38	210	25	66	31
Bad times, early	0.24	248	32	55	38
Bad times, late	0.31	200	30	58	28
Small, rich colleges					
Good times	1.0	0	0	100	0
Bad times, early	0	310	0	90	20
Bad times, late	1.0	0	0	100	0
Small, poor colleges					
Good times	0.54	158	127	15	83
Bad times, early	0.61	101	148	73	52
Bad times, late	0.62	78	151	76	39

cent; administrators are less able to move around from one decision to another. In all these terms, the relative deprivation of the presidents of large, rich schools is much greater, in the early stages of adversity, than that of administrators in other schools.

The large, poor schools are in the worst absolute position under adversity. They have a high level of problem activity, a substantial decision time,[4] a low level of decision-maker mobility, and a low proportion of decisions being made by resolution. But along most of these dimensions, the change has been less for them.

The small, rich schools experience a large increase in problem activity, an increase in decision time, and a decrease in the proportion of decisions by resolution as adversity begins. The small, poor schools seem to move in a direction counter to the trends in the other three groups. Decision style is little affected by the onset of slack reduction, problem activity, and decision time decline; and decision-maker mobility increases. Presidents of such organizations might feel a sense of success in their efforts to tighten up the organization in response to resource contraction.

The application of the model to this particular situation among American colleges and universities clearly depends upon a large number of assumptions. Nevertheless, the derivations from the

---

[4] We have some indirect supporting evidence of an unobtrusive sort. Our original letter requesting cooperation in our studies was mailed to all 42 colleges at the same time. We have recorded the number of days later that an answer was dated in the responding president's office. Since the letters were all mailed (airmail) from California, some of the variation in response time was a function of variation in the time required to deliver the original letter. Most, however, is due to "processing" time in the college or university involved. Forty-one of the 42 colleges responded. The mean and median number of days required for a response from these 41 are shown below for each type of school:

Type of school	Rich		Poor	
	Mean	Median	Mean	Median
Large	20.6	20	44.8	42
Medium	16.3	15	24.7	17
Small	24.1	16	32.9	21

Response times are impressively slow (they ranged from 1 to 78 days), but slowest of all among the large, poor institutions. We might observe also that the one institution from which no reply was received was a large, poor one. The fastest response was from a "president" who reported that since our source book was published his college had gone out of business.

model have some face validity as description of some aspects of recent life in American higher education.

The model also makes some predictions of future developments. As adversity continues, the model predicts that all schools, and particularly rich schools, will experience improvement in their position. Among large, rich schools decision by resolution triples, problem activity is cut by almost three-fourths, and decision time is cut more than one-half. Small, rich schools return to the performance levels of good times. If the model has validity, a series of articles in the magazines of the next decade detailing how President X assumed the presidency of rich school Y and guided it to peace and progress (short decision time, decisions without problems, low problem activity) can be expected.

CONCLUSION   We have tried to translate a set of observations made in the study of some university organizations into a model of decision making in what we have called organized anarchies—that is, in situations which do not meet the conditions for more classical models of decision making in some or all of three important ways: preferences are problematic, technology is unclear, or participation is fluid. The garbage can process, as it has been observed, is one in which problems, solutions, and participants move from one choice opportunity to another in such a way that the nature of the choice, the time it takes, and the problems it solves all depend on a relatively complicated intermeshing of the mix of choices available at any one time, the mix of problems that have access to the organization, the mix of solutions looking for problems, and the outside demands on the decision makers.

A major feature of the garbage can process is the partial decoupling of problems and choices. Although we think of decision making as a process for solving problems, that is often not what happens. Problems are worked upon in the context of some choice, but choices are made only when the shifting combinations of problems, solutions, and decision makers happen to make action possible. Quite commonly this is after problems have left a given choice arena or before they have discovered it (decisions by flight or oversight).

Though the specification of the model is quite simple, the interaction within it is rather complex, so that investigation of the probable behavior of a system fully characterized by the garbage can process and our specifications requires computer simulation.

We acknowledge immediately that no real system can be fully characterized in this way. Nonetheless, the simulated organizations exhibit behaviors that can be observed some of the time in almost all organizations and frequently in some, such as universities. The garbage can model is a possible step toward seeing the systematic interrelatedness of organizational phenomena that are familiar, even common, but that have generally been regarded as isolated and pathological. Measured against a conventional normative model of rational choice, the garbage can process does seem pathological, but such standards are not really appropriate since the process occurs precisely when the preconditions of more "normal" rational models are not met.

It is clear that the garbage can process does not do a particularly good job of resolving problems. But it does enable choices to be made and problems sometimes to be resolved even when the organization is plagued with goal ambiguity and conflict, with poorly understood problems that wander in and out of the system, with a variable environment, and with decision makers who may have other things on their minds. This is no mean achievement.

We would argue that there is a large class of significant situations within universities in which the preconditions of the garbage can process probably cannot be eliminated. Indeed in some, such as pure research, they should not be eliminated. The great advantage of trying to see garbage can phenomena together as a process is the possibility that that process can be understood, that organization design and decision making can take account of its existence, and that, to some extent, it can be managed.

6. The Logic of Choice in American Colleges and Universities

As we have indicated in Chapter 5, the opportunities for choice in a university become complex garbage cans of issues. Debate over the hiring of a football coach can become a debate over the essence of a liberal education. As we have also seen, however, the garbage can is largely a model of argumentation, not of decision making. The manifest processes of choice are procedures for exercising problems as much as for solving them. The argumentation or exercise of problems often has an effect. It helps form the normative background against which individuals and groups act. It is part of the record. But there is more to choice than argumentation. We require a further look at the underlying logic of decision in universities.

Any such examination is, of course, subject to gross overgeneralization. It is quite unlikely that New York University or the University of Illinois will operate in the same way as Ripon College or California Lutheran College. Size and wealth make substantial differences. Such an examination is also subject to simple error. The search for the "real" decision logic is a difficult and often dubious activity, typically contaminated with ideological mythology.

Without denying these problems, we want to try to describe our impressions of the ways in which decision outcomes are produced in some key areas of university internal governance, and particularly our impressions of the presidential role in them. We have based those impressions on the data available to us from the literature and from our interviews.

Specifically, we will consider four domains of decisions that presidents and others agree are important within a modern American college:

1 *The operating budget* The distribution of financial resources among the departments.

2 *Educational policy decisions*   The establishment of curricula and academic organization.

3 *Academic tenure decisions*   The granting of indefinite tenure to individual academic personnel.

4 *Planning*   The development of long-run plans for capital expenditures, academic development, and institutional growth.

As we have seen in Chapter 4, presidents consider fiscal matters, educational policy, and the quality of academic personnel important aspects of their success. Planning is traditionally an important function of executive leadership. These four domains do not include all the decisions made within the university or college that might concern the president. Indeed, some presidents probably devote at least as much time to landscaping and parking. But the four domains are easily recognized by students of colleges as some of the more important activities of educational governance.

Our descriptions of the underlying patterns of decision making in each of these domains are based on our interviews with presidents, chief academic officers (i.e., academic vice-presidents, deans of the college, etc.), chief business and financial officers (i.e., business and financial vice-presidents, treasurers, business managers), and assistants to the president. These interviews were made in our basic 42-school sample and included 41 presidents, 39 chief academic officers, 36 chief business and financial officers, and 28 assistants to the president.

We asked these respondents to describe briefly the processes involved in making operating budgets, academic policy, and academic personnel decisions. We asked them to characterize the long-run plan in the college, what it covered, and how it was developed. We asked them to focus particularly on the role of the president in these activities. The summary descriptions that follow are based primarily on the responses we received.[1]

THE OPERATING BUDGET   Virtually all presidents participate in establishing the annual operating budget. Some presidents go beyond that stage into more active continuing management, but most do not. Thus, by focusing on the annual budget, we capture most of the presidential involvement in operating budget activities.

[1] We are indebted particularly to Nancy Block and Jackie Fry for their work in listening to the taped responses and providing summaries and transcripts of those responses to control our faulty memories.

The operating budget in American colleges and universities can be described in terms of three fundamental accounting flows:

1 The *enrollment cycle* flow. The rate and pattern of enrollment in the college and in the departments depend on the educational program in the school, its reputation, its competitors, and the level of demand for education relative to the supply. Resources come to the university because of the student enrollment. In private universities the main flow is normally through direct tuition charges to the students and their families. Secondary flows from families (donations) and sometimes legislatures (subsidies) depend largely on maintaining or increasing student enrollment. In public colleges and universities the main flow is from legislatures reacting to the number of students enrolled, with secondary flows from tuition and federal subsidies. Resources coming to the university from the student enrollment flow are then distributed by the university to the departments in the operating budget.

2 The *institutional reputation* flow. Presidents and others seek support for the institution from outside agencies. They claim certain properties for the institution (e.g., age, prestige, innovativeness, poverty, uniqueness) as justification for support; or they offer to provide such properties if given the support. Resources come to the school as a function of the cogency of its appeal and the availability of outside resources. The outside agencies include foundations, legislatures, and major donors. Through the magic of endowment, current administrations reap the benefits of past reputations. These resources are then distributed to the departments in the operating budget.

3 The *research reputation* flow. Departments, laboratories, institutes, and individual research workers solicit funds from research support institutions. These are primarily institutions of the federal government (e.g., National Institutes of Health, National Science Foundation, National Aeronautics and Space Administration, the several cabinet-level departments). To a lesser extent they are private foundations (e.g., Ford Foundation, Carnegie Corporation, Sloan Foundation, Rockefeller Foundation). The size of the flow depends on the availability of resources within the particular domain of the department and on the nationally recognized research strength of the department or individual research worker. The resources come directly to the research group, with a fraction flowing to the university generally as overhead.

These three major flows are shown in Figure 10. We have emphasized them as accounting flows because we think the president's role in operating budget decision making is strongly conditioned by the mundane relationship between income and expenditure (see

FIGURE 10 *Major accounting flows determining operating budgets in American colleges and universities*

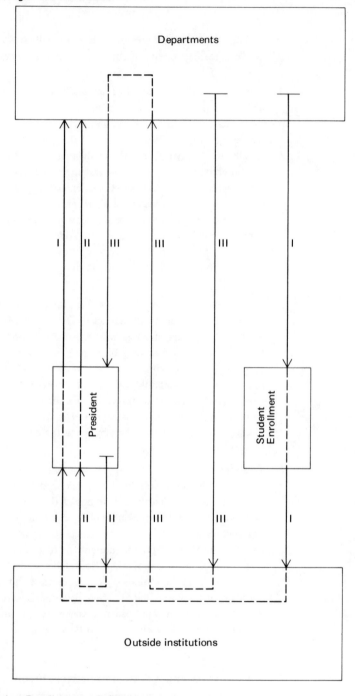

I = Enrollment cycle flow
II = Institutional reputation flow
III = Research reputation flow

Simon, 1967). That fact has been somewhat obscured by the traditions of governmental budgeting with respect to public institutions of higher education. Within those traditions it sometimes appears that income is an "act of God"—or at least of legislatures. But the administrators with whom we talked were quite aware that legislators were de facto parents and that at least 90 percent of the public operating budget is determined by the student enrollment and by some standard formulas, that is to say, by implicit tuition charges.

The dynamics of the flows are such that they substantially restrict presidential influence over the main thrust of the operating budget. Consider first the *enrollment cycle.* We observed two major styles of dealing with income received from student enrollment: (1) direct payment of the tuition or some major fraction of it to the department or school involved; (2) payment to the college and then reallocation on some basis to the departments. Since the departments control enrollments (through the classic departmental control over academic "pricing"—curriculum requirements, grading, and teaching formats), it is hard to see how there can be any really significant difference between the two alternatives in the long run. Control over departmental enrollments gives the departments enormous leverage in the internal bargaining.

The bargaining leverage is attenuated, however, under certain conditions. For example, if the demand for education within the college is strong, and if the amount of teaching delivered per unit of resources is fixed, the flow of resources can be used to influence the flow of enrollment. *If* a president can increase the number of faculty in a department, and *if* that increase does not change the average teaching productivity in the department, he can produce a redistribution of enrollment within the college without changing the overall enrollment. The internal reallocation of resources modifies the implicit prices (e.g., the teacher-student ratio or degree requirements) charged by the various departments in the direction of lowering the prices in the favored departments. If a strong demand for education in the college assures that "outside" competition will not be able to take advantage of the new internal prices, some students will shift from one department to another. Thus, the enrollment flow is brought into equilibrium at a new position determined by the arbitrary reallocation of resources.

The restrictions are rather severe, however. On the one hand, most colleges cannot presume the unconditional student enthusiasm that makes external competition with respect to programs largely irrelevant. On the other hand, among those colleges with strong student demand, only a handful can assume that an increase in resources for a given department will lead that department to increase its attractiveness to students (rather than the obvious alternative of increasing its attractiveness to faculty—for example, by reducing teaching load).

A second attenuation of the bargaining leverage of departments on enrollment occurs in choices between departments that are largely interchangeable from the point of view of student demand. We suspect that the total student demand for courses in sociology and social psychology is more stable than the demand for either one of them, that the total student demand for courses in English and comparative literature is more stable than the demand for either one of them. Waves of students shift fairly easily from one to another as the number of courses offered, the size of classes, and the popularity of teachers change. As a result, it is easier to use a short-run arbitrary flow of resources to increase English enrollment at the expense of comparative literature (and thus to make a stable shift in relative emphasis) than it is to induce a stable shift from physics to English. In this respect, an organization with a large number of departments works in favor of presidential influence.

A third attenuation of departmental leverage is the frequent inability of academic departments to act strategically—particularly during periods of relatively strong outside demand for faculty. In order to use the enrollment cycle as a bargaining device, the department must be prepared to endure some short-run dislocations. It must be prepared to increase enrollment systematically to produce future resources, a procedure that requires coordination within the department and a willingness to incur current costs in anticipation of future benefits. A heavy turnover in faculty makes such a strategy difficult to adopt, since the benefits are unlikely to be realized by the faculty bearing the costs.

In general, the student enrollment flow provides the president with little flexibility. He must, for the most part, ratify the market and approve the allocation of resources in the way dictated by enrollment. He may make marginal variations in that pattern. He may occasionally help to get a new department started. He may, under some conditions, intervene in such a way as to affect demand—for example, by encouraging reduction of requirements so that (under "free trade") a new distribution of enrollment might emerge. He may be able to exploit the difficulties departments have in looking more than one year ahead. With some understanding of the system, in fact, he can probably do more than most academic administrators do. But he acts within a rather tight set of constraints.

The *institutional reputation* flow is a direct contrast with the enrollment cycle. First, it is minor for most institutions. Second, it is the flow most subject to presidential influence. Third, it has a much less dynamic character.

Operating budget resources from the institutional reputation flow (along with their close cousin, the endowment) are minor factors in the budget of most American colleges and universities. However, even at schools at which such resources are quite minor, presidents tend to view them as very important. They are the resources that give the president the greatest sense of control over expenditure. Along with endowment income, they tend to be "his" resources.[2] As the obvious spokesman for the whole institution, the president receives them. Although they are frequently received with commitments on their use, some fraction of them are "free," and some fraction of the committed resources go into already budgeted activities and thereby free other funds.

The relative stability of the institutional reputation flow stems from a long lag in the process. The pattern of expenditures undoubtedly affects the magnitude of the flow, but rarely within the tenure of one president. Changes in the institutional reputation of a college and university attributable to one president normally affect the flow of resources to a subsequent one. In the norrral tenure of a president, the major opportunity for increasing the flow is through merchandising the college, through persuading outside institutions that the college is better than is currently believed or that it might become better. Presidents do that and some have their successes; but it is hard to look at the statistics on endowment over time without concluding that the institutional reputations of American colleges and universities change a good deal more slowly than do their presidents.

Internally, of course, the small size of the short-run effects of presidential action on presidential resources through the institu-

---

[2] At some of the best-endowed universities, endowments flow directly to the subunits in the university rather than to the president. Although those presidents tend to be enthusiastic about the "each ship on its own bottom" ideology, they are also aware of their substantial irrelevance to the expenditures stemming from such independent sources.

tional reputation flow increases presidential independence. Within rather wide boundaries the institutional reputation operating funds can be distributed arbitrarily without affecting the flow of those funds in the succeeding few years. Such a result stems, in large part, from the basic ambiguity within a college of objectives and technology, which can make almost any course of action plausible.

This does not mean that presidents can be capricious. There are other influences on their behavior, and more claims on the money than there is money. In fact, with ambiguous criteria and slow feedback, we might reasonably predict that presidents and other administrators would turn heavily to *social* validation of their resource allocation decisions. A pattern of expenditures becomes legitimate because a large group of people believe it is legitimate. Despite the fact that the intrinsic constraints are weak—indeed because of that fact—presidential behavior is remarkably uniform.

The *research reputation* flow has been the subject of considerable investigation and grief over the past few years. Like the institutional reputation flow, the research reputation flow is a small one for most colleges. Where it does exist, the president is characteristically a minor figure. He does not initiate proposals. He rarely intervenes in them; indeed, he rarely sees them. The presidents with whom we talked did not view themselves as having any significant year-to-year control over that part of the operating budget. Some wished they might have such control but did not view it as a serious possibility except through the "bloc grant" proposals that were gaining some popularity in granting agencies and Congress prior to the major slow-down in the growth of research funds in the late 1960s. The enthusiasm of presidents for institutional grant funding is well documented in the recommendations of such bodies as the Association of Land Grant Colleges, which are technically associations of colleges but actually associations of college presidents.

Not only is the flow outside the control of the president, it is also leverage for others on funds under his control. Outstanding faculty at major institutions control substantial resources directly through research grants; they can and do use that control and the threat of departure (with consequent loss of funds and reputation) as a device for influencing the allocation of other resources. In recent years at major universities the teaching load in physics has very rarely been as great as the teaching load in French.

This research reputation flow is of critical importance to the president of any large, well-known American university. It represents a substantial part of his annual operating budget. It is a basis for attracting and retaining high-quality faculty. It is a primary sign of success as a president. In many terms that the president recognizes as valid, major research grant recipients have higher status than do presidents within the academic community.

The annual operating budget is largely determined by these three flows. But the impact is not the same in all colleges. In fact, we think we can characterize most American colleges and universities rather simply in terms of the extent to which their operating budget depends on the three flows. We will identify four basic budgeting types.

Type A is the university for which the enrollment cycle is relatively unimportant. For most purposes these universities draw upon the institutional reputation and research reputation flows in order to develop their budgets. Income from students is significant, but the colleges are largely shielded from the consequences of enrollment demand by the strong general demand for attendance. Basically, these are the prestigious private universities of the United States, representing about 1 percent of the four-year colleges and universities in the country. In terms of numbers this is clearly an insignificant group. In terms of reputation it includes the giants of American private education.

Type B is the university that relies heavily on both the enrollment flow and the research reputation flow with little (or substantially less) coming from the institutional reputation. These are the major public universities and some private universities in the United States. They represent a major locus of growth in American higher education in the period from 1950 to 1965.

Type C is the college for which research reputation is relatively unimportant. These are the prestigious, small colleges in the United States. Their budgets rely heavily on income from the enrollment cycle and on institutional support and endowment. In terms of numbers of schools and numbers of students, this type is not very common, but it includes the best-known private, liberal arts colleges in the country.

Type D is the college or university for which the enrollment cycle accounts for virtually all the income and operating budget allocations. This is the mean, mode, and median of American higher education. It includes most of the schools and most of the students. In these schools the enrollment market dominates budgeting. Sometimes, for some of them, the demand for education has served to blunt the obviousness of the "customer"; but for most of them most of the time, the budgeting problem is one of finding a set of allocations that produces an educational program that attracts enough enrollment to provide the allocations.

Table 29 shows our estimates of where these types of schools are found in our sixfold division of colleges and universities. What this and our earlier remarks may suggest is the awkwardness of talking about governance at all. Insofar as large parts of the budget —for example, research budgetary items—are not so much decisions as collections of independent agreements assembled for the convenience of the accountants into a common document, we need to reconsider the meaning of decision in a university context. Insofar as other large parts of the budget are embedded in the long-run complications of the enrollment cycle, we need to describe a process that is heavily constrained by "market" factors.

We are also left with some possible interpretations of the problems of budgetary control confronting American college presidents. In particular, we should note:

1 Strong research reputation in the faculty makes weak budget presidents. On the whole, that means that most of the better-known academic institutions will have "weaker" presidents than the less-known institutions.

2 Prestige in the institution makes weak students. Where the demand for entrance is strong, the policy-making force of the enrollment cycle is blunted.[3]

3 Public universities make weak budget presidents. The president of a public university must simultaneously negotiate the appropriations for his operating budget from the legislature or some intervening body and negotiate the allocation of that budget among his departments. The simultaneity and public character of those two negotiations restrict him seriously.

In general, the operating budget of an American university is heavily constrained by accounting procedures, particularly the very elementary requirements of the enrollment cycle. As a result, there are many things that a president cannot do. The presidents with whom we talked were aware of this, particularly within Type

[3] There are many interpretations of the strong positive correlation between prestige of an institution and student unrest. Most of them, correctly in our view, stress factors that have rather little to do with conditions on the campus except as a pretext. We wish simply to add the observation that a school that has 10 outstanding applicants for every place in the freshman class is unlikely to feel enrollment cycle pressure to be attentive to student needs or desires.

	Type	
Size of school	Relatively rich	Relatively poor
Large	A	B
	B	D
Medium	A	D
	B	
	C	
	D	
Small	C	D
	D	

D schools. At the same time, presidents seemed to be somewhat less aware of, or somewhat less interested in, the flexibility the system did offer them. As long as the constraints were met, there was the potential for rather substantial discretionary action. For example, we suspect that many presidents fail or are not willing to distinguish sharply the shifts in the operating budget that will disturb the *total* enrollment from the shifts that will disturb only the internal allocation of that total enrollment. The former are problems; the latter are opportunities.

EDUCATIONAL POLICY DECISIONS

By training, background, and basic commitment, college presidents are academic in orientation. It is natural, therefore, that presidents should have a special concern with academic policy decisions. Most presidents take pride in the academic program of their school and see themselves as performing an important supportive role with respect to that program. They accept credit for new programs and recent changes that they have initiated or supported.

For the most part, however, and particularly in the larger schools, presidents do not appear to have much to say about academic policy. Indeed, the term "policy" is probably somewhat misleading if it conveys a notion of systematic collective decision making. The set of activities that are subsumed under the general term "academic policy" are the organization of academic departments, the organization of the educational program, degree requirements and alternatives, courses and course assignments, and patterns of student education. To describe these as resulting from anything approximating high-level decisions based on policy would be wrong. Presidents and their chief academic subordinates concede that much of the structure of academic policy is determined in the individual departments—realistically, often in the individual classroom.

Formally, academic policy is almost always portrayed as the responsibility of the faculty. By the standard academic constitution, the faculty is granted control over degrees and educational programs. The traditions of faculty control are embedded deeply in the culture of academe. Except in some minor ways, college presidents show little desire to question that tradition. They accept the mythology of "the faculty" even when the size of the institution clearly makes talking about "the faculty" no more sensible than talking about "the students."

At the same time, the presidents recognize that even in a small, liberal arts college the collective decisions of the faculty rarely do more than condition slightly and ratify the actions of the departments and individual teachers. Academic "policy" is the accretion of hundreds of largely autonomous actions taken for different reasons, at different times, under different conditions, by different people in the college. This collection of actions is periodically codified into what is presented as an educational program by the college catalog or a student or faculty handbook.

Consider as a first example of academic policy the academic expectations of faculty and students. What are legitimate programs? What is a legitimate workload? What are legitimate quality and quantity expectations?

These simple working conditions of education are viewed as being primarily the concern of faculty and students. Their importance to parents, or to employers or governmental licensing agencies (particularly in the case of professional education) is for the most part, secondary. As a result, most colleges leave the conditions of education to informal bilateral negotiations between students and faculty. These negotiations take place daily in the classroom, each term in the enrollment and grade lists, and continuously in student-faculty interaction. The results of the negotiation may be formally ratified by the appropriate faculty body, but they often exist simply as a shared understanding within the community. Teachers who enjoy teaching and students who enjoy being taught form enclaves. Teachers who do not enjoy teaching and students who do not enjoy being taught form other enclaves.

The latter coalition is a frequent one. Suppose that a group of faculty views teaching as a job. That is, as something one does in order to be able to do something else (e.g., play golf, sit in the sun, do research). And suppose a group of students views studying as a job; that is, as something one does in order to be able to do something else (e.g., earn a living, sit in the sun, do research). Under such conditions one would expect the bilaterally negotiated educational program to include: (1) a joint agreement to assert that both teachers and students are working very hard and (2) a joint agreement to restrict work. Such agreements are common in American higher education, as they are throughout noneducational work situations. Given the basic organizational situation, the surprise is not that work restriction is practiced, but that work is. If faculty and students had the purely and narrowly self-interested goals of which they are sometimes accused, educational programs would consist of minimally acceptable external façades.

Negotiated work levels are not responsive to conventional bureaucratic interventions. Presidents and others have criticized the resistance of informal agreements to change. The criticism sometimes misses the point. The outcomes of bilateral negotiation between faculty and students are little affected by policy proclamations by presidents or academic councils, although they may be ratified, somewhat inhibited, or modestly stimulated by such machinery. Significant changes appear to result (as, for example, at Berkeley and San Francisco State College) from widespread shifts in faculty and student attitudes. These shifts lead to direct renegotiations at the classroom and department levels that collectively modify the nature of the academic program.

For example, the bilateral bargains between faculty and students appear in recent years to have been renegotiated at some schools in the direction of reducing the traditional scholarship demands on students and faculty and increasing the political demands. Politically acceptable faculty are allowed by students to substitute new criteria and styles of scholarship for the more conventional ones within their disciplines. Politically acceptable students are allowed to substitute ideological development, political activity, or unusual terms of scholarship. These renegotiations of the educational program involve a small minority of students at American colleges and universities, but at a few institutions the number has apparently been large enough to result in appreciable change in the overall educational program.

Whether such changes are viewed as attractive or unattractive, they illustrate the process by which academic policy is actually affected. American college presidents have generally been unwilling or unable to participate significantly in the broad attitudinal changes that underlie such shifts. For the most part, college presidents have not felt they had either the mandate or the platform for producing shifts in the demands that students and faculty make on each other, and have been more inclined to try to make modest bureaucratic limitations on the process than to participate in it.

Consider a second example of academic policy: the structure of general educational requirements (commonly called breadth requirements) imposed on students. This set of rules, by which the claims of liberal education are satisfied, is a persistent source of minor conflict within a college or university and occasionally erupts into a major dispute. Our impression is that faculties struggle with such questions, trying to capture some idea of what a good education is. But since that question is one that few reasonable men can answer with confidence, the outcomes are dominated by three somewhat more mundane considerations:

1   The willingness of students to be coerced into taking courses they would not choose to take independent of the requirement. Students place limits on the proportion of their total studies that can be directed in this way, on the difficulty of the courses that are required, and on the subject matter that may be included.

2   The enrollment needs of various departments. As we have noted above, the enrollment cycle is a major factor in resource allocation. Normally, one cannot have a large French department without large enrollments in French. One cannot support many graduate students as teaching assistants in political science without large enrollments in introductory political science courses. One cannot justify many science laboratories without substantial enrollments in introductory laboratory science courses. An awareness of the virtues of French, political science, and chemistry as elements of a liberal education is facilitated by an awareness of the benefits of enrollments.

3   The desire to have small classes. To have many small classes, the college or university must ordinarily have some large classes that can be taught using modest faculty resources. Two devices of educational policy are used together to accomplish this — required courses and a structure of prerequisites that force enrollments in a few introductory courses. Both are justified — appropriately — in terms of educational considerations. There are reasons why one might require that an educated man have exposure to subjects outside his major field and why one might expect a student to study elementary material before he studies advanced material. How-

ever, the practical considerations of university management almost certainly amplify such beliefs, so that some prerequisites and some breadth requirements are less educationally relevant than they appear to be.

We do not mean to suggest that these considerations are illegitimate. The point is simply that though educational policy discussions are couched in terms of the educational needs of students, they tend to be substantially influenced by the necessities of organizational life in a university. When the chairman of the department of history argues for a required course for all university students in the history of some non-Western society, he need not examine the relative importance of the education (which he believes in) and the implied growth of the history department (which he also believes in). What is good for history is good for the university.

The result is that educational policy, insofar as it is a matter for the general faculty, tends to be a fairly straightforward "logroll" among the major faculty groups. The price of a requirement in humanities is a requirement in natural sciences. The major participants will not ordinarily see it that way, of course. Policy is negotiated without clear distinctions between nobility and necessity.

We observed little inclination among presidents to participate in this logrolling. For the most part, they did not see their interests as being heavily involved; nor did they often have a clear program that was much differentiated from the natural outcome of the logroll. Thus, the two most conspicuous recent trends—the overall reduction in breadth requirements and the strong tendency to eliminate language requirements—have not been affected significantly by presidential action (although through the enrollment cycle such changes have substantial effects within a college or university).

The "major" decisions of academic policy that produce presidential activity are rarely heroic. Presidents sometimes involve themselves moderately in questions of instructional calendars (e.g., quarter versus semester) or in questions of new academic departments or schools (e.g., black studies) or in questions of schoolwide curriculum requirements. In general, the president's role has been relatively unimportant in recent years except in a few cases where he has entered the educational policy arena with limited objectives. Typically, this has been because educational policy has produced an effect on those things that a president does consider important—most notably quiet on the campus, the financial position of the school, and the reputation of the president.

Presidential passivity with respect to academic policy stems, we believe, both from the nature of the process by which that policy is made and from the combination of factors that have dominated college and university life since the Second World War. Institution building, managing growth, and improving the quality of faculty and students have been the heart of the presidential role as defined by the rewards apparently provided and the attributes of a "good president." Contemporary presidents do not consider influence on academic programs a uniquely significant factor in making a successful president. When we asked presidents to describe the reasons for the "success" of the president they viewed as "clearly successful" among their colleagues, consideration of educational policy was mentioned by 23 percent of the respondents and constituted 10 percent of the total list of items mentioned (see Table 12).

Although presidents are educators by experience and by identification, they are not educators by behavior. They notice the anomaly. One of the most reliable complaints of an American college president is the degree to which he is removed from educational matters. He is committed to success in his job. He does not consider academic policy achievements as a major factor in the evaluation of his success. He does not feel he has any serious leverage. He is a nostalgic realist.

ACADEMIC TENURE DECISIONS
Academic tenure, as it has existed for the past 30 years, is a major organizational commitment. Assuming that a faculty member ordinarily receives tenure sometime during his thirties, a tenure decision is essentially a 30-year contract. At present prices the face value of the contract, quite aside from other commitments, is somewhere from $400,000 to $1 million in salary alone. As college presidents have discovered under conditions of budget restrictions, academic salaries are both the largest part of the college budget and one of the parts least susceptible to short-run downward modification.

In addition, tenure is an important symbolic act. Actions on tenure and beliefs about those actions form a major basis for the faculty reward structure within a college. The widespread belief that tenure depends on research productivity has conditioned not only a whole generation of academic workers but also a large number of contemporary theories of academe and its ills. It has been used as an excuse and explanation for bad teaching, bad manners, and bad research.

Whether the excuses, explanations, and beliefs are correct may perhaps be questioned, but it is impossible to question their ubiquity. Moreover, the ritual of the decision process is carefully designed to maintain the beliefs. Each year thousands of department chairmen solicit tens of thousands of letters supporting the claims to tenure made by members of their staff. These letters and other supporting documents are processed through a typically complex series of assessments by faculty committees, departments, deans, executive committees, and provosts until they arrive at the president's desk. At each stage, the process is made to appear more powerful than it is in at least two senses: (1) the rate of moving to tenure is almost certainly higher than believed; and (2) the "failures" are rarely real failures. They succeed later (often at a different school) and often become at least as distinguished in research as those who "succeeded" originally.

In the past quarter-century college presidents have operated under conditions that have made the substance of tenure decisions relatively less important to them than the associated ritual. There are at least seven clear reasons for this:

- First, most of the costs of the long-term contract in a tenure decision are borne by subsequent administrations. Although presidents concern themselves with long-term consequences for the institution—often more than others within the organization—it is natural for those costs to be somewhat less pressing than some others.

- Second, with a high turnover of faculty, the contract is really not a 30-year one. This is particularly true for a school where faculty members are likely to have options for movement.

- Third, with continued inflation and flexible salary schedules, the contract is not as expensive a commitment as it appears, nor as absolute.

- Fourth, with rapid growth, tenure decisions of the past represent a smaller part of the institution's total commitment than would be true under stable conditions. As long as growth is maintained, tenure commitments are balanced by expansion of the nontenured staff.

- Fifth, in some cases the costs have seemed to be largely borne by the federal government through research grants. A senior research star is a good financial investment, not a net cost. Not only can substantial elements of his salary be funded extramurally, he brings additional funds to support others. Although this situation has directly affected only a small minority of the tenure decisions within American colleges and universities, it probably has contributed to a belief that tenure decisions are not, in fact, as costly as they appear to be.

- Sixth, with a shortage of qualified faculty and an active market for faculty, there appears to be no way of maintaining a faculty without granting tenure rather liberally. The alternative, in principle, is higher salary. In many cases, the institutional structure of salary schemes makes such a tradeoff difficult. Even where it does not, few presidents are likely to save future dollars by paying present dollars.

- Seventh, the president has no basis for believing that his judgment is better than the process. Moreover, even if he believes he knows better, he knows that he has little chance to demonstrate the superiority of his judgment in any reasonable length of time.

We would expect presidents of some schools to be more concerned with the substance of tenure decisions than presidents of others. Presidents of schools where turnover of faculty is low and where growth is modest or nonexistent would involve themselves more directly in tenure decisions than would presidents of high-turnover and rapidly growing schools. Although our data from interviews are not adequate to a firm test of such ideas, we believe that they are generally consistent with such conclusions. Relatively active presidents tended to be in the very small handful of prestigious institutions of stable size and in the larger group of stable-sized, low-prestige colleges off the major academic marketplace.

Most of the presidents we interviewed had never rejected a tenure recommendation that came to them through the internal faculty and administrative reviewing process. The overall rejection rate—at the final approval point—appears to be no more than 5 percent and probably closer to 1 percent. Some presidents, though by no means all, tried to involve themselves earlier in the process in order to develop a consensus before the time for their formal action arrived. This was much more characteristic of presidents in small schools than of those in large ones. In larger schools, presidents typically viewed their role in tenure decisions as ratifying the actions recommended by the chief academic officer and the appropriate faculty-administrative committees. This would break down seriously only in the occasional case in which some major part of the president's constituency became activated. Recently, this has almost exclusively involved student protest against the refusal of tenure to a popular teacher and community-trustee protest against the granting of tenure to a politically unpopular professor. Spectacular as such cases sometimes are and as difficult as they may become for a president, they have been and still are infrequent.

We have argued, however, that this situation is based on the seven key reasons listed above. The last 25 years have been a special era in the history of American higher education that appears to be ending or to have ended. Growth rates have slowed considerably. As a result, market demand for faculty and faculty turnover appear destined to be reduced.[4] The rate of growth of research support has declined. All these factors are likely to increase presidential activity in tenure decisions. Through him, both symbolically and perhaps directly, local and internal factors seem likely to become somewhat more important than they have been (e.g., teaching, university service, good collegiality) and cosmopolitan, national, and professional factors somewhat less important. We are likely to have an increase in the number of complaints about "cronyism" or "personal favoritism" and a decrease in the number of complaints about a professor's primary allegiance lying with his outside professional groups.

Although it is hard to imagine that academic tenure decisions will become a major source of attention for most presidents, the ritual considerations associated with tenure will continue to be important. The reputed quality of the faculty and the research standing of the school (two important dimensions to many presidents) can be influenced by creating a climate of belief in the importance of research. This climate has been constructed by emphasizing the research basis for promotion and tenure decisions and by dramatizing the research basis through a system of reports, market offers, research "stars," and the like. For most purposes, the accuracy of a "publish or perish" characterization of the concrete tenure rules is less critical than a wide acceptance of research productivity as a norm of the system.

We would expect to find presidents concerned that the dogma of research be reinforced by the litany of promotion procedures. As the pressures upon presidents have changed (e.g., from students and from sources of funds), we can expect the dogma and the litany to be revised, and the perceived reasons for tenure decisions to

[4] For a discussion of some of the faculty personnel consequences of the end of growth see Kenneth McNeil and James D. Thompson (1971).

shift. With research, teaching, and service standards vague and uncertain, it is particularly important that the president announce that they are being used. And this is not simply a callous strategy of deception. It is also a recognition that if one is going to influence such diffuse things as the research identity of an institution, the influence will come about in large part by changing the pictures of people within the institution, pictures that reveal what those people are good at and what those who are rewarded are good at. A general acceptance of teaching dogmas will probably produce more teaching, even though the changes in peoples' beliefs are almost certain to be greater than the changes in their behavior.

PLANNING Planning is a primary responsibility of executive leadership and is so certified by traditional administrative theory and by innumerable modern treatments. In our interviews, we never heard a president deny the importance and virtue of planning within the college. In many cases they observed that this had not been a function that was well performed within the college previously. In some cases they observed that it was not a function that was easy to perform. But the fundamental value of planning was asserted by all, and in approximately the same terms by all.

Most presidents accepted two basic organizational axioms with respect to planning:

- A primary responsibility of leadership is that of providing broad, general direction to the organization.
- Orderly direction requires a clear specification of objectives, an identification of alternative routes to those objectives, and a choice among those alternatives.

In short, one must have a plan.

Moreover, it was generally accepted that the plan should be comprehensive. It should involve academic planning, fiscal planning, physical planning, personnel planning, research planning, and organizational planning as an integrated and consistent master plan. The frequently recited stories of physical planning that proceeds without attention to the academic plan of the university are seen as horror stories.

Despite this unanimous acceptance of the importance of planning, we saw little evidence of planning in American colleges and universities—at least planning in the terms indicated above. At each of the colleges in our sample we asked presidents and their chief subordinates whether their college had a "plan." We also asked what role the plan played in current decisions. The answers varied somewhat across four main alternatives:

1 Yes, we have a plan. It is used in capital project and physical location decisions.

2 Yes, we have a plan. Here it is. It was made during the administration of our last president. We are working on a new one.

3 No, we do not have a plan. We should. We are working on one.

4 I think there's a plan around here someplace. Miss Jones, do we have a copy of our comprehensive 10-year plan?

Most schools had a capital-physical plan of some sort, most of which were subject to relatively continuous review and revision. Few people were completely satisfied with such planning. Nearly everyone agreed that it rarely took adequate account of "academic" considerations. It was often felt that actual decisions were essentially independent of the plan. There were persistent problems in identifying a rational basis for a particular plan. Nevertheless, such plans were reasonably well accepted and reasonably institutionalized.

In a similar way, many schools had fiscal plans of one sort or another. It was not uncommon to find plans for future operating budgets. Plans for fiscal problems associated with income uncertainties (e.g., endowment earnings, grant income, tuition/enrollment) were common, particularly among nonpublic institutions. In public institutions legislative-administrative tactics seemed to make it impossible to develop serious contingent plans for alternative levels of public appropriations. Plans to deal with cash-flow difficulties (particularly associated with heavy dependence on tuition income) or with the short-term investment of temporary surges of cash were common. Long- and medium-range planning, however, seemed to be very modest and hyperroutine. Other fiscal planning was, for the most part, "technical" in the sense that it did not ordinarily involve considerations beyond the maintenance of the best financial position possible for the institution.

Some schools have academic plans. Some of these are voluminous—the natural consequence of asking each department to prepare a plan and then binding all the documents together without editing. Few administrators thought the academic plans were useful in decision making. On the whole, academic plans seem to suffer from two conspicuous administrative problems: (1) they often had no connection to any decisions that anyone might be called upon to make; and (2) they rejected the idea of scarcity. At best, they were lists of what the various academic departments wished Santa Claus would bring them. At worst, they were fantasies, neither believed in nor intended to be believable.

Presidents believe in comprehensive planning, but do virtually none of it. How do we understand such an inconsistency, and what are its consequences?

We believe that the phenomena of planning—and the corresponding presidential attitudes—are the striking consequences of the inconsistencies between universities as organizations and the models of organizations with which presidents are familiar. Plans, in their usual form, particularly long-run comprehensive plans, presume substantial clarity about goals, substantial understanding of the basic technology of the organization, and substantial continuity in leadership. Universities have none of these, except in the capital-physical-fiscal-planning area. Presidents frequently come to the presidency from outside the organization and are frequently succeeded by someone from outside the organization. Their terms are short relative to the length of time involved in a "plan." Except for their chief officers in business finance, their main subordinates will remain in office for an even shorter period. Boards of trustees are rarely organized to maintain continuity in anything more than general fiscal policies. Presidents emphasize the importance of making a mark on the institution. They have little stake in continuity with the past. They may hope for continuity with the future, but they would have to be extraordinarily naïve to expect their successor to spend much time "implementing" someone else's plan. Despite the obeisance paid it, comprehensive planning has little reality for presidents in the form in which we usually conceive it.

Long-run planning in universities is something other than long-run planning. In particular, we would identify four major things that plans become:

1 Plans become *symbols*. As we have noted, academic organizations provide few "real" pieces of feedback data. How are we doing? Where are we going? An organization that is failing can announce a plan to succeed. An institution that does not have a reactor can announce a plan for one, and is probably valued higher than a university without such a plan.

2 Plans become *advertisements*. What is frequently called a "plan" by a university is really an investment brochure. It is an attempt to persuade private and public donors of the attractiveness of the institution. Such plans are characterized by pictures, by *ex cathedra* pronouncements of excellence, and by the absence of most relevant information.

3 Plans become *games*. In an organization in which goals and technology are unclear, plans and the insistence on plans become an administrative test of will. If a department wants a new program badly enough, it will spend a substantial amount of effort in "justifying" the expenditure by fitting it into a "plan." If an administrator wishes to avoid saying "yes" to everything, but has no basis for saying "no" to anything, he tests the commitment of the department by asking for a plan.

4 Plans become *excuses for interaction*. As several students of planning have noted, the results of the process of planning are usually more important than the plan. The development of a plan forces some discussion and may induce some interest in and commitment to relatively low-priority activities in the departments and schools. Occasionally that interaction yields results of positive value. But only rarely does it yield anything that would accurately describe the activities of a school or department beyond one or two years into the future. As people engage in discussions of the future, they may modify each other's ideas about what should be done today, but their conclusions about what should be done next year are likely to be altered in the interim by changes in personnel, political climate, foundation policy, or student demand.

The side benefits of plans seem enough to sustain talk of planning and a modest level of activity, but not enough to motivate either intense presidential involvement or a communitywide commitment to execute what has been written. As long as education is a process particularly sensitive to the character and individual interests of those who teach and those who study, the direct rewards of planning activity both for presidents and for others can be expected to remain relatively low.

PRESIDENTIAL POWER The American college president plays a far from dominant role in these four conspicuous areas of college decision making. He is important. He has power. The process, however, has a logic that he cannot alter, and normally does not want to alter.

It is unlikely that we can determine how much power the American college president has or should have. Such questions require a specification of a model of executive and administrative power that has proven impossible to make (see March, 1966). However, we can consider some possible reasons why the president's power is an issue and a problem, and we can examine some implications of those reasons. To do this, we will assert that the following propositions are plausible without detailed argumentation or evidence:

- Most people believe in a simple force model of organizational choice. That is, they believe that power (force) is distributed among participants and that decisions are approximated by the weighted average of individual wishes (where the weights are the power indices of the individuals).

- The simple force model of organizational choice accounts for a good deal less of the variation in outcomes than is believed. There are other factors that are relevant in important ways.

- The president both is perceived to have and, in fact, does have more power than most (perhaps all) other participants in college or university decision making.

- Power, the interpretation of power, and the assessment of individual leadership behavior are considered against the background of an egalitarian ideology within the United States.

Notice that the second point is not a direct argument that "power" is distributed more "equally" than is commonly believed. The argument is that a simple force model is incorrect, that there are substantial "nonpower" factors in decisions. Since these are independent of power as reflected in the standard model, they are as likely to help the "weak" as the "strong." Thus, in effect they equalize apparent power.

The decision processes we have described are not easily characterized in simple force terms. Decisions are typically not made by a confrontation of well-organized factions, with victory to the strongest. The factions are not well organized. They are rarely all activated at one time. They rarely have any significant staying power. As a result the American college president is faced with a set of beliefs about the amount of power he should have and the amount of power he does have that assure some resentment toward him. In addition, he is faced with a disparity between his potential power and beliefs about his power that assures his disappointment and the disappointment of others in his ability to act powerfully. He is resented because he is more powerful than he should be. He is scorned and frustrated because he is weaker than he is believed capable of being. If he acts as a "strong" president, he exposes his weakness. If he acts as a "democratic" president, people consider him timid. For the most part, his behavior has only modest impact on beliefs about presidential legitimacy or power.

We can illustrate the situation very simply. In Figure 11 we plot perceptions of power against hierarchical position within the organization. We have simplified considerably by assuming that there is a linear relationship between power and hierarchical position and that the "total power" perceived within the system is fixed, but neither of those simplifications is critical to the argument.

The horizontal line represents the *evaluative* norm within the university. We have portrayed the simple case of a pure egalitarian ideology. The steep line represents the *cognitive* norm within the university. It reflects the attribution of power within the organization. The intermediate line is the *behavioral* situation (the exerciseable power) within the university. It is more steep than the evaluative norm (assertions 3 and 4) and less steep than the cognitive norm (assertions 1 and 2).

Since he is at the top of the hierarchy, the president is represented by the three endpoint values in Figure 11: his *legitimate* power (point *c*), his *actual* power (point *b*), and his *perceived* power (point *a*).

FIGURE 11 *Hierarchical position and perceptions of power within the university*

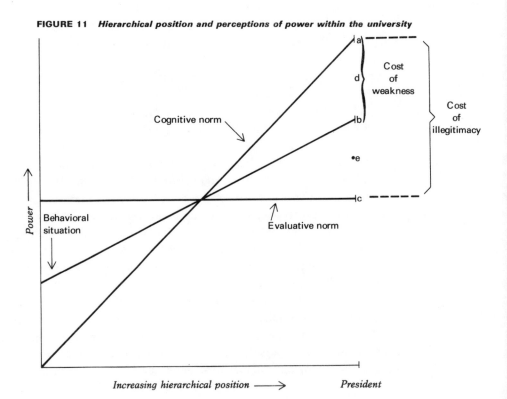

From this it is easy to see that the president is subject to two major costs with respect to power: The first costs are the costs of illegitimacy—the difference between the perceived power of the president and the legitimate power *(a–c)*. According to our assertions, these costs will always exist. The second costs are the costs of weakness—the difference between the perceived power of the president and his actual power *(a–b)*. According to our assertions, these costs will also always exist.

The costs of illegitimacy are realized in resentment toward the office and the person holding it, in pressure to reduce the power of the president, in motivational assumptions about the behavior of presidents (e.g., "power-hunger"). The magnitude of the costs of illegitimacy depends on the extent to which the power model of the university is accepted and the extent to which norms of equality apply.

In general, we would expect to find the degree of acceptance of the power model to increase with the degree of conflict in the organization, the size of the organization, and the average pleasure derived from politics by participants in the organization. We would expect the acceptance of norms of equality to increase with the degree of differentiation between hierarchical status orders and other (e.g., professional) status orders, with the opportunities for exit from the organization provided within the environment, with the degree of public control of the institution, and with the recency of presidential ascension to the office.

The costs of weakness, on the other hand, are paid in criticism for timidity, in disappointment among supporters, and in reduced self-esteem. The magnitude of these costs depends on the extent to which the power model is accepted and on the actual power of the president (or, in effect, the number and scope of other factors in decisions). We would expect the actual power in these terms to increase with the slack in the system. Slack serves as a buffer from exogenous forces. We would expect the actual power to increase when other participants become more dependent on the organization, for example, when exit opportunities decline. We would expect power to increase as the social significance of universities decreases.

This kind of analysis provides an interpretation of one familiar sequence of university events. If slack declines at the same time as the social importance of universities and conflict in them increases, complaints about presidential timidity will increase at a more rapid rate than complaints about presidential illegitimacy (which may in fact decline). Objections to presidential weakness will be particularly notable in large, public institutions. If subsequently the opportunities for exit by other administrators, students, and faculty decline, complaints of both kinds decline; but the decline is most notable with respect to perceptions of the weakness of presidents. Presidents become both stronger and more legitimate, particularly the former.

We can add to the analysis in Figure 11 by considering the president's own perception of the distribution of power. In general, we would expect presidents to see their power as somewhat more than that presumed by the egalitarian norm and as somewhat less than that believed by nonpresidents. What difference does it make?

In our discussion we have assumed that the president's perception of his power has no direct effect on either legitimate power or perceived power. However, it could affect actual power. If the president sees his own power as greater than it actually is (say at point d), the cost of weakness will still be $a-b$ (since his perception cannot change the facts in a positive direction). If, on the other hand, he perceives his power as less than it actually is (point e), he will generally not realize all his actual potential power. The costs of weakness are, in fact, either $a-b$ or $a-e$, whichever is larger. Presidents who underestimate their power and act in terms of that underestimate will not affect their costs of legitimacy (unless the perceptions of power are actually a function of events as well as models) but will affect the costs of weakness.

If the president overestimates his power, he will think he can do something that, in fact, he cannot. If the president underestimates his power, he will think he cannot do something that, in fact, he can. Generally, the former errors are more conspicuous, both to the president and to his audiences, than are the latter. As a result, we would expect ordinary learning to lead the president to reduce his estimate of his own power (though he may easily still overestimate it).

Combining these observations, we obtain the following kind of progression. A president is more likely to overestimate his power in the early years of the presidency than in the later years. This occurs because he is coming to the presidency from the universe of nonpresidential beliefs about presidential power (which tend to be high), because he has high hopes, and because a honeymoon with his audiences makes the costs of illegitimacy less conspicuous. The result is a large power-expectation gap for the president and a large number of errors of attempting to do things he cannot. Over time, the president reduces his estimate of his power as he learns from the errors. His learning reduces the power-expectation gap, decreases the frequency of those errors, increases the (less conspicuous) errors of timidity, and increases the cost of weakness. At the same time, familiarity with the president as president raises the legitimacy of his position among his constituencies, with a resulting decline in the costs of legitimacy. According to this analysis, presidents should ordinarily experience systematic increases in the complaints about their timidity over time and systematic decreases in the complaints about their illegitimacy.

Presidents are not the only actors in the college scene who experience the phenomena we have indicated. In particular, student leaders, faculty leaders, and trustees can be located on Figure 11 in a similar way. If we are substantially correct, the costs of weakness and the costs of legitimacy are less for them, but some of the same phenomena obtain. They will generally find themselves less powerful than they expected and less powerful than their constituents expect them to be.

It is our impression that these phenomena became notable within universities during the 1960s, when two major efforts were undertaken.

The first was an effort to legitimize leadership. Presidents, faculty leaders, student leaders, and trustees undertook active campaigns to establish the legitimacy of their positions. Those took the form of much more extensive consultation by boards of trustees before appointing presidents, of much more active efforts on the part of student and faculty leaders as well as presidents to establish "communication" with their constituents, of serious attempts to act their roles.

The second was an effort to downgrade the standard perceptions of power. Presidents have commented at length on the limitations on their power. So have students, faculties, and trustees. Although they have each tried to explain their own limitations by exaggerating the power of others in the system, the net apparent effect is to reduce the power expectations held by followers. We have tried to indicate some reasons why we believe this general shift in perceptions is a shift in the direction of accuracy. It is also a shift that reduces the pressure on all the leaders within the system.

THE CERTIFICATION OF STATUS The discussion of the power of the president may serve to remind us that university governance is simultaneously a system for making decisions and a system for certifying status. The first of these functions dominates most discussions. We identify the system of governance as the procedures by which major decisions are made. Who is allowed access to the university—as student, faculty member, trustee, donor, employee? How are the scarce financial resources of the university allocated? How do the participants in the university use their time? What are the formats and rules of the teaching function? What research is done? Who is president?

The status certification function of governance is less commonly discussed but is at least as important. For many people, the process and structure of university governance are more important than the outcome—at least within wide ranges of possible outcomes. Participation is not a means but an end. Academic institutions easily become *process-* rather than *output*-oriented. Goals provide scant evidence on whether the output of the decision process within academe is desirable, but participation in the process is a conspicuous certification of status. Individuals establish themselves as important by virtue of their rights of participation in the governance of the institution.

Suppose we consider the implications of a simple hypothesis: Most people in a college are most of the time less concerned with the content of a decision than they are with eliciting an acknowledgment of their importance within the community. We believe that some substantial elements of the governance of universities can be better understood in terms of such a hypothesis than in terms of an assumption that governance is primarily concerned with the outcomes of decisions. Presidents are more insistent on their right to make a decision than on the content of the decision. Faculty members are more insistent on their right to participate in faculty deliberations than they are on exercising that right. Students are more insistent on their right to representation on key decision bodies than they are on attending meetings. Boards of trustees are more insistent on defining the scope of their authority than they are on using it.

Much of the argument is over the symbols of governance. Who has the right to claim power? Since the main symbols of power and status are participation and victory, the university decision-making system is crowded with instruments of participation and claims of victories: committees, faculties, ad hoc groups, reviews, memoranda, votes, meetings, rallies, conferences. The system is typically not crowded with actual participation except where validation of status positions is involved. It is often hard to sustain student and faculty interest in the activities of a committee—even one whose existence they apparently consider a matter of some import—unless some highly symbolic conflict between groups can be arranged. The situation has been captured well in recent years by the picture of distinguished faculty, who rarely before had attended a general faculty meeting, coming to a meeting to discuss whether students should be allowed to attend.

As a system for making decisions, the standard college governance system is open to a number of vital challenges. It is not clear that it has a major role in the outcomes of decisions; that anyone seriously wants it to have such a role; that it is constituted in such a way as to make such a role feasible. The formal structure of governance does, however, provide some gradations of deference and a forum for debating the rights to participation. Not everyone receives as much deference as he might like. Arguments over scarce deference can be just as ferocious and just as serious as arguments over "real" resources. Universities, like countries, may struggle for a long time to decide the participation rights of member groups. But by providing numerous parallel decision systems with numerous levels of overlapping committees, titles, and responsibilities, universities are relatively efficient in reducing conflict over status resources.

By calling attention to the importance of status, we do not intend to demean it. That academic man cares more for his self-respect than for his material well-being (if he does) may not be entirely a vice. And if he does, he may perhaps be excused the luxury of fighting more for the former than for the latter.

Least of all should persons concerned about the substance of university decisions scorn a concern by others in the allocation of status. Such variations in concern form the basis for one of the most common of organizational exchanges—the exchange of status for substance. As Dale Carnegie (1936) has observed, the most natural coalition in the world is between someone who wants to sell pots and pans and someone who wants to be admired. In a world in which most people care more about their self-esteem than they do about what pots and pans are bought, anyone who has the opposite scale of values is in strong trading position. Apparently, universities are such a world. A person who is interested in changing a university has some chance of doing so if he is willing to accord status to others within the community and is able to prevent the decisions in which he is interested from becoming garbage cans for collectively insatiable status concerns.

CONCLUSION The examples of decisions we have chosen are intended to be representative of significant issues in modern university life. They suggest some serious limitations in our metaphorical descriptions of presidential roles. Those descriptions are, as we noted in Chapter 4, heroic in their view of presidential importance. The portrait of reality we have sketched in the last two chapters includes a more limited presidential role. A president probably has more power than other single individuals but except for a very few cases presidents do not appear to dominate directly the decision making in their institutions. They face a poorly understood and rather tightly constrained managerial world. In that world they contribute important ritual legitimacy to some decisions and they play a significant role in the certification of the status of other participants. Their ability to control decision outcomes is often less than expected by those around them and by themselves.

The mismatch between expectation and reality is not news to the presidents. They experience the limitations of their role. Presidents accept the conventional description of the role in part because they have no alternative and in part because heroic expectations about presidents are characteristic of others with whom they deal. To question those expectations significantly would raise a large number of complications not only in the life of a president but also within the extended social network within which he operates.

7. The Organization of Time

College presidents are busy. The presidents with whom we talked, as well as the presidents reported in other studies and in the daily newspapers, describe their jobs as demanding in terms of time and energy. The people around them—students, faculty, administrators, trustees, and external contacts—make a similar assessment. By every report, the job is physically and emotionally exhausting. There is not enough time. There are too many people to see. There are too many things to do.

Not only do presidents report themselves overloaded, they also describe themselves as being unable to attend adequately to the "important" aspects of their jobs.

Most incumbents testify that they find it difficult, if not impossible, to direct their efforts towards being most influential in the area where they perceive their greatest responsibility—*providing purpose and direction for their institutions.* Although they work a long and tiring week, they are forced to divide their time to attend to a multiplicity of functions and, as a consequence, they find their success diminished by relatively inconsequential problems (Perkins et al., 1967, stress in original).

By self-report and by the comments of outside observers, the college president is overworked and misworked.

The unanimity of the reports is persuasive. At the same time, however, it is puzzling. Colleges and universities vary substantially in size, wealth, characteristics of their clientele, and heterogeneity, and in the size, organization, and efficiency of their staffs. Across all this variation, their presidents work approximately the same busy, subjectively impossible schedule. It seems remarkable that every president is working about the same amount of time, and it seems remarkable that every president experiences about the same sense of frustration in the misallocation of his effort. Yet, from available reports, that appears to be the case.

* For an empirical update on presidential time allocation, see Appendix E written by James R. Glenn, Jr., and James G. March for this edition.

In effect, we have a pair of mysteries. On the one hand presidents complain about the demands on their time. On the other hand, they do not seem to do much about them. On the one hand, presidents are physically and emotionally active. On the other hand, their impact on such things as operating budgets, academic policy, academic personnel decisions, and long-run planning is modest.

What is a president doing? How is his time organized? Where is he during the day? Whom does he see? These are the questions to which we now turn in an effort to understand the presidential role. It is, as we shall see, not an exotic story. The mysteries we have noted stem more from curiosities in the usual interpretations of the role than from the role itself. The pattern of presidential activities is rather ordinary executive behavior. It is heavily regulated by social expectations within the organization and by the president himself, follows a fairly simple daily and weekly cycle, and is moderately sensitive to differences in college size. This is about what we would expect of any executive role, particularly in an organization in which goals and technology are unclear. It is neither mysterious nor particularly surprising—except when contrasted with a thoroughly improbable specification of a model of managerial behavior.

THE AGGREGATE DISTRIBUTION OF EFFORT The average workweek reported by presidents in New York is more than 60 hours (Perkins et al., 1967).[1] Our own estimates are that presidents work, on the average, about 50 to 55 hours from Monday to Friday. Assuming that 5 to 10 hours is a reasonable estimate of the average working weekend, the two estimates are consistent. The American college president works about 20 hours more per week than the average one-job wage earner.

Sixty hours is a long week. It is also familiar. Self-reports of faculty workweeks in the United States regularly produce estimates of about 60 hours of work per week on the average (University of California, 1970). Within the academic culture the 60-hour week is apparently a strong convention. As we have noted earlier, college presidents are academics. A 60-hour normal week is unlikely to seem inappropriate to them or to their associates, even though the

[1] This chapter draws heavily on two major sources of data. The first is a study made for the Board of Regents of the State University of New York (Perkins et al., 1967, pp. 27–35). The second study is one made by us of the calendars of our basic sample of presidents on two days in the spring of 1970. The details of the procedures for that study are reported in Appendix D. The former study was limited to New York State and included junior college presidents. The latter study used our national sample and did not include junior colleges.

presidential 60 hours may seem longer and more exhausting than the faculty 60 hours.

Presidents certainly are working hard, by any reasonable standards of work in contemporary American culture. To examine what they are doing with their time we asked four simple questions about their calendars:

1 Where do presidents spend their time?

2 In what size groups?

3 With whom?

4 At whose initiative?

Where Do Presidents Spend Their Time? Table 30 shows our estimates of the distribution of presidential time according to location. These estimates are based on the study of presidential calendars (see Appendix D) and reflect our standard estimating procedures (see Appendix A). The average president spends about 47 percent of the normal workday (from 8:00 A.M. to 6:00 P.M.) on the campus, 14 percent of his time in town but not on the campus, 16 percent of his time at home, and 22 percent of his time out of town.[2] The amount of presidential travel is obviously

[2] The statistic on the percentage of time spent out of town is comparable with two other estimates available to us. First, in the New York study (Perkins et al., 1967) presidents were asked how many days they spend "away from the campus" each year. Since most of the time spent "in town but not on campus" in our study consists of a few hours spent off campus on days in which the president spends most of his time on campus, we assume that the 30 to 31 days estimated by the New York college and junior college presidents for the time they are "away from campus" is approximately comparable to the time our calendar study indicates presidents are out of town. If we assume a workyear of about 275 days, the New York study estimates 11.1 percent of a president's time is spent out of town.

Second, we asked each of the secretaries in our sample to estimate the number of days that the president would be away from the campus ("out of town") during the two weeks immediately following our visit to the college. The estimated number of days away from the campus from their responses is 1.5 days per week. Thus, the secretaries estimate that the president will spend about 27.3 percent of the next two workweeks "out of town." These predictions seem to be considerably higher than the actual time reported in the calendar study or the time estimated by presidents.

On the whole, we are inclined to consider the calendar reports as more reliable than either of the other two estimates. We think it reasonable to expect presidents to underestimate their time away from campus (particularly retrospectively in the context of an official state study) and to expect secretaries to overestimate it when looking forward. In addition, Jenny Cloudman has suggested to us that since secretaries acquire additional independence, responsibility, and authority when presidents are gone, they may overestimate the expected frequency of his absence.

substantial, but it is not extraordinary by the standards of modern executives. Similarly, the amount of time presidents spend away from the campus but "in town" is probably greater than that spent by most other individuals in the college organization but not greater than that spent by other chief executives of substantial enterprises.

	Estimates from
Location	*42-college sample*
At home	16%
Own office	35
Other on campus	12
Other in town	14
Out of town	22

TABLE 30
Proportion of total time spent by presidents (according to secretarial logs), by location, 8 A.M. to 6 P.M.

College presidents follow a fairly conventional work pattern, but there is an "academic" flavor to the conventionality. The habits of faculty life are extended to administrative life. This is exemplified particularly by the blurring of the distinction between office hours and home hours. Even during regular work hours, presidents spend two-thirds as much time at home as they do "out of town." One-sixth of the 8 A.M. to 6 P.M. workday is spent at home. This consists primarily in time after 5:00 P.M., and around noon. Presidents and their secretaries tend to list the "normal" workday as being from eight to six, but behaviorally its office phase appears frequently to end around five o'clock. Many presidents often have lunch at home. In addition, throughout the day—and particularly after noon—about one president in 10 can be expected to be at home.

Although we do not have data that will permit us to be sure, we believe that the statistical pattern is not the result of a few presidents regularly spending large shares of their time at home. Rather we think it stems from most presidents having variable work patterns. They appear sometimes to work at the office from seven in the morning until midnight. On other days, they do not really come to the campus before ten, or they leave the office by three. They often work at home on the so-called "paperwork" of letters, reports, and the preparation of speeches.

Presidents spend about half of their time on the campus, three-fourths of that in their own offices. Thus, the average president spends 25 to 30 hours a week at the college. As we shall see, most of that time is spent talking to people. Despite this, according to the study of New York presidents, the typical individual who wants to see a president can anticipate a delay of three or four days for an appointment (Perkins et al., 1967).

The sign on the office door says "President." Since, as we have seen in Chapters 5 and 6, the president has less than complete control over the system, we would speculate that a president devotes a considerable portion of the time of his day to three traditional royal activities: (1) the reception of petitions, (2) the giving of formal assent, and (3) the certification of position. These are important functions. They address themselves to fundamental difficulties in an anarchic decision system. An obscure decision process inhibits the airing of discontent, the legitimation of action, and the social ranking of participants.

In What Size Groups Do Presidents Spend Their Time?
Table 31 shows our estimates of the group sizes within which presidents function during the 8 A.M. to 6 P.M. workday. Although the data from the New York study are somewhat different from those obtained from our sample, the differences are modest enough to give us some confidence that the average president spends almost half of his working hours in groups in which there are at least two other persons, a little more than one-fourth of his time meeting a single person, and about one-fourth of his time alone.

TABLE 31 *Proportion of time spent by presidents (according to secretarial logs), by number of persons present*

Number of persons present	Estimates from New York study	Estimates from 42-college sample (8 A.M. to 6 P.M.)
President alone	28%	25%
One other person	25	35
Two or more others	48	40

The presidency is a social job, based heavily on interaction with other people. We exaggerate that phenomenon somewhat by focusing on the normal workday. Both secretaries and presidents report that the work done at home (as distinct from the work done at the office) is characteristically individual paperwork. Nevertheless, we think it is clear that a college president in the United States can expect to spend, on the average, seven to eight of the 10 hours between eight in the morning and six at night engaged in talk.

In Table 32 we show three sets of estimates of the way in which presidents allocate their time to different groups. The first set of estimates is from our study of secretarial calendars. The second set of estimates is from a somewhat similar study of the logs of 24 New York State presidential secretaries. The third set of estimates was made from a sample of 180 New York college presidents.[3]

TABLE 32 *Proportion of time spent by college presidents with various categories of persons (when presidents are not alone)**

Various categories of persons	Estimates from secretarial logs (42-college sample)	Estimates from secretarial logs (N.Y. State presidents)	Estimates by N.Y. State presidents themselves	
Outsiders	32%	41%	31%	[35%]
Constituents	28	26	38	[31]
Trustees	8	8	6	[6]
Students	9	5	11	[6]
Faculty	11	13	21	[19]
Administration	40	34	31	[34]
President's office	6			
Academic administration	18			
Nonacademic administration	16			
TOTAL	100	101	100	[100]

* These estimates exclude situations in which the president is alone or with his family, but otherwise include his whole (24-hour) weekday. In order to compare the two studies, some collapsing of categories has been necessary, but the two sets of categories were independently quite similar.

These aggregate data suggest that presidential behavior, as reflected in contact patterns, is broadly consistent with the presidential characterization of the role as being a mixture of administrator (dealing with hierarchical subordinates), political leader (dealing with constituents), and entrepreneur (dealing with bankers, customers, and suppliers). Although contacts rarely fall into only one of these categories, and the match is somewhat crude, we can locate the president in terms of his relative attention to the three roles.

[3] The New York study, as we have noted, includes two-year as well as four-year college presidents (Perkins et al., 1967). These data are not broken down by type of college in the report. On the basis of some closely related data we have been able to make some approximations to the results that obtain for four-year New York State presidents. These estimates are shown in square brackets. No comparable breakdown is available for the secretarial logs from the New York study.

This is done in Figure 12 which displays the relative attention to the three roles.

Figure 12 shows eight points:

A is a hypothetical president whose contact patterns describe him as an "administrator."

P is a hypothetical president whose contact patterns describe him as a "political leader."

E is a hypothetical president whose contact patterns describe him as an "entrepreneur."

O is a hypothetical president whose contact patterns describe him as dividing his time equally among the three roles.

X1 is the average president described by the data from our 42-college sample.

X2 is the average president described by the data from the New York State secretarial log study.

X3 is the average president described by the data from the New York State questionnaires of presidents.

X4 is the average president described by our (square bracketed) estimates of the four-year president in the New York questionnaire study.

The most obvious conclusion from the results is that all the studies show college presidents as dividing their time somewhat equally among the three roles. In this sense at least, aggregate presidential behavior is consistent with the aggregate presidential descriptions of the role.

Contrary to some modern impressions, college presidents do not spend very much time talking to students or faculty. They talk to students about as much as they talk to trustees and less than they talk to faculty (that is, faculty who do not hold administrative positions). Between 5 and 10 percent of their contacts are with students, mostly with student officers. Another 10 to 15 percent of presidential contacts are with faculty who do not hold administrative positions. When we asked presidents and their chief administrative subordinates how many students were present at the last group meeting of any kind involving the president, the answer 87 percent of the time was "none." From the point of view of a typical business organization, this amount of contact with "workers" is undoubtedly high. From the point of view a president who feels pressed for time, it may seem overwhelming. But the total time spent with faculty and students is about equivalent to one working

FIGURE 12 *The balance of attention to three of the presidential roles in four studies of contact patterns*

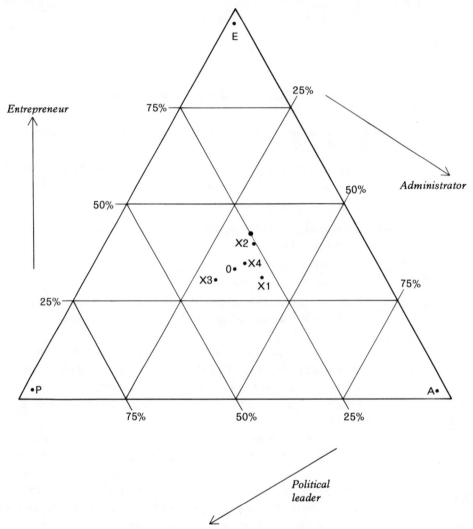

day per week. If the modern college president is overloaded with people to see, it is not because of an extraordinarily large contact load with respect to students or faculty.

We call attention to the level of contact with students and faculty partly because it is sometimes somewhat controversial but also partly because presidents appear systematically to overestimate it. As Table 32 shows, the questionnaire responses of presidents in New York State show them devoting an average of 32 percent of their contacts to students and faculty, while their secretaries estimate it at 18 percent of the contacts. It is probably true that secretaries "see" fewer of the faculty and student contacts of a president than he does. That will account for part of the difference. But it is probably also true that presidents report themselves as having more contact than they do—both because it is normatively appropriate for them to have such contact and because the contacts are more memorable than some of the others.

There are some further features of the contact patterns that are instructive. On the average, presidents have slightly more contact with their academic administrative subordinates than they do with their nonacademic administrative subordinates. If we compute the ratio of the number of contact hours devoted to academic administrators to the number of contact hours devoted to nonacademic administrators, the average ratio is 1.12. For every contact with a nonacademic administrator, the average president has 1.12 contacts with an academic administrator.

In a similar fashion we can compare the number of contacts the president has with those members of the community whose identifications are primarily academic (i.e., students, faculty, academic administrators) to those members of the community whose identifications are primarily nonacademic (i.e., president's office, nonacademic administrators, trustees, outsiders). In this sense, the average ratio of academic contacts to nonacademic contacts is 0.56. For every contact with a member of the president's office, nonacademic administrator, trustee, or outsider, the average president has 0.56 contacts with a student, faculty member, or academic administrator.

Finally, we have computed a statistic on the extent to which a president consults his faculty directly, rather than through an academic administrator. Like the president, academic administrators are overwhelmingly from the faculty. They often identify with the faculty as much as with the administration. They are often treated as spokesmen, or at least as conduits, for faculty opinion. The ratio of presidential contacts with academic administrators to contacts directly with faculty reflects the extent to which the consultation of the faculty occurs "through channels." On the average, the academic "through channels" ratio is 1.64. That is, for every contact with a faculty member without administrative rank, the average president has 1.64 contacts with academic administrators.

As we indicated in the preceding section, college presidents spend a very large proportion of their time either talking to people or listening to them. They exist in a verbal world. In this respect, the job is a rather natural one for someone with an academic background. It demands an ability to produce oral wisdom, to enjoy verbal encounter, and to sustain interest in prolonged exercises in discussion and conversation. When they are not talking or listening, presidents are likely to be reading or writing. The time that we have described as "alone" is often a time for correspondence, for telephone calls, for reading reports, and for preparing reports and speeches.

What do they talk about? Presidents classify conversations with administrative subordinates as dealing primarily with the everyday problems of administrative life. Respondents in the New York study (Perkins et al., 1967) identified most of their time with subordinates as "administrative planning," an acceptable short description of the meetings at which administrators review for each other their problems and their intentions, seek to avoid problems of coordination or conflict, and formally ratify decisions.

Conversations with trustees and with many external contacts are heavily related to financial concerns within the college, with the general problems of persuading the outside world that the university is a reasonable institution to support or with the mutual acknowledgment of position by president and outside contact.

Conversations with students (other than student officers) and faculty are primarily a mix of personal consultations, complaint sessions, and background discussions. Despite all the publicity attached to major student-president confrontations and faculty-president confrontations, most presidential contacts with these groups are completely unspectacular. Presidents are invited to meetings; presidents see students or faculty members who seek favors, reassurance, or emotional support.

Who Controls the Pattern? The pattern of time allocation that we have described is not primarily a result of presidential design. There are wide variations in access to the president. The buffers of assistants, subordinates, secretaries, and wives regulate the flow of contacts. Further, the traditions of life in academe and in hierarchical organizations moderate the flow of demands on him. The president's time is clearly rationed, but very few of the presidents with whom we talked had a serious sense that *they* were doing the rationing or that there was any particular logic to the resultant distribution of attention.

Most contacts with the president are not initiated by the president. In the course of our interviews on the campuses of our 42-college sample, we asked presidents and others to give us information about the "last contact" the president had with various types of people (e.g., students, trustees). In particular, we asked how the contact happened. Was it initiated by the president? Was it initiated by the other person? Was it a casual meeting? Was it a regularly scheduled meeting?

Table 33 shows the responses. Apparently about 30 percent of the average president's contacts (excluding his contacts with "outsiders," for whom we have no information) are initiated by him. This varies from about 35 to 40 percent of the contacts he has with student officers, administrators, and trustees to only 7 to 20 percent of his contacts with ordinary students and faculty. Only in the case of his chief administrative subordinates does the president initiate a higher share of the contacts than are initiated by the other person involved.

This does not necessarily mean that 70 percent of the president's schedule is outside his control. Clearly, he has some choices in which initiations from others he accepts. Clearly, he can, in principle, regulate the total stream of contacts by relatively modest initiations. We do not believe that is what is happening, however. Rather we believe that a large share of the presidential life is regulated by personal contacts and a large share of those personal contacts are regulated by outside initiative.

These aggregate statistics on the allocation of time by the president are consistent with a picture of a president who is basically reacting to others, who leads a busy, verbal life, and who divides his time relatively equally among the administrative, entrepreneurial, and political roles of the job. Before we turn to an examination of the implications of these data for interpretations of presidential styles, however, we should examine some variations among presidents. Thus far we have limited our attention to the "average" president. In the next two sections we consider the sources of differences in presidential time allocation.

TEMPORAL VARIATIONS IN ALLOCATION

For the most part, studies of work have limited the concern with temporal pacing to the more extreme cases — to assembly line pacing and to other highly structured activities that sometimes seem alien to the human spirit. Such a limitation is unnecessary. Normal life is regulated by the calendar and by the clock. We are all clock watchers. Although there are variations between and within cul-

TABLE 33 *Percentage of last contacts between presidents and others, by type of contact initiation*

Type of contact initiation	Student officers, editors, etc. (1)	Other students (2)	Faculty adminis- trators (other than the chief) (3)	Other faculty (4)	Trustees (5)	Chief adminis- trative officers (6)	For all these contacts (i.e., excluding outsiders) (7)
Casual meeting	6	44	14	36	22	16	21
Initiated by the president	39	19	36	7	36	36	30
Initiated by the contact	44	38	45	43	36	28	36
Regularly scheduled meeting	11		4	14	6	20	13
TOTAL	100	101	99	100	100	100	100

(1) Based on the (unweighted) responses of the 18 presidents who reported their last student contact was with a student officer, editor, or other official of the student body.

(2) Based on the (unweighted) responses of the 16 presidents who reported their last student contact was not with a student officer, etc.

(3) Based on the (unweighted) responses of the 22 presidents who reported that their last faculty contact was with a faculty member who also held an appointment as a department chairman or dean.

(4) Based on the (unweighted) responses of the 14 presidents who reported that their last faculty contact was with a faculty member who did not have an administrative position.

(5) Based on the (unweighted) responses of 36 presidents.

(6) Based on the (unweighted) responses of 39 chief academic officers, 36 chief business officers, and 28 assistants to the president.

(7) An estimate based on weighting the other columns in terms of the relative frequency of contact with the several groups (see Table 32).

tures, most of us lead reasonably reliable lives. We celebrate weekends. We eat and sleep according to a fairly regular schedule. Presidents are not particularly unusual in this regard.

A president's life is orderly. Presidents sleep at night and work during the day. They arise in the morning, have breakfast, and go to work, arriving there around eight. About noon they stop for lunch, returning to the office about 1:30. They work until about five or six o'clock, then go home for dinner. After dinner they read, write a little, spend time with their families, or perhaps go out to a meeting before retiring.

Figure 13 shows our estimates of where presidents are over the course of an average workday. Although we have accurately described the model day above, there is substantially more variability than our "conventional" picture seems to suggest. As a result, we should note two features of the pattern of presidential locations over the day that are not reflected well in the modal description. First, although presidents are more likely to be working at the office than any other single place during most of the day, most of them are elsewhere before 9:00 A.M., after about 4:30 P.M., and from about 11:30 A.M. to about 2:30 P.M. Second, presidents are substantially more likely to be in their offices in the before-lunch period than in the after-lunch period. After lunch there is a good chance that they will be found elsewhere on campus or around town.

The pattern of presidential locations shown in Figure 13 is closely

FIGURE 13 *Percentage of presidents at four locations, by hour of the day*

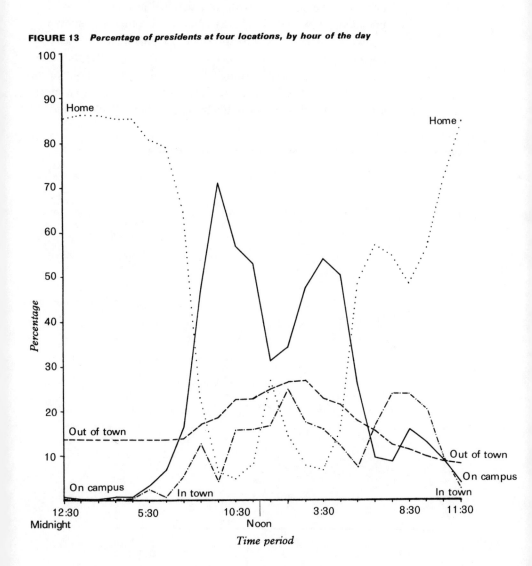

related to the way in which the presidents organize their day with respect to the three major roles we have identified. Although a president has a heterogeneous schedule, the three roles of administrator, politician, and entrepreneur are not found in equal mixes throughout the day. If we consider the share of presidential contacts that are with (1) administrative subordinates, (2) constituents, and (3) outsiders through the day, we find that presidents tend to be administrators in the morning, to deal with their external world at noon, to return in the afternoon to administration, but to switch to the political role increasingly in the later stages of the afternoon and early evening. This pattern is detailed in Figure 14, where the president's time path in the distribution of contacts is shown.

Figure 15 shows how the president divides his time between being alone, meeting with one person, and meeting with groups. After a brief period in early morning when he is likely to be alone or meeting with a single other person, the president moves into a morning schedule in which he is unlikely to find himself alone and quite

FIGURE 14 *Daily time path of presidents in contact-pattern role space*

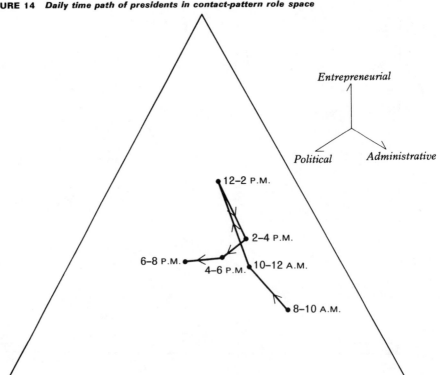

FIGURE 15 *Percentage of presidents in groups of various sizes, by hour of day*

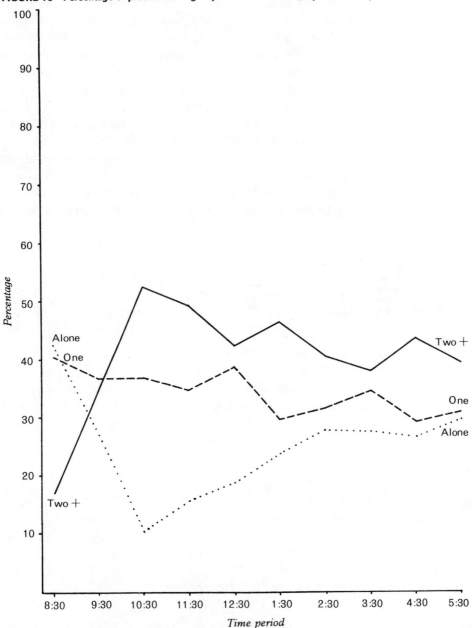

likely to find himself meeting with groups. By 10:30 A.M. only 10 percent of the presidents are alone. During the day, group time declines, time alone increases.

The daily pattern apparently has a weekly variant that is quite similar. Since our study of presidential calendars involved only two days (Tuesday and Friday), we cannot make a detailed examination of the weekly cycle. Nevertheless, we can observe some consistent variations. Table 34 shows the differences between Tuesday and Friday. Friday is clearly more of a constituency day; presidents are more likely to be on campus (particularly at some place other than their own office), and are more likely to meet with constituents (particularly trustees and faculty). The end of the week, like the end of the day, is a time for seeing the constituents. The combination of the daily and weekly cycles results in a late Friday (4 P.M. to 6 P.M.) in which 51 percent of the contacts are with faculty, students, or trustees and only 14 percent are with administrators.

TABLE 34
Allocation of time estimated from secretarial logs (8 A.M. to 6 P.M.), comparison of two days

	Friday	*Tuesday*
Where the president is		
Home	19%	13%
On campus	50	44
In town (not on campus or home)	11	17
Out of town	19	25
With whom he has contact		
Administrative subordinates	37%	42%
Constituents	34	23
(Trustees)	10	7
(Students)	9	9
(Faculty)	15	7
Outsiders	28	35
How many people he is with		
Zero	24%	25%
One	34	34
Two or more	41	40

Taken collectively, the data indicate an orderly pattern of activities in the presidential schedule. There is substantial variance. Presidents may be doing almost anything at almost anytime. However, there is an underlying tendency toward a daily and weekly cycle in the pattern of activities. The regularity of these temporal variations suggests that presidents play their different roles at different times and in different places. They follow a standard daily and weekly cycle in their work, attending to administrative matters first.[4]

The pattern undoubtedly reflects, in part, the limited degrees of freedom in a tight schedule. Once mornings have been committed to administrative meetings, other things are forced to another time. At the same time, the president's life appears to be organized in a way that indicates a priority he shares with his contacts. Extracurricular activities for students, departmental service for faculty, community service for trustees are all attended to after one is through "working" for the day or the week. Such activities thus come disproportionately at the end of the day and the end of the week—they are not really quite "play" but also not quite "work." Contact with the president is a special activity to be engaged in after the normal routine of the day is completed. It suggests the analogy of a cocktail party. Few cocktail parties are scheduled early in the morning or early in the week either—and perhaps for the same general reasons.

Although we have no data to confirm it, we believe that the presidential day and week are both characterized by a temporal movement from relatively programmed activity to relatively unprogrammed activity; from relatively precise problems to relatively diffuse problems; from relatively stable, repetitive relations to relatively less stable, less repetitive relations; from relatively technical administrative roles to relatively royal, symbolic roles.

The movement is conventional and is consistent with "Gresham's Law of Planning" (March & Simon, 1958). Highly-structured activity, such as administration, will take priority over less-structured activity, such as reflection or broadranging discussion. In this case, nonetheless, it seems somewhat perverse. Assuming that the usual human factors of work efficiency as a function of fatigue apply to college presidents, they will exhibit an "efficiency" curve that approximately parallels their administrative activity curve. They and their contacts are likely to be at their least efficient levels when they are pursuing the relatively diffuse, unprogrammed problems of entrepreneurial and political roles; on the other hand, both presidents and their contacts seem to suggest by the time

[4] With such a perspective it may be interesting to note that the data also indicate that the typical early morning pattern is to meet with nonacademic administrators first and then with academic administrators.

priorities they establish that if "first things come first," then "politics" is an activity of lesser importance.

The "average" president is a convenient and not entirely misleading fiction. There is enough consistency in time allocation patterns across a relatively wide range of types of schools to indicate that the major implications we can draw about the way presidential time is organized may be true across the whole range of collegiate institutions. There are, however, some differences.

First, as we show in Table 35, presidents of "rich" colleges are more likely to be out of town than are presidents of "poor" colleges; presidents of poor colleges are more likely to be in town but not on campus than are presidents of rich colleges. Reputation, status, and resources affect the day-to-day mobility of college presidents.

TABLE 35
Proportion of time spent by presidents (according to secretarial logs), by locations and subsample, 8 A.M. to 6 P.M.

	Type of school					
Location	*Large rich*	*Medium rich*	*Small rich*	*Large poor*	*Medium poor*	*Small poor*
Home	17%	10%	15%	21%	18%	15%
On campus	53	62	51	50	49	43
*In town**	15	8	7	21	17	14
Out of town†	14	20	26	8	15	27

*Includes local transit.
† Includes out-of-town transit.

Second, presidents of small colleges are more likely to be found out of town than are presidents of large colleges. Partly, this is because large colleges tend to be in larger communities than small ones. As a result, "in town" has a different functional significance for institutions of different sizes. As one would expect from such reasoning, large-college presidents spend more time "in town" than do small-college presidents (although those differences are not as great as in the rich-poor case).[5]

Third, as we show in Figure 16, there are some differences in the relative weight attached to the three major presidential roles. Presidents of larger schools seem to spend more time in administrative and less time in entrepreneurial roles than do presidents of smaller schools.

[5] There are no major differences among the various types of schools in the proportion of time presidents spend on the campus or at home. This seems to be fairly constant across size and wealth categories. If anything, large-school presidents are home or on campus more than small-school presidents.

FIGURE 16 *Differences in contact patterns by size of school*

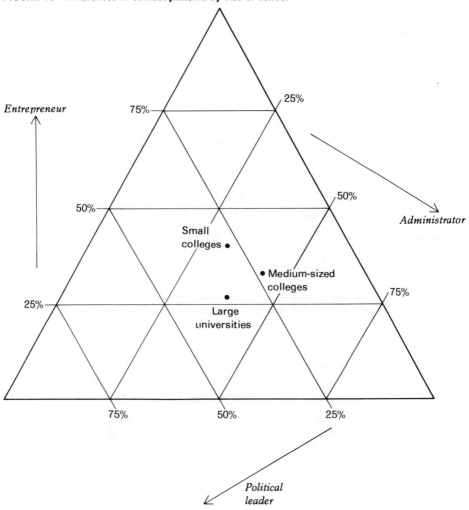

Fourth, as we show in Table 36, size affects the pattern of contacts with subordinates. In large schools, presidents spend much more time with academic administrators than they do with nonacademic administrators. In small schools, presidents spend much more time with nonacademic administrators than they do with academic administrators.

Fifth, as we show in Table 37, the amount of presidential time devoted to "academics" (i.e., academic administration, faculty, and students) relative to the amount of contact with others in-

TABLE 36 *Ratio of number of contacts with academic administrators to number of contacts with nonacademic administrators*	*Size of school*

Size of school	Ratio of number of contacts
Large	2.61
Medium	1.82
Small	0.69

creases with size. Presidents of small schools have relatively less contact with the "academic" part of the organization than do presidents of larger schools.

TABLE 37
Ratio of number of contacts with academics* to number of contacts with nonacademics†

Size of school	Ratio of number of contacts
Large	0.83
Medium	0.70
Small	0.43

* Refers to students, faculty, academic administrators.
† Refers to president's office nonacademic administrators, trustees, external.

Sixth, as we show in Table 38, presidents of small schools are more likely than presidents of larger schools to talk directly with faculty rather than to communicate through academic administrators. At least in this sense, the larger, and particularly the medium-sized, schools are more bureaucratic. Since there are more faculty in the larger schools, this means that as size increases, there is a sharp decline in the likelihood of an individual faculty member having contact with the president.

TABLE 38
Ratio of number of contacts with academic administrators to number of contacts with faculty

Size of school	Ratio of number of contacts
Large	2.08
Medium	3.12
Small	0.98

Seventh, as we show in Table 39, presidents of large schools are less likely to deal with people one at a time than are presidents of small or medium-sized schools. They are more likely to be alone. Both of these seem to reflect a greater personalization of relations in smaller schools.

TABLE 39		Size of school		
Proportion of presidential time spent by number of persons present and size of school	*Number of persons present*	*Small*	*Medium*	*Large*
	President alone	22%	25%	37%
	One other person	35	38	17
	Two or more others	43	37	46
	TOTAL	100	100	100

Most of these differences are modest. There are very substantial similarities in contact patterns and the utilization of time among presidents across a wide range of size and wealth. Within size categories there is variation. Though the differences are extremely large, they do cast some additional light on the presidency. Consider in particular the size effects we have noted:

Presidents of larger schools are more likely to:

- Be "in town."
- Spend time in administrative roles rather than entrepreneurial roles.
- Spend time with academic administrators rather than nonacademic administrators.
- Spend time with "academics."
- Interact with faculty through academic administrators rather than directly.
- Deal with people in groups rather than singly.
- Be alone.

We think this set of results can be summarized in terms of two major size effects. In the first place, presidents of larger schools are turned somewhat more "inward" than presidents of smaller schools. Although by a number of standard measures of status large-school presidents have higher status than small-school presidents and might be expected to have a more "cosmopolitan" perspective, their organizational behavior is actually more tightly linked to the university and (within the university) to the academic activities of the university. From this point of view, the standard academic experience of college presidents (see Chapter 2) probably prepares them better for a large-school presidency than for a small-school presidency.

In the second place, the presidency of a larger school is less personal. More of the interactions are in groups or via written communication (when presidents are "alone," they are mostly writing, talking on the phone, and reading correspondence and reports). A higher proportion of the communications flow through administrative channels. Large universities are large bureaucratic organizations in the forms of interaction they produce. Their styles are different from the personal styles of the typical academic department. From this point of view, the standard academic faculty experience of college presidents probably prepares them better for a small-school presidency than for a large-school presidency.

As we showed in Chapter 4, there is considerable agreement among presidents on the images they have of the job. They see it as a combination of administrator, institutional entrepreneur, and political leader. We also noted, however, that there are some differences among presidents in the secondary overtones they provide to that picture. Specifically, we were able to divide our sample of presidents into two groups: one group with a relatively authoritative interpretation of the combination of roles and a second group with a relatively mediative interpretation. This image orientation is strongly related to the size of the college or university. Large-school presidents are much less likely to have a mediative interpretation of their role than are small- or medium-sized-school presidents.

As we also saw in Chapter 4, presidents who hold the typical large-school image of the presidency have higher expectations of another administrative job, lower expectations of a return to the faculty, and less direct faculty contact; lay greater emphasis on the role of planning; are more likely to describe meetings with subordinates as "advisory" rather than as making "formal" decisions; and as signs of presidential success are inclined to stress quiet and respect of the faculty and community more heavily and educational programs less heavily. Similarly, when we look at their organization of time, we discover that presidents with a relatively authoritarian view of the presidency are more likely to be in town, to deal with people in groups rather than singly, to be alone, to spend time with "academics," to interact with faculty through administrators rather than directly, and to spend more time with students and trustees relative to faculty. These results are summarized in Tables 40, 41, and 42.

TABLE 40
Proportion of time spent by presidents (according to secretarial logs), by persons involved (when president is not alone), by role orientation of president

	Role orientation of president	
Persons involved	Relatively authoritative	Relatively mediative
Administrative	37%	41%
President's office	7	8
Academic administrators	21	16
Nonacademic administrators	9	17
Constituents	32	27
Trustees	12	7
Students	13	8
Faculty	7	12
Outsiders	32	32

TABLE 41
Critical contact ratios, by role orientation of president

	Role orientation of president	
Contact ratios	Relatively authoritative	Relatively mediative
Academic administrator–nonacademic administrator	2.3	1.0
Faculty–academic administrator	0.35	0.71
Academic-nonacademic	0.69	0.57
Students-faculty	1.8	0.68

TABLE 42
Proportion of time spent by presidents, by number of persons present and role orientation of president

	Role orientation of president	
Number of persons present	Relatively authoritative	Relatively mediative
President alone	27%	23%
One other person	21	35
Two or more others	52	42

IMPLICATIONS FOR THE PRESIDENCY

These data on the ways college presidents spend their time suggest that the allocation of time on the job is regulated by six major factors:

1 *The size of the school* Presidents in relatively large schools develop a style that is both somewhat more "local" to the college and somewhat less personal. They see their job in somewhat more authoritarian and some-

what more academic terms. Presidents in relatively smaller schools use a style that is oriented less to the internal operation of the school and is somewhat more personal. They see their job in somewhat more mediative and in somewhat less academic terms.

2   *A daily and weekly cycle*   Presidents do administration first in the day and first in the week, switch to their external roles later in the day and later in the week, and reserve their time increasingly for "political" activities as the day draws into the evening and the week draws into the weekend.

3   *General expectations within the culture*   Presidents work a normal workweek that is approximately the same as that reported by faculty members. The structure of their workweek depends heavily on the initiations of others.

4   *Role expectations of presidents*   Presidents expect (and feel that others expect of them) that they will be administrators, politicians, and entrepreneurs. They divide their time more or less equally among the roles. Presidents, and the others around them, expect presidents to perform the royal functions of hearing petitions, granting formal assent, and confirming positions.

5   *The ambiguity of the job*   Neither presidents nor the people around them have much idea about the relationship between success and presidential behavior. Unable to point to serious attributes of success, they learn to point to attributes of "effort."

6   *The pleasures of presidents*   Presidents generally enjoy and seek out the emotional perquisites and the acknowledgment of office. This phenomenon directly affects the overall pattern of time allocation by the president.

The result of the operation of these factors is a familiarly inextricable combination of "myth" and "reality." The objective situation of presidents is largely built on the beliefs they bring to the job and share with their associates. Those beliefs are not exotic. The utilization of time by presidents is not bizarre. It stems from a series of daily and hourly judgments that are individually unspectacular and mostly unexceptionable. Yet, most presidents and most observers of the presidency are unhappy with the overall allocation of time that results.

As we noted at the outset, any consideration of the ways in which presidential time is allocated must confront both the reality and curiosity of presidential complaints. Presidents feel misused. Most of the presidents with whom we talked appeared to feel rather little control over their schedules. They felt themselves to be the victims of the pressures upon them and the limitations of time and their own energies. Too many people asking too much too often. Too many "trivial" activities that had to be engaged in. No time for thinking or reading or initiating action.

The complaints seem legitimate, but they are—at least to some degree—curious. How can a president recognize a disparity between what "ought" to be done and what "is" being done with his own time and be unable to reduce the disparity? Why is it impossible for a president to organize his own schedule? Why does he do "trivial" things, knowing that they are trivial? Why does he fail to spend time thinking or initiating action if that is what is important? What strange organizational and personal processes have captured the president? Why can't a president say "no"?

In part, the college president has difficulty saying "no" because he has no normatively legitimate basis for substituting his judgment on the way his time should be allocated for the pattern of expectations among his colleagues and contacts. As we have said repeatedly, the university is an organization that does not know what it is doing. Its goals are ambiguous and its technology obscure. As a result, there is no way that a president can demonstrate, either to others or to himself, that an alternative pattern of attention would (or did) result in improved performance.

We believe that the workload and the distribution of that workload among contacts, among styles of activities, and among places reflects the predominately social specifications of the job. Presidents work hard. Many of them are tired. Many of them report the inordinate demands on their time. Few of them ask why they accept the demands. Few of them act decisively to eliminate the demands. They seem to believe that the presidential report card has two components: effort and performance. Performance is largely an act of God or at least not clearly under the control of the president. If the president works hard, he may still face a financial, student, or faculty catastrophe. But if he doesn't work hard, he will be treated as a failure in any event.

Presidents satisfy the norms with respect to how long they will work, with whom they will interact, when they will meet them, and where. As a result, we observe a rather strong element of mundaneness in the daily and weekly cycle of presidents. Their hours are regular, though long. We observe a tendency to separate the various aspects of the presidential role into separate time segments. Administration, politics, and entrepreneurship are equal,

but separate, aspects of the job. We observe a strongly social flavor to the organization of time. Time is organized in terms of people, rather than problems.

These regularities and the norms that they reflect also suggest
that there is a certain element of mythology in presidential assertions on the misallocation of presidential time. College presidents
read. They are aware that the grandeur of executive leadership
is rarely reflected in the realities of their job as they know it. They
suspect—in some grand sense—that this inconsistency stems partly
from some overall misallocation of effort. Yet each of the daily
opportunities available to revise that misallocation is passed by
because there is no way to claim persuasively that today's small
unit of time should be spent in a different way. A belief in the mis-
use of time is a part of the presidential creed but not a basis for
presidential action.

The dilemma is sustained by the people around the president.
Everyone seems to accept the dogma that the president is overworked and misworked. Nevertheless, neither the president's
administrative subordinates, nor his constituents, nor his patrons
are prepared to act in terms of such a dogma. Both in terms of the
status that contact with the president provides and in terms of the
minor favors that a president can grant, the president's attention
is a scarce resource of value to those around him. Anyone in the
system who claims a position of importance, or who aspires to
one, supports his claim by his association with the president.
Legislators, local businessmen, alumni, student politicians, faculty
politicians, social and community leaders, newspaper reporters,
subordinates, secretaries, bankers, and neighbors enjoy their contacts with the president. Few of them believe—and there is no
profound reason why they should believe—that presidential attention to the ill-defined, contradictory, and diffuse global purposes
of the university would be more efficacious to them or to the general
good than attending to their immediate needs.

At the same time, we believe the college president has difficulty
saying "no" because much of the time he does not really want to
do so. The latent absurdity of being the executive leader of an
organization that does not know what it is doing haunts the presidential role. That sense of absurdity is somewhat ameliorated by
a pattern of attention that reinforces a feeling of reality for the role.
This means a busy schedule, the press of work, the frequent reminders of the fact that one *is* the president, the attention to minor
things one *can* do.

The organization of presidential attention can be viewed partly as a response to a very serious personal problem faced by anyone in the role of leader in an organized anarchy. It is almost impossible for a president to secure meaningful information on the quality of his performance in the presumptive terms of executive evaluation. Since the objectives of the organization are unclear, how can we say that the organization is successful? If we have difficulty in assessing the success of an organization, we necessarily have difficulty in assessing the quality of executive leadership in terms of output variables. As a result, presidents and others need to look for other reminders of the quality of leadership. They find these indicators in the process rather than in the outcomes of the process.

The college president is an executive who does not know exactly what he should be doing and does not have much confidence that he can do anything important anyway. His job is the pinnacle of his success, and he has been—by the standards of most of his contemporaries and colleagues—a quite successful person. Consciously or not, presidents organize their time in such a way as to maintain a sense of personal competence and importance in a situation in which that is potentially rather difficult. They make themselves available to a large number of people whose primary claim is simply that they want to see the "president." Counter to most other evidence, such interactions remind the president that he is the boss. Similarly, presidents preside over otherwise largely pointless meetings, for the process of presiding involves a subtle reassertion of primacy.

We also believe that presidents work long hours in large part because they enjoy them. We are growing accustomed now to the possibility that some women may prefer work life to home life. We should not be too surprised to discover data consistent with the possibility that some men have similar preferences. The cultural conventions of family life and the moralistic obligations of high status should not obscure the rather obvious point that, on the average, persons holding positions such as a college presidency will find their work roles comparatively flattering and pleasurable relative to their family roles, even if they have by most standards a happy and productive family life. College presidents work long hours because they are successful, not the other way around.

That leadership is a form of consumption as well as a factor in production is a proposition familiar to students of organizations and leaders for many centuries. It does not demean the college presidency to note that the modern college or university is conspicuously a place in which we would expect leadership as consumption to be particularly important. Despite the recent jokes and literature, it is a reward. Rewards are earned in the past, savored in the present.

If our analysis is correct, some recent proposals for reform of the college presidency are misdirected. These proposals have placed considerable emphasis on reducing two aspects of the presidential allocation of attention. The first is the presidential overload. The second is the way in which reaction drives out action. The standard recommendation for dealing with presidential overload and the shortage of presidential initiative is to increase presidential staff or to arrange some kind of dual or tripartite presidency. Although we believe that reorganization and staff strengthening of the presidency may be possible, we believe that much of the discussion misunderstands the nature of the overload.

It is a mistake to see the pattern of presidential attention as a burden imposed on a reluctant leader by an unreasonable group of associates. As long as presidents continue to use the metaphors they do to describe the organization and their role, as long as the university continues to have ambiguous goals and poorly specified technologies, and as long as the presidency is the top of the promotion ladder for a career in academic administration, the process will be difficult to change. The president will be very likely to work long hours and to devote a large share of that time to meeting with people on their demand and within the framework of socially defined legitimate claims on him—regardless of the size, organization, or quality of the staff with which he works. We see very little evidence in the calendar data or in our interviews that the overload on the president is related in any consistent way to the apparent complexity of the problems facing the institution, to the size of the staff available to the president, or to the organization of the presidency.

Most presidents would prefer a slightly—even substantially—different world, but not at the cost of undermining their own conceptions of themselves as competent and important individuals. If we wish to change the pattern of activities by presidents, we will need to change the orientation presidents have to their jobs, themselves, and the relationship between the two. We will need to define some reasonable expectations by associates. Without such changes, the time demands on presidents in the future will be as they have been in the past, largely independent of the problems they face or the help they have.

8. Presidential Tenure

As we have developed our interpretation of the college presidency over the preceding chapters, two themes seem particularly conspicuous. The first is the idea that the presidency is heavily regulated by social norms and conventional expectations. The world in which presidents live is a world of considerable potential ambiguity made manageable by the superimposition of conventions. The second is that there is a fair disparity between the models presidents have available to them for interpreting their roles and their actual experience in the roles. What happens in universities seems to be less a consequence of either bureaucratic or political management than is implicit in usual discussions of presidential leadership.

Within this world, presidents come and go. They serve for some years and then are fired, quit, retire, or die. According to some theories, they serve longer terms if they solve the problems of the presidency—or if they are not presented with good job alternatives. Presumably, they serve shorter terms when the combination of their own competences, will, and the problems of the day lead to observable failures in solving the problems—or when the attractions of new jobs call them away.

Whether such theories are correct, there is something to be learned from an examination of the best external evidence we have on the presidential experience: the length of his term in office.[1]

[1] Most of the analysis in this chapter is based on an examination of the presidents from 1900 to 1971 in the 42 schools within our basic sample. With the help of the respective staffs, we have reconstructed the tenure history of the presidency in these schools during the twentieth century. The data are nearly complete. Since some of the 42 schools were founded later than 1900, a complete data set would cover 2,570 presidential years. We have information on years of tenure in 2,557 (99.4 percent) of those cases, and information on the age of the president in 2,507 (97.9 percent). In the manner detailed in Appendix A, "Procedures for Estimating Various Statistics for the Universe of Presidents," we have used these data to make estimates about the universe of presidents and the universe of students' presidents.

* For an empirical update on presidential tenure, see Appendix F written by James R. Glenn, Jr., and James G. March for this edition.

The tenure expectancy of a president is of considerable personal relevance to him. Presidents talk about it, ordinarily with a grim smile. It is also of considerable theoretical significance to the student of organizational leadership. By understanding some of the dimensions of presidential exits, we understand something of the nature of the university and how it organizes its leadership.

In this chapter we ask what happens to presidents after they take office. How long do they serve? What are the patterns of departures? Where do they go after the presidency? Why do they leave the presidency? What are the implications of an analysis of presidential tenure for the role of the president? The questions are familiar ones. They have been the focus of considerable interest and speculation in recent discussions of the presidency. Within the limits of the data available, we have tried to construct a first approximation to an understanding of presidential tenure and the careers of presidents during and after the presidency. We then try to use that first approximation to consider the ways in which the tenure and career structure pose problems for presidents and for the organizations they lead.

THE MEASUREMENT OF TENURE It is clear that we need to talk about the tenure of college presidents in order to discuss the role intelligently. What is less obvious is that the discussion of tenure is itself a difficult task. Indeed, a good discussion of tenure presumes a good theory of the presidency — as much as the other way around.

We can illustrate the problem by examining a rather common observation about the American college presidency — that the tenure of American college presidents decreased abruptly during the 1960s. Statements to that effect have appeared fairly frequently in recent years.[2] Although as early as 1960, Selden was examining the reported drop in presidential tenure, most of the attention to the phenomenon has come later and appears to be based on three kinds of data:

- The wide public coverage of troubles on the campus, the difficulties of presidents in dealing with those troubles, and the difficulties of trustees in replacing presidents.

- The reported estimate that about 300 of the 2,500 colleges and universities (including junior colleges) in the United States are currently looking for new presidents.

[2] See for example, *New York Times*, May 11, 1969, section 4, p. 14; March 15, 1970, p. 66; April 26, 1970, p. 56; July 19, 1970, p. 1.

- Kerr's (1970) analysis of the years in office of presidents of universities belonging to the Association of American Universities. Kerr found that the mean number of years that sitting presidents had been in office was 10.9 in 1899, 9.5 in 1929, 7.7 in 1939, 7.4 in 1959, and 5.9 in 1969. The median dropped from 7 years in 1929 to 2 years in 1969.

We believe that many of the inferences being drawn from these data are subject to question. They often appear to be cases of interpreting verbal conclusions rather than the studies themselves. This is particularly obvious in discussions of "average tenure." What does "average tenure" mean? We can imagine a number of quite different meanings that can be given to a concept of "average tenure" or to some aggregate measure of tenure distribution. For example, here are five:

1 *The backward cohort* The distribution of tenures for presidents completing their term in a particular year. Thus the average tenure (in this sense) for 1972 is the average number of years served by presidents leaving office in 1972. The distribution is knowable in 1972.

2 *The forward cohort* The distribution of tenure for presidents beginning their terms in a particular year. Thus the average tenure (in this sense) for 1972 is the average number of years served by presidents assuming office in 1972. This distribution is knowable at some point (about 35 years later). It may be estimated in 1972.

3 *Additonal tenure* The distribution of additional tenure for presidents now in office. Thus the average tenure (in this sense) for presidents in office in 1972 is the average number of years served between 1972 and the date of leaving the presidency. This distribution is knowable at some later date, but it may be estimated in 1972.

4 *Completed tenure* The distribution of completed tenure for presidents in office on a particular date. Thus the average tenure (in this sense) for 1972 is the average number of years in office for all presidents in office in 1972. This distribution is knowable in 1972.

5 *Full tenure* The distribution of full tenure (completed plus future) for presidents in office on a particular date. Thus average tenure (in this sense) for 1972 is the average number of years in the full term of office for all presidents in office in 1972. This distribution is knowable only later but can be estimated in 1972.

We believe that most people who talk about the tenure of college presidents really mean "full tenure," the "forward cohort," or "additional tenure." That is, they want to know either what the expected total tenure of presidents now in office is, or what the expected tenure of presidents recently appointed is, or how much longer presidents now in office can expect to serve. It is remarkable that none of the studies known to us report any of these statistics. What they generally report are quite different statistics — either the backward cohort or completed tenure. The latter, in particular, has been inexplicably labeled as "life expectancy" in several popular discussions of the presidency with a resulting major underestimation of the true expected (full) tenure.

What does it mean to say that "average tenure" is changing? Recent reports of presidential tenure are being used to suggest that one or more of the following assertions is true:

- *Assertion 1* Presidents now taking office can expect to have (on the average) shorter tenures than presidents taking office in some earlier year (e.g., 1952). (This is decreasing forward cohort tenure.)

- *Assertion 2* Presidents currently in office can expect to remain in office (on the average) fewer years than could the group of presidents holding office in some earlier year. (This is decreasing additional tenure.)

- *Assertion 3* Presidents leaving office currently are leaving office earlier than would have been expected when they came into office. (This is decreasing backward cohort tenure.)

- *Assertion 4* Presidents currently in office will have shorter tenures (on the average) than presidents who were in office at some earlier year. (This is decreasing full tenure.)

It should be noted that these are not equivalent statements. In fact, the full tenure statistic (computed by finding the average total tenure of presidents in office in a particular year) will yield substantially higher numbers than the forward cohort statistic (computed by finding the average tenure of presidents assuming office in a particular year). This is not a statistical freak. It stems from the fact that the average full tenure of presidents currently in office is conceptually quite different from the average tenure of a cohort of presidents assuming office in a particular time period. The magnitude of the difference between the two statistics depends on the amount of variation in the length of tenure. In the case of college presidents, there is considerable variation. As a result, the average full tenure of presidents in office in a particular year is notably higher than forward cohort average tenure.

It should also be noted that none of the four assertions is possible without a theory of presidential tenure. Each requires us to estimate some unknown distribution. Either we need to estimate the expected future tenures of new or current presidents or we need to estimate the tenures that would have been expected of currently exiting presidents. Either estimate requires assumptions about the nature of presidential careers. For example, we may need to make some assumptions about the age distribution of presidents and the extent to which tenure is dependent on age. In the latter part of this chapter we will try to sketch the rudiments of such a theory. As we will see there, the data indicate that we will require a theory more complicated than the implicit one currently used to justify assertions about changing average tenure.

As the above remarks suggest, the analysis of presidential tenure is a good deal more complex than would be indicated by reading some recent discussions of the presidency. It is a theoretical and statistical problem requiring more data than are currently available. Nevertheless, we have tried to make the best assessment we can. We will try to detail that assessment in the remainder of this section, but we can anticipate the major conclusions here:

It seems probable that the tenure expectations of American college presidents, as a whole, are now about what they have been through most of the twentieth century. Tenure was higher during the 1930–1945 period than earlier or subsequently. There have been long-run changes within schools that have shown considerable growth. In general, however, there has not been any dramatic change in recent years in any of the terms outlined in our four basic assertions. That is, *we do not believe there is evidence of any major recent shifts in the expected tenure of new presidents, or the expected additional or full tenure of current presidents, or that departing presidents are leaving office much earlier than would have been expected.* There have been some recent changes. But these appear to us to have been more conspicuously changes in the reasons why presidents leave office and in the interpretations made of their departures than in the amount of time presidents should be expected to serve.

Most of the data on which perceptions of declining tenure are based involve considering the *average completed tenure* of a sample of presidents as an index of the *expected additional tenure* in the same sample. For example, an analysis of the time trends in the average length of service of American Association of Universities (A.A.U.) presidents currently in office (Kerr, 1970) is cited as evidence of one or more of our four basic assertions above. It is usually taken as self-evident that average completed tenure and average additional tenure covary. We easily assume that the change in average completed tenure results from changes in some conditions that will also result in a change in average additional tenure. Few commentators on the tenure of presidents have questioned the assumption that these two measures are positively correlated. Yet it is a strong assumption. It directly implies that presidents are being exposed, over a prolonged interval of years, to a severe sort of retirement-producing disease that all presidents are roughly equally likely to contract. Since full tenure is the sum of completed and additional tenure, this view implies that full tenure is highly variable. If it were not, for example if full tenure were fixed or had very small variance, the correlation of completed and additional service years would be strongly negative. There are alternative suppositions that are quite as plausible. For example, we might argue that the disease involved is transient, and perhaps one particularly likely to affect presidents of advanced tenure. On this view it is possible for the completed tenure statistic to drop drastically as a relatively small number of long-term presidents leave the sample. Full tenure, however, could remain relatively unaffected, and the additional tenure of a group of current presidents would therefore be higher rather than lower.

Several items of data bear on the choice between these two views. In Figure 17 we show the plot of average completed tenure of American college presidents and average additional tenure since 1900 as we estimate them from our sample. Figure 18 shows the same plots for the average completed tenure and average additional tenure of an average college student's president. In both cases the average tenure is unknown after 1951 because at least one president in our sample who was in office in 1951 is still in office. Inspection reveals that there are frequently short periods in which completed tenures decline simultaneously with an *increase* in additional tenures. Moreover, a detailed examination of three of the four cross-sectional years that we studied in Chapter 2 (1924, 1939, and 1954) shows that the correlations of completed and additional tenures are .076, − .234, and − .320. Finally, the variation in the full tenure statistic is moderately large. Using the 167 full tenures in our historical sample, the estimated mean is 10.28 years and the estimated standard deviation 7.05.[3]

[3] The correlations count rich and large colleges more heavily than their frequency in the population of all colleges, since they are based on unweighted data. Also see Chapter 2, footnote 1, for information on the size and overlapping membership of the cross sections. The 1969 cross-section correlation cannot be given since additional tenure is unknown. Two still sitting presidents were omitted in calculating the 1954 correlation.

FIGURE 17 *Average additional and completed tenure in twentieth century (president weights)*

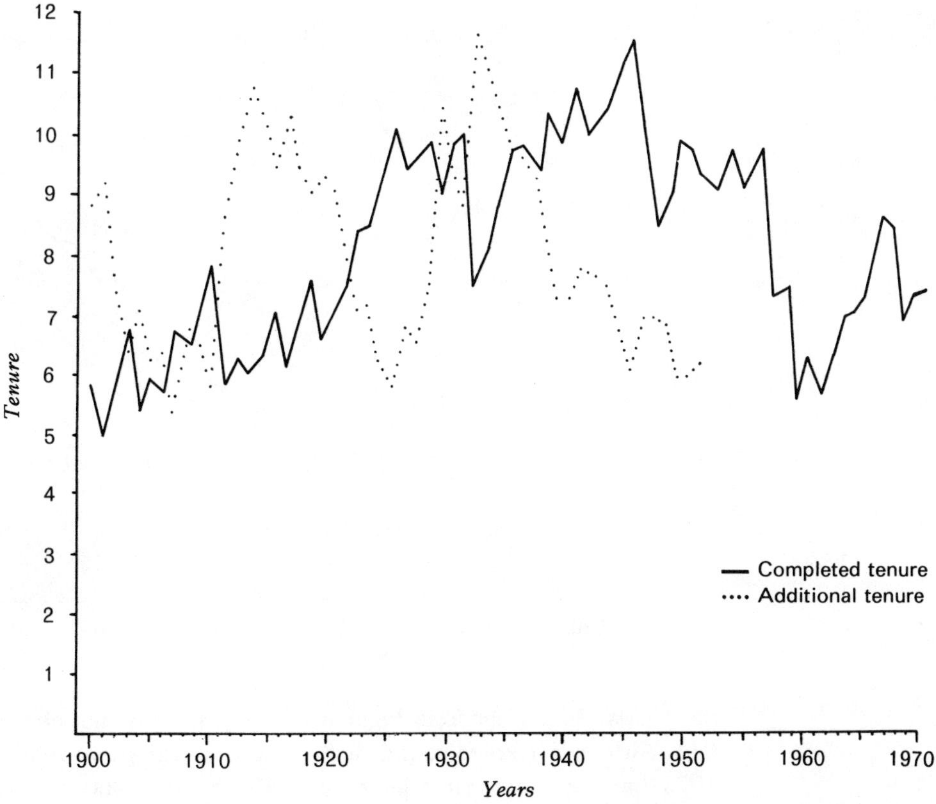

Taken together, these data hardly provide a strong basis for preferring the first view to the second. It seems unlikely that some sort of short-tenure disease is becoming endemic among presidents. It seems more plausible to us to view the system as having suffered a transient shock, opposite in direction to and shorter and less severe than that experienced in the Depression-war interval. Historically, the average completed tenure statistic has not been positively correlated with the additional tenure statistic. In fact, although the correlations are low, the best predictive use that can be made of that statistic is to argue that declines in average completed tenure will mean an increase in average additional tenure. This assertion is, we believe, distinctly counter to most recent inferences about that statistic.

There is another anomaly. The "student unrest" interpretation of presidential tenure would suggest a drop in completed tenure during

FIGURE 18 *Average additional and completed tenure in twentieth century (student weights)*

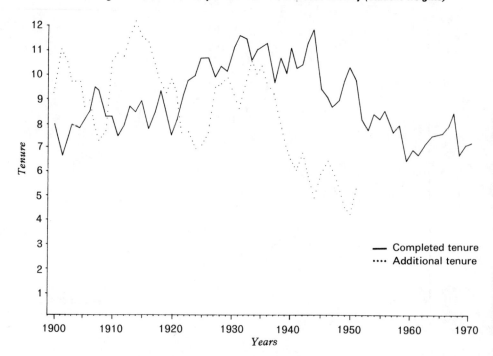

the 1960s. As is clear from Figures 17 and 18, we do not observe that. Although average completed tenure dropped from 1945 to 1970, the drop came primarily in the 1950s, not the 1960s. During most of the 1960-1970 period, we estimate that average completed tenure among American college presidents was generally rising.[4] If average completed tenure is a signal, it is a signal of something that predates the troubles of the 1960s (as, indeed, the student unrest may also be).

We believe that the sharp changes shown in the A.A.U. data (Kerr, 1970) stem from two factors: (1) the special character of the universities represented there (we will turn below to some special features of presidential tenure in large universities); and (2) a short-term transient. The usual argument has been that the very recent

[4] Selden (1960) and Ferrari (1970) each estimate mean completed tenure of college presidents. Selden made an estimate of 8.1 years for 1959 presidents; Ferrari made an estimate of 7.8 years for 1967–68 presidents. The Ferrari estimate is consistent with our own; the Selden estimate is not (although it would be consistent with our estimate for 1956–57). If we accept these estimates, the mean completed tenure is virtually unchanged during the 1960s.

sharp drop in median completed tenure among A.A.U. presidents indicates a low "life expectancy" of presidents. An examination of the backward cohort does not support such a view. The median full tenure of the 23 A.A.U. presidents who left office in the 1966–1969 period (i.e., those whose departure resulted in the low median completed tenure of their successors) was 11 years.[5] Recently, departing A.A.U. presidents have served about as long as one would expect a typical American college president to serve.

The conclusion can be extended to the general population of colleges. We can compare two different groups of college presidents. The first group is the immediate *predecessors* of *all current* presidents. The second group is the immediate predecessors of *new* presidents. If the life expectancy of presidents were dropping, we would expect the immediate predecessors of new presidents to have served shorter terms on the average than the immediate predecessors of all presidents. Such a comparison can be made by using two substantially simultaneous studies. Ingraham (1968) found that the mean full tenure of the predecessors of *all* current presidents (among four-year, accredited schools) was 11 years. Bolman (1965), using a very similar—though smaller—sample, found that the mean term in office of predecessors of *newly named* presidents was 12 years. Such data clearly do not support the hypothesis of recents drops in tenure expectations.[6]

We conclude that changes in college president full tenure have been substantially less than we have been led to believe and different in cause. Average completed tenure and average additional tenure are, as we would expect from their negative correlation, more variable than their sum, the average full tenure.

During most of the twentieth century the median college president has served about 10 years. The major general exception to the stability of median full tenure is the longer median full tenures achieved by presidents who held office during the Depression of the 1930s or during the Second World War. Median tenure now

[5] We are grateful to Clark Kerr for providing us with the raw data from his analysis.

[6] In fact, any procedure that looks at recently changing presidencies weights low-tenure institutions (if there are such) somewhat more than high-tenure institutions. As a result, we would expect the Ingraham (1968) estimates to be slightly higher than the Bolman (1965) estimates if there were no change. The fact that the Bolman estimates are slightly higher suggests that, if anything, recent changes have been in the other direction.

appears to be about what it was before 1930. Our estimates of the median tenure acheived by four different cohorts of presidents are shown in Table 43.

TABLE 43
Estimated
median full
tenures of
college
presidents
assuming office
during four
different time
periods

Time period	Estimated median full tenure of all college presidents	Estimated median full tenure of all students' college presidents
1900–1914	8	9
1915–1929	10	11
1930–1944	14	12
1945–1959	10	9

The aggregate data, however, conceal some significant variations by size of school. In Figure 19 we plot the median full tenures over time of presidents of schools that were — in 1968 — large (over 9,000 students), medium (1,500 to 8,999 students), and small (under 1,500 students). There has apparently been a significant long-term decline in the tenure of presidents of universities that are now large. Although our estimates for subsamples are based on smaller numbers (minimum $n = 10$) and subject to significant sampling error, we estimate that the median tenure of large-school presidents has declined enough to move them from the top to the bottom of the scale.

Schools that were relatively small in 1968 are, for the most part, schools that have experienced relatively modest and relatively gradual growth. They include 92 percent of the schools and enroll 58 percent of the students in four-year schools in the United States. The large schools are disproportionately schools that have grown substantially over the twentieth century — and particularly since 1945. Although the data base for these subsample estimates is thin, we think it is reasonable to speculate that relatively rapid growth in an institution tends to reduce presidential tenure; relative stability in size tends to increase tenure. This is consistent with the rise in tenure during the Depression and war years, with the long-term decline in tenure in currently large schools, and with the postwar decline in tenure in the average school.

Growth is, of course, heavily correlated with other things — heterogeneity, personnel turnover, reputation, slack, exit opportunities, visibility, and external funding, to mention only a few. It is not easy to be sure that growth is itself significant. If, how-

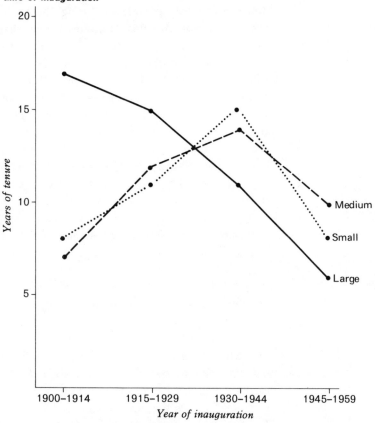

FIGURE 19 *Median full tenures of college presidents, by size of school and by time of inauguration*

ever, growth tends to reduce average presidential tenure, then the end to rapid expansion of four-year school enrollment in the United States should lead to a slight rise in the average full tenure of college presidents in the next decade.

The disaggregated data also indicate that the rise in full tenure during the 1930s and 1940s is more significant than it originally appeared. It was partially obscured by the steady decline among larger schools. Our estimate of the median tenure of presidents who *left office* in the 1930–1944 period is 18 years. Some of our confusion over tenure comes from seeing postwar tenure as abnormally low rather than the 1930–1944 tenure as abnormally high.

The changes in the schools that experienced rapid growth over the century and the changes of the 1930–1944 period are apparent exceptions to a general stability in tenure expectations among American college presidents during the twentieth century. The recent crises on American campuses have changed some aspects of the job for some presidents. They have changed the dramatic interpretations written by observers. They have affected the lives of some presidents in important ways. But simple linking of campus unrest with the life or exit of most presidents appears unlikely. It seems to us a confusion of the important drama of personal tragedy with the actuarial reality of tenure to see conclusive evidence of major changes in presidential tenure in the retirement of President Nathan Pusey from Harvard at the age of 63 after 18 years, or of President Grayson Kirk from Columbia at the age of 64 after 17 years. The impact of campus crises on the overall tenure picture is about comparable to the impact of a flood in Louisiana on the overall life-expectancy tables for the United States.

Overall, average presidential tenure is about what it has been throughout most of the twentieth century, except for the 1930–1944 period. If there is a decrease, it is small and can best be explained as the consequence of highly localized campus transient effects and the long-term impact of growth throughout the schools. We do not believe there has been a dramatic recent shift in the time presidents are serving or will serve in the future. We believe that new presidents can expect to serve about 10 to 12 years, as presidents have served in the past, and as recently retiring presidents have. We believe the most likely trend over the next few years is a slight upturn in presidential tenure associated with greater stability in college size.

DEPARTURE RATES AND THE CAREER SURFACE
We have tried to suggest some of the complexities involved in understanding the tenure of college presidents. Even such an apparently simple question as the probable term of office of an entering president requires not only a more careful specification of the meaning given to "tenure" but also a better understanding of the processes by which presidents leave office. As a first step toward a theory of presidential tenure, we have attempted to construct a *career surface* for presidents.

The career surface is a simple map of *age- and tenure-specific departure rates* from the presidency. In principle, it is possible to determine for each college president at any point in time his age and the length of time he has been in office. For any combination of age and tenure (e.g., age of 60 years, tenure of 5), we may count the number in two groups: *(a)* the number of presidents leaving office at that age and tenure; and *(b)* the number of presidents attaining that age and tenure. Then $b-a$ is the number of presidents passing successfully into the next year of life and service; and a/b is the age- and tenure-specific departure rate—the fraction of all presidents reaching a particular age and tenure point who leave at that point.

If we know the age- and tenure-specific departure rates for each combination of age and tenure, we can display them as "heights" above the age-tenure plane. The idea of a career surface defined in terms of age- and tenure-specific departure rates for presidents is central to our discussion of presidential tenure in the next two sections. We will try to show how it can be used to examine some important attributes of the role, to estimate the consequences of choosing presidents or assuming office as a president at a particular age, to discuss the implications of movement from one presidency to another, and to identify some critical career path problems of the college presidency.

MODES OF DEPARTURE FROM THE COLLEGE PRESIDENCY

In order to look at the career surface pattern of departures from the presidency, we believe it is necessary to distinguish five different ways by which a presidency is ended:

1 By replacement of an "acting" or "interim" president

2 By departure, through death or retirement, after age 65

3 By death before age 65

4 By transfer to the presidency of another college

5 By resignation or dismissal

Each of these modes of departure involves a different process, and pooling them into a single summary statistic is potentially confusing. We are, of course, primarily interested in the last mode. But before we can consider the pattern of resignation or dismissal, we must "clean" the data by eliminating the impact of the others.

Acting Presidents

Trustees sometimes appoint an acting, or interim, president to hold office while they seek a person for the job. In some cases, such appointments are formalized later into regular, "permanent" positions as president. More typically, however, they are planned tenures of less than a year, sometimes extended into a second year.

Our data indicate that the post-World War II use of acting presidents has been considerably greater than the prewar use and that acting presidents are most common in large schools. We estimate that the chance that a college or university in the United States would have an acting president (or some other interim administrative arrangement) on January 1 in a particular year has been about 0.02 over the past 70 years. Since 1945, it has been about 0.04, and in large universities since 1945, it has been about 0.06. There is no sign that the use of acting presidents increased in the 1960s over the level of the previous decade.

A theory of presidential tenure should attend to the interim presidency, but as a separate phenomenon. The use of an acting president presumably reflects a feeling on the part of trustees that it is impossible to find a suitable presidential replacement in the time between the resignation of a president and the date at which that resignation becomes effective. This apparent insufficiency of available time may come in turn from decreases in the "leadtime" given by departing presidents, from increases in the amount of consultation that is felt obligatory by the trustees before a new appointment is made, or from decreases in the attractiveness of obvious candidates for the position. Both size (because of the more complicated problems of consultation that larger schools present) and the effects of growth may yield an increase in the number of acting presidents observed.

Acting presidents confuse presidential tenure statistics. Occasionally, they are counted as "vacancies" when estimating the number of schools looking for presidents, and as "presidents" when estimating the tenure expectations of college presidents. The acting president is clearly a short-term president. Since 1900 only about 20 percent have been in office on January 1 in two consecutive years. If the use of acting presidents increases notably, it will become necessary to examine the acting president in his own right; but he should not be confounded with the regular appointee. So long as the current situation exists—in which the acting presidency is clearly differentiated by title and public expectations as well as by a low rate of conversion into the regular position—we think the acting president phenomenon should be treated separately from a consideration of the tenure of college presidents. As a result, we have removed the clearly identified acting president from our data before conducting our analysis of tenure.

Departure after Age 65   It is clear from our data that the rate of departure from the presidency changes rapidly when a president reaches his mid-sixties. Although some presidents have continued to hold office into their eighties and some presidents do not start their terms until their late sixties, as presidents reach normal retirement age and normal life expectancy, departure rates become overwhelmingly a function of age rather than years of service. The presidency is a job, and most occupants leave it relatively quickly after they reach the age of retirement, if they reach that age.

A theory of departure from the presidency must attend to exits through retirement or death after retirement age. We will obviously need to assess the chance that a president will reach age 65 in office before we can estimate the chance that a president will depart after that age. We can, however, estimate that historically the chance that a randomly selected school in a randomly selected year would have a president who would subsequently depart at, or after, age 65 is 0.26. The chance that a randomly selected student in a randomly selected year would have attended a school presided over by a president who reached 65 in office is 0.39.[7]

As is obvious from the difference between the two estimates above, the chance that a school has a president who will still be in office at age 65 is much greater for larger schools than for smaller. It is much greater for rich schools than for poor schools. As might have been guessed from our previous discussion about the lengthening of tenures in the 1930–1944 period, it was much greater during that period than it was before 1930 or after 1944. These results are summarized in Table 44.

TABLE 44
Chance that the president of a randomly selected college in a randomly selected year will still be in office at age 65, by type of college, by time

Type of school	1900–1929	1930–1944	1945–1970*	1900–1970*
Large, rich	65%	97%	17%	54%
Medium, rich	53	93	57	64
Small, rich	02	49	29	24
Large, poor	20	66	26	33
Medium, poor	31	52	28	35
Small, poor	08	44	15	18
All (institutional weights)	18	50	23	26
All (student weights)	35	68	26	39

* An underestimation stemming from the assumption that all current presidents who are not yet 65 will leave office before they are 65.

[7] Note that this is not the proportion of all presidents who will depart after 65. This estimate weights presidents by their length of service in order to assess the chance that a sitting president will be in office at 65.

Regardless of how likely it is for a modern president to reach age 65 in office, it seems clear that a theory of departures after that age is not particularly complex. The departure rates are very high. Presidents retire. Presidents die. This year the chances are about one in four that a random college has a president who will leave office at 65 or later.

Death Before Age 65

Presidents sometimes die in office before they reach 65. We have examined the pattern of deaths in office to assess the probability of a job-specific pattern of mortality. As nearly as we can determine, there is none. Mortality in office appears to be a function of age (as would be expected). We see no signs that it is a function of either the kind of school or the number of years of tenure (once age is controlled). The job is not, strictly speaking, a "killing" job. A theory of presidential tenure needs to attend to death as a moderately important mode of exit from the presidency, but no new theory of *presidential* death appears to be required. As a result, we have excluded exits by death from our analysis.

Transfers to Other Presidencies

Some presidents leave one college presidency to take another. In our sample of twentieth-century presidents, 13 came to a job at one of our sample institutions from another presidency; 4 left one of the sample institutions to go to another college or university presidency.[8]

The theoretical and statistical significance of transfers from one presidency to another is potentially quite large.[9] If each vacancy in a presidency is filled by transfer from another presidency, an initial vacancy due to some other factor (e.g., a death) produces a whole chain of vacancies.[10]

In order to examine the impact of vacancy chains in our total picture, we must answer two questions:

[8] This tabulation is limited to cases in which a president resigns from his position at one school to move immediately to a new presidency. It excludes cases in which there is an interval of other work.

[9] See White (1970) for a detailed application of the idea that job vacancies move through a system as opposed to the usual notion that men move through jobs.

[10] For example, if one-half of all vacant presidencies are filled by transfer from another presidency, then 100 presidential deaths will result in 50 vacancies (as 50 presidents move to fill half of the positions vacated by death). Filling these 50 will result in 25 more vacancies. And so on. It can be shown that the number of vacancies produced by a vacancy chain in which there is a fixed proportion ($1/k$) of transfers approaches $n/(k-1)$ where n is the number of

- What factors affect variations in the magnitude of the transfer effect?
- What is the pattern of transfers?

In fact, we probably need to respond to the second of the questions before we can do much with the first.

Since no studies have yet been directed specifically at the issue of vacancy chains within the ranks of college presidents, our examination of the pattern of transfers is necessarily based on inferences from a few other studies and a close look at the rather modest number of cases in our own sample. Nevertheless, the picture seems to be consistent and to make reasonable theoretical sense.

First, most transfers seem to be movements "up" the status hierarchy of colleges and universities. Consider two obvious indices of university status: size and wealth per student. If we consider the 17 cases of presidential movement in our sample, we find the pattern of movement shown in Table 45. Presidents seem clearly to move up with respect to size; the case of wealth is less clear but in the same direction. Overall, only one transfer was to a definitely "inferior" school.

TABLE 45
Relative size and wealth of the new schools of transferring presidents

Wealth	Size	
	Up	*Down*
Up	7	3
Down	6	1

Second, the age distribution of presidents coming to office from another presidency is different from that of other presidents at their accession to office. Transferring presidents are older on the average. In our cross sections, the mean age of accession of transferring presidents was 48.8 (median 48). This is about three years older than the overall average age (see Chapter 2).

Third, the mean length of tenure in the first presidency (before transfer) is 8.4 years. The median is 8 years. This is two or three years shorter than the average term.

additional vacancies produced by outside events (in the case of our example, by death). Thus, in our example, the 100 vacancies created by death produce a total of another 100 new vacancies. The number of such additional vacancies depends heavily on $1/k$ the rate of transfers. It measures the strength of this "multiplier effect" upon any vacancies produced by our other processes.

Thus, the pattern for transferring presidents is fairly clear. They enter their first presidency at a slightly younger age (median 40) than most, transfer to their second presidency after about 8 years, at which time they are slightly older than the average incoming president (median 48). The transfer is a promotion. They go to a school that is rated as "better" in some conspicuous sense than the one from which they have moved.

What difference does the pattern make? On the one hand, it complicates the problems of estimating the transfer rate among presidents. We will return to that point in a moment. On the other hand, it introduces some predictable variations in the observed departure rates and attributes of presidents in different kinds of schools and at different times. Suppose, for example, that we had three status classes of schools ("high," "middle," "low"), that transfers took place only between adjacent classes and only "up," that all three classes had the same rate of vacancies by external forces like death or internal forces like disaster, that all three classes were the same size, and that the transfer rate was 10 percent. Then we would end up with the results portrayed in Table 46 (for every 300 "natural vacancies"). The total vacancy rate will be lowest in the high-status schools and highest in the low-status schools.[11]

TABLE 46
Consequences for vacancies of differential rates of transfer by presidents of different type schools

Type school	Vacancies by other causes	Vacancies by transfer
High	100	
Middle	100	10
Low	100	11

When we turn to the factors affecting variations in the magnitude of the transfer effect, we also find some plausible results. The tendency for transfers to be "promotions" explains the fact that we find substantially more transfers *into* our sample of schools than transfers *out*. Our sample is a stratified one and has more high-status

[11] Notice, however, that this assumes that the vacancies produced by the vacancy chain are additional vacancies rather than substitutes. It is, of course, quite possible that the presidents who transfer are not, in fact, increasing the vacancy rate but are precisely those who would be leaving the institution in any event. In such a case, transfers would have the effect of changing the kind of jobs taken by departing presidents but would not increase the rates of departure in lower-status schools. We do not have adequate data to differentiate between the two alternative hypotheses.

(i.e., rich and large) colleges than would be expected by chance.[12] Because of the modest number of cases involved, we cannot place much confidence in our estimates with respect to presidential transfers, but we believe that the proportion of presidencies *filled* by presidents from another school varies from less than 1 percent in small, poor schools to over 20 percent in large, rich schools. The proportion of presidencies *terminated* by transfer varies from less than 1 percent in large, rich schools to over 10 percent in small, poor schools.

This pattern, moreover, is subject to fluctuations over time. Ferrari (1970) examined the proportion of current presidents who had been presidents elsewhere as a function of the number of years they had been president (thus effectively the year of their accession to their current presidency.) Because his sample looks backward from current presidents, his numbers are biased increasingly downward as one goes back in time and attempts to estimate the number of presidents in a particular year who came from another presidency. Nevertheless, they are instructive. In Table 47 the low numbers for tenures over 15 years can probably (though not with certainty) be discounted, but the smaller percentage of presidents who have started their second presidencies in the most recent five years is both striking and, if anything, likely to underestimate a change

TABLE 47 Percentage of presidents who were previously presidents elsewhere, by tenure	Number of years in office	Percentage from other presidencies
	New	3
	1–5	6
	6–10	10
	11–15	10
	16–20	5
	Over 20	4

SOURCE: (Ferrari, 1970).

in the direction of substantially fewer transfers. Similarly, if we look at our data, we see a clustering of transfers in certain time periods. For the most part, high rates of presidential transfers appear to be associated with relatively boom times in colleges and universities.

[12] Again, we refer the reader to Appendix A for a discussion of sampling and estimation procedures.

We think it is fair to speculate that during "good" times it is relatively easy to establish a favorable reputation as a college president, and trustees are more inclined to promote another president. During "bad" times, a college president must be substantially better or luckier to establish a favorable reputation, and the rate of transfer drops.

Resignation or Dismissal We have tried to differentiate the special features of acting presidents, death, retirement, and transfer to another presidency largely in order to examine the data with respect to resignation and dismissal without contamination by other factors. The other factors are important to presidential tenure. In Table 48 we have pooled our previous estimates to provide a composite picture of the chance that a randomly selected current president will be an acting presi-

TABLE 48
Estimated proportions of current presidents who are acting presidents or will terminate their tenures after age 65, by death before 65, or by transfers to another presidency

Presidents	Proportion of all presidents	Proportion of students' presidents
Acting presidents	4%	4%
Will still be in office at age 65	28	32
Will die in office before age 65	10	9
Will transfer to another presidency	6	3
TOTAL	48	48

dent, will still be in office at 65, will leave his position by dying before 65, or will move to another presidency. As will become clear below, such estimates are subject to error since they presume stability in the resignation and dismissal pattern as well as in the age distribution of presidents; but they give an approximation to the chance that tenure will be concluded by the relatively straightforward processes of death, retirement, promotion to another presidency, or the end of an interregnum. The chance is about one-half for an average president in a given year.

For the rest, it might seem useful to differentiate "resignation" from "dismissal," but this appears to be extraordinarily difficult. In fact, we believe it would be misleading. Very few presidents are officially dismissed. In almost all cases there appears to be a mixture of "pull" and "push" that is the result of a relatively long-term, relatively subtle procedure of accommodation between the president and his environment. The ambiguity of the organization is transmitted in a natural way to the ambiguity of departure.

Thus, we turn to the strange mixture of such phenomena as "failure," "aging," "time in office," and "disasters in the college" that is a part of every recent discussion of the tenure of college presidents. If we assume that presidential tenure is systematically connected to the length of time a man is in office, or to his age, or to some interaction between the two, or to some interaction between one or the other of those factors and some external events, then we are interested in understanding what we have called the career surface of presidents.

A career surface, as we defined it earlier in this chapter, shows the age- and tenure-specific departure rates estimated for a group of presidents. Within our data we simply cannot examine variations in the career surface over time or over types of schools. As we have indicated above, we think that there are some differences over time and across schools. Departure rates are generally higher under conditions of growth than under conditions of size stability. As a result, a definitive study of the career surface will require a much larger historical sample than ours. Our present effort is limited to identifying some general features of that surface by pooling all our subsample data without regard to time.

Figures 20 and 21 show the two differently weighted, estimated career surfaces for college presidents if we ignore acting presidents,

FIGURE 20 *Empirical career surface (president weights)*

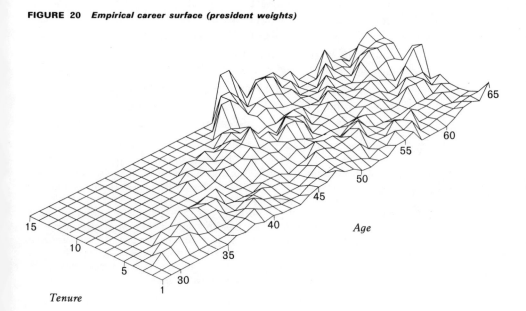

FIGURE 21 *Empirical career surface (student weights)*

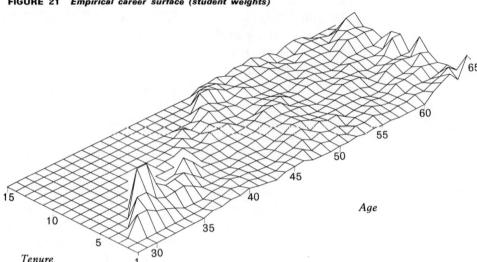

death, and retirement after age 65.[13] (We have not removed transferring presidents, but they represent only four cases in the data.)

Although the details of these surfaces are somewhat complicated, some important main features of the picture are not. There appears to be both an age and a tenure effect. Neither effect is monotonic. Rather, they appear to reflect some "preferred" ages and tenures for departure. With respect to age, there is something like a 15-year wave with peak departure rates at about 35, 50, and 65. The age-troughs occur at about 42 to 43 and about 57 to 58. With respect to tenure, there appears to be a series of five-year waves of similar shape but increasing amplitude. The peaks occur at 4, 9, and 14 years of service.

Figures 22, 23, and 24 show a hypothetical approximation to the career surface. Figure 22 shows the hypothesized age wave. It is a symmetric wave with a 15-year period. Figure 23 shows the hy-

[13] The career surfaces are based on averaging procedures to compensate somewhat for the thinness of the data. The points shown in the figures are generated by taking the mean of the 3 × 3 parallelogram surrounding the point. That is, the value shown for the departure rate at age 44, tenure 3, is actually the mean of nine points: 42,2; 43,2; 43,3; 44,2; 44,3; 44,4; 45,3; 45,4; 46,4. We have also used a different smoothing procedure that pools the data from five points surrounding the reference point in such a way that no two points are derived from source data involving the same president. In that case, the value for point 44,3 would be the mean of five points: 43,4; 44,4; 44,3; 44,2; 45,2. The alternative smoothing procedure results in a somewhat different appearance of the surface, but it has the same main features.

FIGURE 22 *Hypothetical age-departure wave*

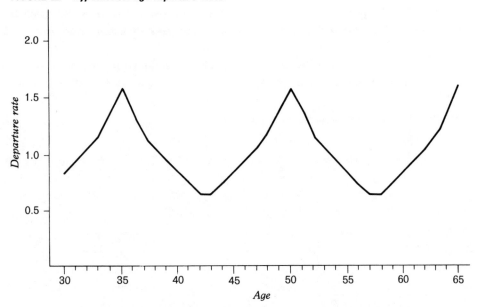

FIGURE 23 *Hypothetical tenure-departure waves*

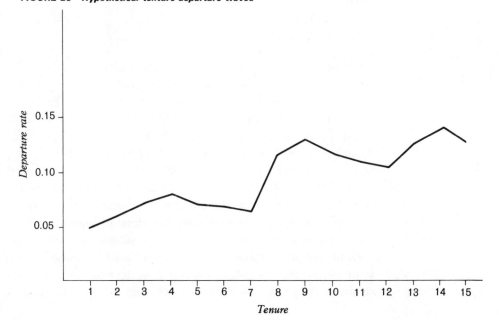

pothesized years-of-service waves. They are five-year waves with peaks at 4, 9, and 14 years. The departure rates within each five-year cycle are proportional to the peak departure rate within that cycle.

Figure 24 shows the resulting combined theoretical career surface over starting ages from 30 to 65 and tenures up to 15 years.

FIGURE 24 *Theoretical career surface*

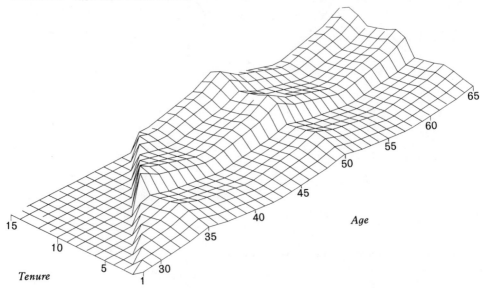

In this surface we assume that the age wave and the years-of-service wave are independent and that they are multiplied to produce a departure rate. The hypothesized departure rates on our theoretical surface have, as would be expected, substantially lower variance than do the departure rates estimated from our sample. The results are, however, as close as we believe we can come to understanding the surface in relatively simple terms at this time. The theoretical points show correlations of .412 and .229 with the estimates obtained from the historical data portrayed in Figures 20 and 21.

If the theoretical surface we have described in Figure 24 is, in fact, a reasonable first approximation to a presidential career surface, our theories of presidential tenure may need to be much more "norm-dependent" than we had believed. At the outset of our thinking about tenure, we were led to such theories as "over time a president wears out his welcome with important groups," or "weaker presidents are weeded out first, so the longer the tenure, the better the average president and the lower the chance of departure."

Such hypotheses have some truth in them. There clearly are factors other than age and tenure waves that determine presidential departure rates. However, in our rush to find causality in the everyday events of presidential life, we appear to have systematically underestimated the importance of age and tenure norms. Presidents are much more likely to leave at about age 50 than they are at ages 43 or 57. Presidential departures are also keyed to length of service in a way that suggests an implicit term of office that is five years long (with decreasing prospects of renewal). Here as elsewhere in our investigation of the presidential role, we observe the apparent impact of social expectations in the regulation of life.

We can derive some general properties of presidential tenure expectations by examining the career surface more thoroughly. Since presidents age one year with each additional year of service as president, a president's walk across the career surface follows a line that originates on the O-tenure edge at the age of starting the presidency and proceeds on a 45-degree angle, with age and tenure each increasing a year at a time. By examining these 45-degree angle "career paths," we can elaborate some of the implications of the career surface. Prospective presidents are invited to study their own futures by walking the line appropriate to their starting age.

In order to explore this surface, we have examined the effects of age at accession on presidential tenure expectations. Table 49 shows some statistics from the cumulative distribution of tenures (according to the theoretical surface) for presidents assuming office at ages 30 to 64. Because of the 15-year age wave, there are actually only 15 distinct distributions. If our theoretical approximation is close to correct, age at accession makes some difference to the tenure expectations. Table 49 shows some illustrative indicators of the difference in the distributions:

- Median tenure. This varies from 8 years to 10 years. It is slightly higher for presidents assuming office around age 36 or age 52 than it is for presidents assuming office about age 30 or 45.

- Mean tenure. In a similar fashion mean tenure varies from 8.8 to 11.0 years (for presidents assuming office before they are over 60 years of age).

TABLE 49 *The effect of age at assumption of the presidency on tenure (according to theoretical surface in Figure 24)*

Age at assumption of the presidency	Median tenure	Mean tenure*	Most likely tenure	Probability of serving at least:			Probability of still retaining office at age:		
				5 years	10 years	15 years	55	60	65
30	8	10.4	4	0.73	0.42	0.27	†	†	†
32	8	10.4	3	0.68	0.45	0.28	†	†	†
34	10	10.5	1	0.71	0.51	0.28	†	†	†
36	10	10.8	14	0.77	0.54	0.24	†	†	†
38	10	11.0	9	0.81	0.54	0.23	†	†	†
40	9	10.9	9	0.83	0.49	0.22	0.22	†	†
42	9	10.6	8	0.80	0.42	0.23	0.29	†	†
44	8	10.5	4	0.76	0.42	0.26	0.37	†	†
46	8	10.4	4	0.70	0.43	0.27	0.48	0.31	†
48	9	10.4	2	0.69	0.47	0.28	0.60	0.40	†
50	10	10.7	1	0.74	0.53	0.27	0.74	0.53	0.27
52	10	10.7	†	0.79	0.54	†	0.89	0.69	0.36
54	10	10.7	†	0.83	0.52	†		0.79	0.44
56	9	10.2	†	0.82	0.44	†		0.88	0.55
58	†	9.6	†	0.78	†	†		0.96	0.65
60	†	8.8	†	0.73	†	†			0.73

*Since the theoretical surface deals only with tenures up to 16 years, we have assumed that the mean tenure of presidents who have a tenure of at least 16 years is 22 years. This is the estimate we make from our historical data.

† Not possible to establish from theoretical surface.

- Most likely tenure. The modal term varies radically from one starting age to another. Note, however, that the probability of the most likely tenure being the actual tenure is almost always less than 0.10.

- Probability of serving a term of at least 5, 10, or 15 years. In general, if one wants to maximize the chances of serving at least five years, one should start around age 40 or 54. However, such ages tend to minimize the chances of serving at least 15 years. The ages that maximize the chances of survival for at least 15 years, conversely, tend to minimize the chances of serving at least five years.

- Probability of serving at least until age 55, 60, or 65. As we have noted earlier, the way to retire from a presidency is to begin it late. A president must come to office no sooner than his forty-seventh birthday if he wants at least a 50–50 chance of being in office when he is 55. If he wants a 50–50 chance of staying in office until he is 65, he should delay starting until he is 55 years old.

We show in Table 50 the additional tenure expected for presidents having a given age and completed tenure. This life-expectancy table is only an approximation to a genuine actuarial table. It is based on a theoretical career surface. Although we believe that surface captures many of the features of the true surface, it is no better than a first approximation. Where our data are rich enough to compare estimates of tenure expectancy obtained from the theoretical surface with estimates of tenure expectancy obtained from our sample, the estimates are close; but we cannot assert with confidence that a larger sample would confirm the theoretical surface, or the expectations, in detail.

From these tables we can generate a variety of simple survival recommendations for presidents. If the career surface is correct, a would-be president may want to time his arrival at the presidency so as to control (somewhat) his probable departure.

In the same spirit, we can examine possible strategies of two-school presidents. Given that a president is in office and started his term at a given age, what is the best age to switch? A two-school president follows a path across the career surface that starts at the O-tenure edge at the age for starting the first presidency, follows the 45-degree line until he shifts presidencies, then returns to the O-tenure edge, and finally continues on a new 45-degree line. We are looking for the best such course. Suppose that the president wishes to maximize the chances of serving a total of at least 15 years in the two jobs. Then we can determine the best age to change presidencies in order to maximize the chances of serving at least 15 years under the departure rates of the theoretical surface. The remarkable fact is that the best time to shift presidencies is after eight years of service in the first presidency, regardless of the initial age of starting. Moreover, the chance of making it to 15 years of combined tenure does not depend on starting age. (The unconditional chance of reaching 15 years without a switch ranges from 0.22 to 0.27.) It may also be noteworthy that we found eight years of service in the first presidency to be the median service of presidents who transfer. If our career surface estimates are correct and if presidents who move from one pres-

TABLE 50
Expected
additional
tenure for
presidents of
given age
and completed
tenure
(theoretical
suface)

| | | | | | Completed years of tenure | | | | |
Age	0	1	2	3	4	5	6	7	8
28	10.53	9.84							
29	10.50	9.86	9.26						
30	10.45	9.86	9.35	8.81					
31	10.38	9.84	9.41	8.97	8.46				
32	10.35	9.86	9.45	9.11	8.71	8.06	'		
33	10.40	9.97	9.54	9.23	8.95	8.40	7.66		
34	10.53	10.22	9.80	9.49	9.26	8.81	8.16	7.29	
35	10.69	10.52	10.21	9.95	9.73	9.30	8.74	7.96	7.82
36	10.85	10.57	10.36	10.20	10.02	9.63	9.11	8.44	8.34
37	10.93	10 54	10.27	10.20	10.12	9.79	9.33	8.73	8.65
38	10.99	10.54	10.18	10.03	10.04	9.83	9.45	8.91	8.86
39	11.00	10.50	10.11	9.86	9.76	9.67	9.42	8.97	8.94
40	10.94	10.38	10.00	9.70	9.49	9.30	9.18	8.88	8.88
41	10.81	10.18	9.81	9.50	9.24	8.94	8.72	8.57	8.66
42	10.64	9.96	9.54	9.23	8.95	8.61	8.28	8.04	8.20
43	10.53	9.84	9.31	8.95	8.67	8.32	7.94	7.58	7.63
44	10.50	9.86	9.26	8.79	8.46	8.10	7.71	7.29	7.25
45	10.45	9.86	9.35	8.81	8.36	7.94	7.53	7.09	7.03
46	10.38	9.84	9.41	8.97	8.46	7.90	7.42	6.95	6.90
47	10.35	9.86	9.45	9.11	8.71	8.06	7.42	6.88	6.84
48	10.40	9.97	9.54	9.23	8.95	8.40	7.66	6.93	6.87
49	10.53	10.22	9.80	9.49	9.26	8.81	8.16	7.29	7.15
50	10.69	10.52	10.21	9.95	9.73	9.30	8.74	7.96	7.82
51	10.85	10.57	10.36	10.20	10.02	9.63	9.11	8.44	8.34
52	10.71	10.31	10.27	10.20	10.12	9.79	9.33	8.73	8.65
53	10.76	10.30	9.93	10.03	10.04	9.83	9.45	8.91	8.86
54	10.72	10.21	9.86	9.59	9.76	9.67	9.42	8.97	8.94
55	10.51	9.92	9.69	9.43	9.20	9.30	9.18	8.88	8.88
56	10.21	9.56	9.33	9.18	8.95	8.64	8.72	8.57	8.66
57	9.87	9.16	8.90	8.73	8.61	8.31	7.96	8.04	8.20
58	9.60	8.88	8.48	8.28	8.14	7.96	7.63	7.25	7.63
59	9.36	8.67	8.26	7.91	7.75	7.54	7.33	6.96	6.89
60	8.77	8.11	8.09	7.74	7.42	7.18	6.94	6.69	6.67
61	8.24	7.60	7.56	7.63	7.30	6.89	6.60	6.32	6.45
62	7.75	7.12	7.06	7.11	7.25	6.81	6.34	6.00	6.13
63	7.37	6.76	6.59	6.62	6.74	6.80	6.30	5.76	5.86
64	6.98	6.41	6.30	6.23	6.33	6.36	6.40	5.81	5.76
65	6.53	6.00	6.00	6.00	6.00	6.00	6.00	6.00	6.00

9	10	11	12	13	14	15
8.23						
8.58	8.27					
8.83	8.58	8.17				
8.94	8.75	8.42	7.91			
8.89	8.76	8.51	8.10	7.73		
8.70	8.60	8.41	8.10	7.82	7.48	
8.32	8.27	8.13	7.90	7.71	7.46	7.00
7.84	7.89	7.80	7.62	7.51	7.36	7.00
7.35	7.48	7.50	7.37	7.32	7.27	7.00
7.03	7.03	7.14	7.12	7.14	7.18	7.00
6.89	6.76	6.72	6.80	6.97	7.10	7.00
6.85	6.69	6.51	6.41	6.71	7.01	7.00
6.89	6.73	6.50	6.24	6.36	6.82	7.00
7.15	6.98	6.74	6.40	6.37	6.65	7.00
7.75	7.50	7.21	6.85	6.78	6.91	7.00
8.23	7.92	7.56	7.16	7.03	7.07	7.00
8.58	8.27	7.85	7.39	7.18	7.14	7.00
8.83	8.58	8.17	7.65	7.36	7.22	7.00
8.94	8.75	8.42	7.91	7.54	7.31	7.00
8.89	8.76	8.51	8.10	7.73	7.39	7.00
8.70	8.60	8.41	8.10	7.82	7.48	7.00
8.32	8.27	8.13	7.90	7.71	7.46	7.00
7.84	7.89	7.80	7.62	7.51	7.36	7.00
7.35	7.48	7.50	7.37	7.32	7.27	7.00
6.62	7.03	7.14	7.12	7.14	7.18	7.00
6.47	6.31	6.72	6.80	6.97	7.10	7.00
6.33	6.22	5.99	6.41	6.71	7.01	7.00
6.04	6.13	5.96	5.66	6.36	6.82	7.00
5.93	5.98	6.03	5.78	5.67	6.65	7.00
6.00	6.00	6.00	6.00	6.00	6.00	7.00

idency to another are otherwise subject to the career surface of presidents as a whole, the average transferring president chooses his time to move in such a way as to maximize his chances of having a combined tenure of 15 years. We doubt that new jobs appear or that presidents move in quite such a calculating way; but whatever the process, the outcome has a certain rational elegance.

TABLE 51
Best age to change presidencies and probability of tenure of 15 or more years as calculated from theoretical surface of Figure 24

If the initial starting age is:	*Then, the best shifting age is:*	*And the probability of serving at least 15 total years is:*
30	38	0.40
35	43	0.41
40	48	0.40
45	53	0.40
50	58	0.41
55	63	0.40

Finally, we can examine the effect of shifts in the age distribution of presidents on their tenure expectations. It is clear from Table 49 that the tenure distribution associated with each starting age varies. As a result, if the career surface does not change, shifts in the distribution of starting ages would produce shifts in the distribution of tenures. The nature of those shifts is obviously not monotonic. That is, raising or lowering the average starting age for presidents does not necessarily raise or lower the tenure expectations. Moreover, an inspection of Table 49 reveals that small consistent shifts in the age distribution will have only modest impact on the tenure distribution. A substantial effect would require that starting ages be lumped heavily in a few of the ages that are relatively distinctive with respect to the tenure distributions they produce. Such an event seems unlikely.

PRESIDENTIAL TENURE THE PRESIDENCY

In order to use the statistics on presidential tenure to help us understand the role better, we need to pursue the departure pattern further. In an earlier section (see p. 165) we have identified the major processes by which presidents leave the presidency and the actuarial characteristics of that movement. In this section we attempt to look more closely at where presidents go when they leave the presidency and at the logic of presidential tenure.

If the past experience is a reasonable predictor, about 40 percent of the current American college presidents will terminate their presidencies after age 65 or through death before that age. Another 15 percent will leave the presidency before age 65 but will not move from the presidency to a new full-time job. Thus, historically, about 55 percent of the time American colleges have had presidents who made the presidency a terminal position. This proportion is about the same across all our size and wealth categories and has stayed approximately constant through the years.

The statistic is, however, potentially quite misleading. It does not mean that *any* president has a 55 percent chance of having the presidency be his last job. The best way to make the presidency a terminal position is to start it late in life. A president who begins the presidency after 55 has a much better than 55 percent chance of making it his final job. A president who starts the presidency before 45 has a much less than 55 percent chance.

Table 52 shows the distribution of postpresidential jobs for presidents as we estimate that distribution from an examination of the 1924, 1939, and 1954 cohorts of presidents in office. About 14 percent of college presidents move from the presidency to another position in academic administration. Some of these take other presidencies. The number of presidents who transfer to another presidency appears to vary strongly with "good times" for higher education and with the size and wealth of the school, but overall (at least in our samples) it represents a distinct minority of all the postpresidential careers in academic administration. Presidents are more likely to go to other academic jobs than to another presidency. Except for those who go on to another pres-

TABLE 52 Estimated distribution of presidents among postpresidential careers for presidents in office in 1924, 1939, 1954*		
Postpresidential careers	*Proportion of all presidents*	*Proportion of all students' presidents*
Terminal position	55%	61%
Academic administration	13	15
Faculty	14	11
Ministry	8	2
Business, government, foundations, etc.	10	12
TOTAL	100	101

* These figures do not include the presidents in office in 1954 who were still in office in 1970 (about 15 percent of the 1954 total).

idency, presidents who end their presidencies by going to another position in academic administration almost invariably take positions that are identified as having less social status, prestige, and power than the presidency they left.

About 10 percent of presidents subsequently take a position in government, business, nonprofit organizations, or similar activities. This is more characteristic of presidents of large universities than it is of presidents of smaller schools. The positions are widely varied; but like the bulk of the academic administrative positions to which presidents move, the positions in business, government, and foundations usually enjoy less prestige than the presidency from which the individual has come. The shift is, in most standard terms, a shift from a better job to a poorer one.

The remainder of the presidents return to the faculty or the ministry. Since this route is much more common among small and medium-sized schools (where it represents about half of all exits other than those through death or retirement) than among large schools (where it is rare), our estimates of the proportion of college presidencies that are terminated in this way (21 percent) is substantially larger than our estimate of the proportion of students who have presidents who will return to the faculty or ministry (13 percent).

The faculty-minister position in the administrative hierarchy of a college plays a unique role. In most terms it is clearly a step down; but at least within some academic subcultures, it is an accepted and acceptable place for administrators to go when they end their administrative careers or when they interrupt those careers for a few years. It is a position of status and perquisites close enough to those of most administrators, and in independence sufficiently exceeding that of most administrators, to make it an attractive alternative—particularly for a relatively young academic with professional standing. Moreover, the ideology of academe and the ideology of organized religion reinforce the belief that an administrative career—however extended—is simply an interlude in a faculty or ministerial career.

The ideology is subject to some legitimate joking. The idea that life as a member of the faculty or as a parish priest is what all administrators would like if it were not for the sense of obligation they feel to their jobs is largely nonsense, but the talk about the glories of faculty or ministerial life in comparison with administration also serves a number of purposes. Among these, the ideology, and the structure it supports, permit a relatively smooth "downward" movement in the career path.

The result is that the American college and university fairly routinely make "workers" out of "middle executives." For some fairly obvious reasons, this "de-administration" works better with administrators relatively low in the hierarchy (e.g., chairmen) than it does with those relatively high (e.g., presidents); and it works better with relatively short-term administrators than it does with those who have spent a long time on an administrative career path.

From Table 52 we can calculate where presidents who leave the presidency for other jobs go. From those figures, we estimate that historically 29 percent have gone to other positions in academic administration, 31 percent have gone to the faculty, and 40 percent have gone to other jobs. We also asked current presidents where they thought they would go if they left their present job. From their responses we estimate that 40 percent of current presidents expect (or would report they expect) to go to other positions in academic administration, 23 percent expect to return to the faculty, and 38 percent expect to go to other jobs if or when they leave the presidency.

In aggregate, these expectations seem to be quite consistent with experience, but when we look at the variation by subsamples, there are some interesting anomalies. From 40 to 45 percent of the presidents of large schools "expect" to return to the faculty; only 8 percent of the small-school presidents do. On the other hand, 50 percent of the small-school presidents expect to move to another position in academic administration (35 percent of them "expect" another presidency). The aggregate statistics conceal subsample variations that are distinctly at variance with past experience.

Either the world has changed radically, or college presidents are remarkably unperceptive, or our question elicited something other than the serious expectations of presidents. We doubt that almost half of the large- and medium-sized-university presidents in the United States seriously expect to return to the faculty when they leave the presidency. Those figures appear to be inflated by ideology, romance, and evasion. On the other hand, we think the "professional administrator" style of response from the small-school presidents comes closer to reflecting a common self-image—one that is obviously subject to disappointment unless the rates of turnover and transfer in college presidencies become much greater than they have been either in recent years or throughout the twentieth century.

The signs of administrative professionalism that one sees in some small-college circles presuppose a career structure that does not presently exist. It is not hard to predict some disposition on the part of these presidents—and those who would like to be—to develop a normative base for a stronger tradition of academic administrative careers. Two elements of such a base are a belief in short terms for presidents and a belief in a distinct professional competence appropriate to higher education. Some of the ease with which small-college presidents, their academic subordinates, and professional students of higher education administration have accepted the idea that presidential tenure has shortened recently may be attributable to an awareness that each presidential casualty is someone else's opportunity to fill a vacancy. And the reality of a professsion of higher education administration is probably more readily accepted by people who qualify for the profession than by those who do not.

Why Do Presidents Go?
What underlies this pattern of departures? That is, can we make any set of plausible assumptions that will explain both the career surface we have described (see pp. 172–182) and the postpresidential careers we have just discussed? We believe that we can. In particular, we believe that we can help to clarify the mystery of why so many presidents voluntarily leave the presidency for jobs that are lower in status, and that we can contribute thereby to a better understanding of what the presidency is all about.

We believe that the key to understanding the career path of the college president is to recognize that what we describe as a "career" is, in fact, a series of relatively independent events:

- Academics enter administration rather casually and proceed through it one step at a time as plausible vacancies occur and without much attention to the long-term path or its implications.

- The momentum of vacancies in positions—particularly during periods of growth—moves individuals from one position to another rather frequently. Tenure at each administrative position before reaching the presidency is usually relatively brief (on the order of three to seven years).

- Most presidents achieve the presidency at a relatively young age: 15 to 25 years before normal retirement.

- For most college presidents, the presidency is the capstone of their careers. It is the highest position within the profession in which they have spent their entire adult lives. It is the best job they ever have had, or ever will have.

The combination of these features yields a group of presidents whose experience in administration and whose sense of personal progress dictate that they should leave the presidency, but for whom *there is no better place to go.* Relative to their understanding of the pacing of an academic administrative career, they reach the presidency too early in life. Their ages and tenures are such that the presidency occurs as the *step to* their final position rather than *as* the final position.

What happens, then, is a combination of two interacting phenomena. The first is the hard-headed realism of a college president faced with career choices in the last part of his life. The second is the regulation of social norms.

Part of the reason that presidents leave the presidency at a relatively rapid rate around age 50 is that they reach the *age of last opportunity,* after which the quality of jobs for which they qualify starts to deteriorate rapidly. Let us suppose that presidents, in effect, make choices about alternative jobs each year by calculating the expected value (in terms of money, prestige, power, or other similar dimensions of executive positions) of their alternatives of the moment.

In addition, suppose that presidents believe:

- Each job has a fixed value each year. That is, each year one holds a particular job, one receives a certain benefit from it that is independent of the number of years it has been held.

- Jobs are ordered. In particular, the value of the presidency is greater than any other job, and the other jobs also vary in value.

- The probability of *being able to continue* in the presidency from year to year is less than that associated with alternative jobs (e.g., faculty).

- The probability of *being able to move* from the presidency to another specific job is dependent on how old one is (after about age 50). The older one is, the less the value of the jobs to which one can move.

This model helps us to see the dilemma of the president. If he were certain of retaining his presidency until retirement, he would not leave it for another job. However, he is not certain. Moreover, according to the model the value of the best job he can obtain when he leaves the presidency is dependent on his age. The older he is, the less valuable the best alternative. Thus, he has to balance the chance that he can retain the presidency against the continuing reduction in alternatives available to him. The expected value of the lower status job is very likely to be higher than the expected value of the higher status job—particularly just before the age at which people in this professional group are defined as too old for important jobs. The greater the uncertainty about continuing in the presidency, the greater the difference in the expected values.

These beliefs of the president are supplemented by academic norms about presidential tenure. We were struck in our interviews with presidents by the degree to which they felt (1) that they had no real postpresidential alternatives (see page 185) and (2) that presidential tenure should be 7 to 10 years (unless they had already exceeded that figure). We asked each of the presidents in our interviews how much longer he expected to remain in office. By adding his expected additional tenure to each president's already completed tenure, we obtain the full tenure expectations shown in Table 53. In general, presidents expect either to retire from the job or to leave after a tenure of 10 years or less. They behave as though they are caught in the logic of promotion even after they are at the top.

TABLE 53
Tenure expectations reported by 42 current college presidents

No response	*Expect to serve until retirement*	*Expect to serve a total of*		
		0–6 years	*7–10 years*	*over 10 years*
10	12*	7	10	3*

*Two of the three presidents who expect to serve more than 10 years already have done so. Seven of the twelve who expect to retire already have served over 10 years.

Others around the president behave in a similar fashion. The norm of 7- to 10-year terms for presidents is now accepted by many trustees, faculty, subordinates, and students. For them, of course, the contradiction is less profound. It is the departing president who has to figure out what to do with himself. The sooner, the better from the point of view of some key subordinates. As a result, they build a structure of expectations within which the president acts. The structure is reflected in the tenure ridges on the career surface. Presidents are not exactly driven out the door by the dogma of approved tenure, but their own momentum is not much inhibited by the attitudes of the group around them.

This combination of personal experience, social convention, and simple rationality leads a fair number of presidents to move rather voluntarily to a lesser job or to early retirement. It produces the tenure and age waves of the career surface, as well as the peak departure rates we noted in our discussion of the surface (see Table 49). It now remains only to see whether a closer look at the pattern of departures in terms of the career surface will shed some light on the secondary tendency of that ridge to lie along a line on which the sum of age and tenure is constant.

In Figure 25 we have shown on the age-tenure plane the departures of all presidents in our three cross sections (1924, 1939, 1954) who did not retire or die but who left the presidency prior to age 65. We note that a line on the career surface defined as a constant sum of tenure and age is also a line intersecting each career line at which a president is halfway in time from his starting age to

FIGURE 25 *Postpresidential careers of college presidents by age and tenure at time of resignation**

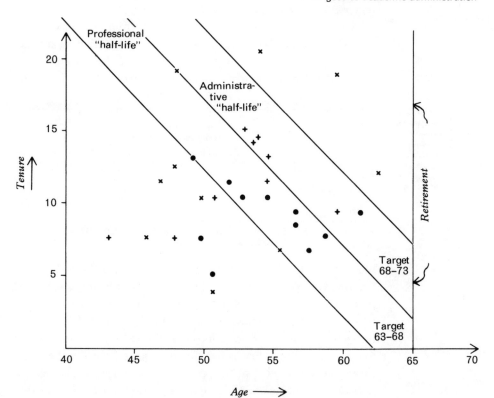

* = goes to business, government, or foundation
● = goes to faculty or ministry
+ = goes to academic administration

*For presidents in the sample who were in office in 1924, 1939, or 1954 and who did not die in office, retire, or leave office after age 65

a possible "target" retirement age (i.e., the sum). If all presidents saw retirement age as the same and timed their departures from the presidency so that they would have as much time on the new job as they had on the presidency, departures would be located along the constant sum line equal to the presumed retirement age.

In Figure 25 there is some suggestion that such a view is not far off. We have distinguished three different types of departures from the presidency:

1   Departures to return to the faculty or ministry

2   Departures to go to another position in academic administration

3   Departures to go elsewhere

If we assume that the target retirement age for the faculty or ministry is 65.5 ± 2.5 and the target retirement age for academic administration is 70.5 ± 2.5, we can define two peak departure regions for those kinds of departures.

The remarkable fact is that departures from the presidency to the faculty, ministry, and academic administration occur overwhelmingly as such an idea would predict. Table 54 summarizes the results. It is as though a president, consciously or not, said to

TABLE 54
*The relation between the timing of presidential departures and the places presidents go**

	Exits to:		
Exits during:	*Faculty or ministry*	*Academic administration*	*Other*
Professional "half-life"	8	1	1
Administrative "half-life"	1	7	1
Other	2	3	8

* For presidents in the sample who were in office in 1924, 1939, 1954, and who did not die in office, retire, or leave office after age 65.

himself that he should leave the presidency when he had as many "productive" years left in his life as he had already spent in the presidency. The idea is not as peculiar as it may seem. It simultaneously "justifies" the tenure in both jobs (each by the tenure in the other) and provides a natural solution to the problem of how to divide something that is too long into parts: Cut it in the middle. From the point of view of "career planning," the president leaves the presidency in the same kind of natural way that he arrived there, by a series of sensible compromises with life as it exists at the time.

CONCLUSION   As Clark Kerr (1970) has pointed out, college presidents have a history of discontent, part of which is traceable to the main features of presidential careers. In our judgment, most of those features have been substantially stable over most of the twentieth century and show few signs of recent abrupt change. These features are particularly painful for that group of presidents who start their presidencies before they are 45. These individuals, presumably the most articulate, aggressive, competent, and lucky of the presidents, have little chance of retiring from their office or of moving from their job to a better one. They will eject themselves, or possibly be ejected, from the best job they will ever have at a time when they see their own capabilities as impressive.

What produces discontent among presidents, of course, does not necessarily produce discontent among others or damage to the institution. It is quite possible that the best president for a college or university is a young man and that the best tenure is relatively brief. Even a relatively "young" president is older than most of his "constituents." Times change more rapidly than a man is normally able to. The vitality of the administrative organization might require a relatively rapid turnover of presidents. Certainly, each of those arguments has plausibility. If true, they suggest that the "villain" for the president is not the college or the career paths of presidents but the president's unfortunate post-50 status and activity needs.

What are the consequences for the organization of the pattern of presidential and postpresidential careers we have outlined? What difference does it make if a president knows that the pinnacle of his personal-social success and the forward-justification of his life will be over in his early fifties? At the outset, we should recognize that the president is hardly unique in this respect. In fact, he shares these problems with an impressive list of people: mothers, generals, rock musicians, football stars, scientists, U.S. Presidential assistants, prostitutes, and others.

All of these face early retirement or its emotional equivalent. All are forced at a relatively early age to accept that they are "over the hill." What difference does it make to their behavior *before* retirement? In the present career structure of American higher education, the major cost of having young, relatively short-term presidents is buried in some features of presidential style. This is particularly true in large universities, where a graceful exit to the faculty or ministry is less likely.

The effects are as predictable for mothers, generals, prostitutes, entertainment figures, and scientists as they are for presidents. They are also familiar to anyone who studies the phenomena associated with retirement, whenever it occurs. They are probably more severe in movie stars than in college presidents.

First, we would expect a president to resent the inexorability of his departure and to act as though the event can, by some act of will or invention, be avoided. The closer he comes to the departure, the more concerned he becomes about having a mistake precipitate the exit. The closer he comes to departure, the more he wants to be surrounded by people and situations that serve to remind him that he is the president.

Second, we would expect a president to be subject to anticipatory nostalgia. No matter what he does after he leaves the presidency, a president's memories will have a disproportionate emphasis on his life as president. It is not a period to be learned from, smiling later about one's many mistakes. It is a period to be remembered, a time to apply the wisdom previously learned, and not a period for which the record can show "promise" or "learning." The record must be written in such a way as to show "delivery" and "achievement." Like the general, the college president knows he is unlikely to have a second war to remember. He must construct his record now.

Third, we would expect a president to develop "cooling out" strategies. Somehow the departure needs to be made tolerable. A resignation needs to be made subjectively plausible. Presidents will behave so as to make the job unpleasant in ways that do not detract from their basic subjective perception of success in it. We would expect them to make themselves intolerably busy—and increasingly so as they approach resignation. They would see the demands on them as increasingly conflictual—and make them so— particularly as they come closer to the time for resignation. They grow tired or sick.[14]

We think that a career system that places these kinds of pressures on presidents is relatively costly in terms of lost leadership.

[14] We cannot choose decisively between a theory that says presidents leave because they find the job intolerable and a theory that says they make the job intolerable because they anticipate leaving; but we think the pattern of departures from the presidency suggests at least that the intolerable character of the job is as much an effect as a cause of the president's departure. We should also note that the somewhat more optimistic, more career-oriented responses of small-college presidents (see pp. 185–186) may be partly a function of their comparative youth. "Cooling out" has not yet begun for many of them.

It is also costly in terms of the corruption of the lives of presidents and those around them. Since the complications arise from the interaction among presidential expectations, models of personal achievement, and the structures of careers, we can imagine improving the situation by changing presidential beliefs or by changing the system. We think the greater hope lies in modifying presidential attitudes and the academic mores on which they are built.

At the same time, however, we suspect that academic organizations might want to reexamine the benefits and costs of insisting on youth in a president. In many respects, the main advantages of youth are relevance and ambition. Relevance is likely both to be attenuated by the prepresidential career filter and to be transitory; and ambition is likely to sour with a realization of postpresidential career options. In fact, one of the major dilemmas of the American college presidency is the ambition trap. Although becoming president typically requires ambition, ambition is badly served by the presidency—and the presidency is badly served by ambition.

9. Leadership in an Organized Anarchy

The college president faces four fundamental ambiguities. The first is the ambiguity of *purpose*. In what terms can action be justified? What are the goals of the organization? The second is the ambiguity of *power*. How powerful is the president? What can he accomplish? The third is the ambiguity of *experience*. What is to be learned from the events of the presidency? How does the president make inferences about his experience? The fourth is the ambiguity of *success*. When is a president successful? How does he assess his pleasures?

These ambiguities are fundamental to college presidents because they strike at the heart of the usual interpretations of leadership. When purpose is ambiguous, ordinary theories of decision making and intelligence become problematic. When power is ambiguous, ordinary theories of social order and control become problematic. When experience is ambiguous, ordinary theories of learning and adaptation become problematic. When success is ambiguous, ordinary theories of motivation and personal pleasure become problematic.

The Ambiguity of Purpose

Almost any educated person can deliver a lecture entitled "The Goals of the University." Almost no one will listen to the lecture voluntarily. For the most part, such lectures and their companion essays are well-intentioned exercises in social rhetoric, with little operational content.

Efforts to generate normative statements of the goals of a university tend to produce goals that are either meaningless or dubious. They fail one or more of the following reasonable tests. First, is the goal clear? Can one define some specific procedure for measuring the degree of goal achievement? Second, is it problematic? Is there some possibility that the organization will accom-

* For a further discussion of this topic, see Appendix G written by James G. March.

195

plish the goal? Is there some chance that it will fail? Third, is it accepted? Do most significant groups in the university agree on the goal statement? For the most part, the level of generality that facilitates acceptance destroys the problematic nature or clarity of the goal. The level of specificity that permits measurement destroys acceptance.

Recent discussions of educational audits, of cost-benefit analysis in education, and of accountability and evaluation in higher education have not been spectacularly successful in resolving this normative ambiguity, even in those cases where such techniques have been accepted as relatively fruitful. In our judgment, the major contributions (and they are important ones) of operational analysis in higher education to date have been to expose the inconsistencies of current policies and to make marginal improvements in those domains in which clear objectives are widely shared.

Similarly, efforts to infer the "real" objectives of a university by observing university behavior tend to be unsuccessful. They fail one or more of the following reasonable tests. First, is the goal uniquely consistent with behavior? Does the imputed goal produce the observed behavior and is it the only goal that does? Second, is it stable? Does the goal imputed from past behavior reliably predict future behavior? Although it is often possible to devise a statement of the goals of a university by some form of revealed preference test of past actions, such goal statements have poor predictive power.

The difficulties in imputing goals from behavior are not unique to universities. Experience with the complications is shared by revealed preference theorists in economics and psychology, radical critics of society, and functionalist students of social institutions. The search for a consistent explanation of human social behavior through a model of rational intent and an imputation of intent from action has had some successes. But there is no sign that the university is one of the successes, or very likely to become one.

Efforts to specify a set of consciously shared, consistent objectives within a university or to infer such a set of objectives from the activities or actions of the university have regularly revealed signs of inconsistency. To expose inconsistencies is not to resolve them, however. There are only modest signs that universities or other organized anarchies respond to a revelation of ambiguity of purpose by reducing the ambiguity. These are organizational systems without clear objectives; and the processes by which their objectives are established and legitimized are not extraordinarily sensitive to inconsistency. In fact, for many purposes the ambiguity of purpose is produced by our insistence on treating purpose as a necessary property of a good university. The strains arise from trying to impose a model of action as flowing from intent on organizations that act in another way.

College presidents live within a normative context that presumes purpose and within an organizational context that denies it. They serve on commissions to define and redefine the objectives of higher education. They organize convocations to examine the goals of the college. They write introductory statements to the college catalog. They accept the presumption that intelligent leadership presupposes the rational pursuit of goals. Simultaneously, they are aware that the process of choice in the college depends little on statements of shared direction. They recognize the flow of actions as an ecology of games (Long, 1958), each with its own rules. They accept the observation that the world is not like the model.

The Ambiguity of Power

Power is a simple idea, pervasive in its appeal to observers of social events. Like *intelligence* or *motivation* or *utility,* however, it tends to be misleadingly simple and prone to tautology. A person has power if he gets things done; if he has power, he can get things done.

As students of social power have long observed, such a view of power has limited usefulness.[1] Two of the things the simple view produces are an endless and largely fruitless search for the person who has "the real power" in the university, and an equally futile pursuit of the organizational locale "where the decision is *really* made." So profound is the acceptance of the power model that students of organizations who suggest the model is wrong are sometimes viewed as part of the plot to conceal "the real power" and "the true locus of decision." In that particular logic the reality of the simple power model is demonstrated by its inadequacy.

As a shorthand casual expression for variations in the potential of different positions in the organization, *power* has some utility. The college president has more potential for moving the college than most people, probably more potential than any one other person. Nevertheless, presidents discover that they have less power

[1] For anyone who wishes to enter the literature, see by way of introduction Raymond Wolfinger (1971*a*, 1971*b*), and Frederick W. Frey (1971).

than is believed, that their power to accomplish things depends heavily on what they want to accomplish, that the use of formal authority is limited by other formal authority, that the acceptance of authority is not automatic, that the necessary details of organizational life confuse power (which is somewhat different from diffusing it), and that their colleagues seem to delight in complaining simultaneously about presidential weakness and presidential willfulness.

The ambiguity of power, like the ambiguity of purpose, is focused on the president. Presidents share in and contribute to the confusion. They enjoy the perquisites and prestige of the office. They enjoy its excitement, at least when things go well. They announce important events. They appear at important symbolic functions. They report to the people. They accept and thrive on their own importance. It would be remarkable if they did not. Presidents even occasionally recite that "the buck stops here" with a finality that suggests the cliché is an observation about power and authority rather than a proclamation of administrative style and ideology.

At the same time, presidents solicit an understanding of the limits to their control. They regret the tendency of students, legislators, and community leaders to assume that a president has the power to do whatever he chooses simply because he is president. They plead the countervailing power of other groups in the college or the notable complexities of causality in large organizations.

The combination is likely to lead to popular impressions of strong presidents during good times and weak presidents during bad times. Persons who are primarily exposed to the symbolic presidency (e.g., outsiders) will tend to exaggerate the power of the president. Those people who have tried to accomplish something in the institution with presidential support (e.g., educational reformers) will tend to underestimate presidential power or presidential will.

The confusion disturbs the president, but it also serves him. Ambiguity of power leads to a parallel ambiguity of responsibility. The allocation of credit and blame for the events of organizational life becomes — as it often does in political and social systems — a matter for argument. The "facts" of responsibility are badly confounded by the confusions of anarchy; and the conventional myth of hierarchical executive responsibility is undermined by the countermyth of the nonhierarchical nature of colleges and universities. Presidents negotiate with their audiences on the interpretations of their power. As a result, during the recent years of campus troubles, many college presidents sought to emphasize the limitations of presidential control. During the more glorious days of conspicuous success, they solicited a recognition of their responsibility for events.

The process does not involve presidents alone, of course. The social validation of responsibility involves all the participants: faculty, trustees, students, parents, community leaders, government. Presidents seek to write their histories in the use of power as part of a chorus of history writers, each with his own reasons for preferring a somewhat different interpretation of "Who has the Power?"

The Ambiguity of Experience

College presidents attempt to learn from their experience. They observe the consequences of actions and infer the structure of the world from those observations. They use the resulting inferences in attempts to improve their future actions.

Consider the following very simple learning paradigm:

1 At a certain point in time a president is presented with a set of well-defined, discrete action alternatives.

2 At any point in time he has a certain probability of choosing any particular alternative (and a certainty of choosing one of them).

3 The president observes the outcome that apparently follows his choice and assesses the outcome in terms of his goals.

4 If the outcome is consistent with his goals, the president increases his probability of choosing that alternative in the future; if not, he decreases the probability.

Although actual presidential learning certainly involves more complicated inferences, such a paradigm captures much of the ordinary adaptation of an intelligent man to the information gained from experience.

The process produces considerable learning. The subjective experience is one of adapting from experience and improving behavior on the basis of feedback. If the world with which the president is dealing is relatively simple and relatively stable, and if his experience is relatively frequent, he can expect to improve over time (assuming he has some appropriate criterion for testing the consistency of outcomes with goals). As we have suggested earlier,

however, the world in which the president lives has two conspicuous properties that make experience ambiguous even where goals
are clear. First, the world is relatively complex. Outcomes depend
heavily on factors other than the president's action. These factors
are uncontrolled and, in large part, unobserved. Second, relative
to the rate at which the president gathers experimental data, the
world changes rapidly. These properties produce considerable
potential for false learning.

We can illustrate the phenomenon by taking a familiar instance
of learning in the realm of personnel policies. Suppose that a manager reviews his subordinates annually and considers what to do
with those who are doing poorly. He has two choices: he can replace an employee whose performance is low, or he can keep him
in the job and try to work with him to obtain improvement. He
chooses which employees to replace and which to keep in the job
on the basis of his judgment about their capacities to respond to
different treatments. Now suppose that, in fact, there are no
differences among the employees. Observed variations in performance are due entirely to random fluctuations. What would the
manager "learn" in such a situation?

He would learn how smart he was. He would discover that his
judgments about whom to keep and whom to replace were quite
good. Replacements will generally perform better than the men
they replaced; those men who are kept in the job will generally
improve in their performance. If for some reason he starts out being
relatively "humane" and refuses to replace anyone, he will discover
that the best managerial strategy is to work to improve existing
employees. If he starts out with a heavy hand and replaces everyone, he will learn that being tough is a good idea. If he replaces
some and works with others, he will learn that the essence of
personnel management is judgment about the worker.

Although we know that in this hypothetical situation it makes
no difference what a manager does, he will experience some subjective learning that is direct and compelling. He will come to
believe that he understands the situation and has mastered it. If
we were to suggest to the manager that he might be a victim of
superstitious learning, he would find it difficult to believe. Everything in his environment tells him that he understands the world,
even though his understanding is spurious.

It is not necessary to assume that the world is strictly random
to produce substantially the same effect. Whenever the rate of

experience is modest relative to the complexity of the phenomena and the rate of change in the phenomena, the interpretation made of experience will tend to be more persuasive subjectively than it should be. In such a world, experience is not a good teacher. Although the outcomes stemming from the various learned strategies in the personnel management example will be no worse because of a belief in the reality of the learning, the degree of confidence a manager comes to have in his theory of the world is erroneously high.

College presidents probably have greater confidence in their interpretations of college life, college administration, and their general environment than is warranted. The inferences they have made from experience are likely to be wrong. Their confidence in their learning is likely to have been reinforced by the social support they receive from the people around them and by social expectations about the presidential role. As a result, they tend to be unaware of the extent to which the ambiguities they feel with respect to purpose and power are matched by similar ambiguities with respect to the meaning of the ordinary events of presidential life.

The Ambiguity of Success Administrative success is generally recognized in one of two ways. First, by promotion: An administrator knows that he has been successful by virtue of a promotion to a better job. He assesses his success on the current job by the opportunities he has or expects to have to leave it. Second, by widely accepted, operational measures of organizational output: a business executive values his own performance in terms of a profit-and-loss statement of his operations.

Problems with these indicators of success are generic to high-level administrative positions. Offers of promotion become less likely as the job improves and the administrator's age advances. The criteria by which success is judged become less precise in measurement, less stable over time, and less widely shared. The administrator discovers that a wide assortment of factors outside his control are capable of overwhelming the impact of any actions he may take.

In the case of the college president all three problems are accentuated. As we have seen earlier, few college presidents are promoted out of the presidency. There are job offers, and most presidents ultimately accept one; but the best opportunity the typical president can expect is an invitation to accept a decent version of administrative semiretirement. The criteria of success in academic administration are sometimes moderately clear (e.g., growth, quiet on campus, improvement in the quality of students and faculty), but the relatively precise measures of college health tend neither to be stable over time nor to be critically sensitive to presidential action. For example, during the post-World War II years in American colleges, it was conventional to value growth and to attribute growth to the creative activities of administrative leaders. In the retrospective skepticism about the uncritical acceptance of a growth ethic, we have begun to reinterpret a simple history that attributed college growth to the conscious prior decision of a wise (or stupid) president or board. The rapid expansion of higher education, the postwar complex of student and faculty relations and attitudes, and the massive extension of governmental subsidies to the research activities of colleges and universities were not the simple consequences of decisions by Clark Kerr or John Hanna. Nor, retrospectively, does it seem plausible to attribute major control over those events to college administrators.

An argument can be made, of course, that the college president should be accustomed to the ambiguity of success. His new position is not, in this respect, so strikingly different from the positions he has held previously. His probable perspective is different, however. Success has not previously been subjectively ambiguous to him. He has been a success. He has been promoted relatively rapidly. He and his associates are inclined to attribute his past successes to a combination of administrative savoir-faire, interpersonal style, and political sagacity. He has experienced those successes as the lawful consequence of his actions. Honest modesty on the part of a president does not conceal a certain awareness of his own ability. A president comes to his office having learned that he is successful and that he enjoys success.

The momentum of promotion will not sustain him in the presidency. Although, as we have seen, a fair number of presidents anticipate moving from their present job to another, better presidency, the prospects are not nearly as good as the hopes. The ambiguities of purpose, power, and experience conspire to render success and failure equally obscure. The validation of success is unreliable. Not only can a president not assure himself that he will be able to lead the college in the directions in which others might believe, he also has no assurance that the same criteria will be applied tomorrow. What happens today will tend to be rationalized tomorrow as what was desired. What happens today will have some relation to what was desired yesterday. Outcomes do flow in part from goals. But goals flow from outcomes as well, and both goals and outcomes also move independently.

The result is that the president is a bit like the driver of a skidding automobile. The marginal judgments he makes, his skill, and his luck may possibly make some difference to the survival prospects for his riders. As a result, his responsibilities are heavy. But whether he is convicted of manslaughter or receives a medal for heroism is largely outside his control.

One basic response to the ambiguities of success is to find pleasure in the process of presidential life. A reasonable man will seek reminders of his relevance and success. Where those reminders are hard to find in terms of socially validated outcomes unambiguously due to one's actions, they may be sought in the interactions of organizational life. George Reedy (1970) made a similar observation about a different presidency: "Those who seek to lighten the burdens of the presidency by easing the workload do no occupant of that office a favor. The 'workload'—especially the ceremonial work load—are the only events of a president's day which make life endurable."

LEADER RESPONSE TO ANARCHY The ambiguities that college presidents face describe the life of any formal leader of any organized anarchy. The metaphors of leadership and our traditions of personalizing history (even the minor histories of collegiate institutions) confuse the issues of leadership by ignoring the basic ambiguity of leadership life. We require a plausible basic perspective for the leader of a loosely coupled, ambiguous organization.

Such a perspective begins with humility. It is probably a mistake for a college president to imagine that what he does in office affects significantly either the long-run position of the institution or his reputation as a president. So long as he does not violate some rather obvious restrictions on his behavior, his reputation and his term of office are more likely to be affected by broad social events or by the unpredictable vicissitudes of official responsibility than by his actions. Although the college library or administration building will doubtless record his presidency by appropriate portraiture or plaque, few presidents achieve even a modest claim to attention 20 years after their departure from the presidency; and those who are remembered best are probably most distinguished by their good fortune in coming to office during a period of collegiate good times and growth, or their bad fortune in being there when the floods came.

In this respect the president's life does not differ markedly from that of most of us. A leadership role, however, is distinguished by the numerous temptations to self-importance that it provides. Presidents easily come to believe that they can continue in office forever if they are only clever or perceptive or responsive enough. They easily come to exaggerate the significance of their daily actions for the college as well as for themselves. They easily come to see each day as an opportunity to build support in their constituencies for the next "election."

It is an old story. Human action is frequently corrupted by an exaggeration of its consequences. Parents are intimidated by an exaggerated belief in their importance to the process of child-rearing. Teachers are intimidated by an exaggerated belief in their importance to the process of learning. Lovers are intimidated by an exaggerated belief in their importance to the process of loving. Counselors are intimidated by an exaggerated belief in their importance to the process of self-discovery.

The major consequence of a heroic conception of the consequences of action is a distrust of judgment. When college presidents imagine that their actions have great consequences for the world, they are inclined to fear an error. When they fear an error, they are inclined to seek social support for their judgment, to confuse voting with virtue and bureaucratic rules with equity. Such a conception of the importance of their every choice makes presidents vulnerable to the same deficiencies of performance that afflict the parents of first children and inexperienced teachers, lovers, or counselors.

A lesser, but important, result of a heroic conception of the consequences of action is the abandonment of pleasure. By acceding to his own importance, the college president is driven to sobriety of manner. For reasons we have detailed earlier, he has difficulty in establishing the correctness of his actions by exhibiting their consequences. He is left with the necessity of communicating moral intent through facial intensity. At the same time, he experiences the substantial gap between his aspirations and his possibilities. Both by the requirements of their public face and by their own intolerant expectations, college presidents often find the public enjoyment of their job denied to them.

The ambiguities of leadership in an organized anarchy require a leadership posture that is somewhat different from that implicit in most discussions of the college presidency. In particular, we believe that a college president is, on the whole, better advised to think of himself as trying to do good than as trying to satisfy a political or bureaucratic audience; better advised to define his role in terms of the modest part he can play in making the college slightly better in the long run than in terms of satisfying current residents or solving current problems. He requires an enthusiasm for a Tolstoyan view of history and for the freedom of individual action that such a view entails. Since the world is absurd, the president's primary responsibility is to virtue.

Presidents occupy a minor part in the lives of a small number of people. They have some power, but little magic. They can act with a fair degree of confidence that if they make a mistake, it will not matter much. They can be allowed the heresy of believing that pleasure is consistent with virtue.

THE ELEMENTARY TACTICS OF ADMINISTRATIVE ACTION

The tactics of administrative action in an organized anarchy are somewhat different from the tactics of action in a situation characterized by clearer goals, better specified technology, and more persistent participation. Nevertheless, we can examine how a leader with a purpose can operate within an organization that is without one.

Necessarily, any presentation of practical strategies suggests a minor Machiavellianism with attendant complications and concerns. There is an argument that strategies based upon knowledge contribute to administrative manipulation. There is a fear that practical strategies may be misused for evil ends. There is a feeling that the effectiveness of the strategies may be undermined by their public recitation.

We are aware of these concerns, but not persuaded by them. First, we do not believe that any major new cleverness that would conspicuously alter the prevailing limits on our ability to change the course of history will be discovered. The idea that there are some spectacularly effective strategies waiting to be discovered by some modern Machiavelli seems implausible. Second, we believe that the problem of evil is little eased by know-nothingness. The concern about malevolent manipulation is a real one (as well as a cliché), but it often becomes a simple defense of the status quo. We hope that good people interested in accomplishing things will find a list of tactics marginally helpful. Third, we can see nothing in the recitation of strategic recommendations that changes systematically the relative positions of members of the organization. If the strategies are effective, it is because the analysis of organization is correct. The features of the organization that are involved are not likely to change quickly. As a result, we would not anticipate that public discussion of the strategies would change their effectiveness much or distinctly change the relative positions of those (e.g., students, presidents) who presumably stand to profit from the advice if it is useful.

As we will indicate later in this chapter, a conception of leadership that merely assumes that the college president should act to accomplish what he wants to accomplish is too narrow. A major part of his responsibility is to lead the organization to a changing and more complex view of itself by treating goals as only partly knowable. Nevertheless, the problems of inducing a college to do what one wants it to do are clearly worthy of attention. If presidents and others are to function effectively within the college, they need to recognize the ways in which the character of the college as a system for exercising problems, making decisions, and certifying status conditions their attempts to influence the outcome of any decision.

We can identify five major properties of decision making in organized anarchies that are of substantial importance to the tactics of accomplishing things in colleges and universities:

1 Most issues most of the time have *low salience* for most people. The decisions to be made within the organization secure only partial and erratic attention from participants in the organization. A major share of the attention devoted to a particular issue is tied less to the content of the issue than to its symbolic significance for individual and group esteem.

2 The total system has *high inertia.* Anything that requires a coordinated effort of the organization in order to start is unlikely to be started. Anything that requires a coordinated effort of the organization in order to be stopped is unlikely to be stopped.

3 Any decision can become a *garbage can* for almost any problem. The issues discussed in the context of any particular decision depend less on the decision or problems involved than on the timing of their joint arrivals and the existence of alternative arenas for exercising problems.

4 The processes of choice are easily subject to *overload.* When the load on the system builds up relative to its capabilities for exercising and resolving

problems, the decision outcomes in the organization tend to become increasingly separated from the formal process of decision.

5   The organization has a *weak information base*. Information about past events or past decisions is often not retained. When retained, it is often difficult to retrieve. Information about current activities is scant.

These properties are conspicuous and ubiquitous. They represent some important ways in which all organizations sometimes, and an organization like a university often, present opportunities for tactical action that in a modest way strengthen the hand of the participant who attends to them. We suggest eight basic tactical rules for use by those who seek to influence the course of decisions in universities or colleges.

Rule 1: Spend time. The kinds of decision-making situations and organizations we have described suffer from a shortage of decision-making energy. Energy is a scarce resource. If one is in a position to devote time to the decision-making activities within the organization, he has a considerable claim on the system. Most organizations develop ways of absorbing the decision-making energy provided by sharply deviant participants; but within moderate boundaries, a person who is willing to spend time finds himself in a strong position for at least three significant reasons:

- By providing a scarce resource (energy), he lays the basis for a claim. If he is willing to spend time, he can expect more tolerant consideration of the problems he considers important. One of the most common organizational responses to a proposal from a participant is the request that he head a committee to do something about it. This behavior is an acknowledgment both of the energy-poor situation and of the price the organization pays for participation. That price is often that the organization must allow the participant some significant control over the definition of problems to be considered relevant.[2]

- By spending time on the homework for a decision, he becomes a major information source in an information-poor world. At the limit, the information provided need have no particular evidential validity. Consider, for example, the common assertions in college decision-making processes about what some constituency (e.g., board of trustees, legislature, stu-

[2] For a discussion of this point in the context of public school decision making, see Stephen Weiner (1972).

dent body, ethnic group) is "thinking." The assertions are rarely based on defensible evidence, but they tend to become organizational facts by virtue of the shortage of serious information. More generally, reality for a decision is specified by those willing to spend the time required to collect the small amounts of information available, to review the factual assertions of others, and to disseminate their findings.

- By investing more of his time in organizational concerns, he increases his chance of being present when something important to him is considered. A participant who wishes to pursue other matters (e.g., study, research, family, the problems of the outside world) reduces the number of occasions for decision making to which he can afford to attend. A participant who can spend time can be involved in more arenas. Since it is often difficult to anticipate when and where a particular issue will be involved (and thus to limit one's attention to key times and domains), the simple frequency of availability is relatively important.

Rule 2: Persist. It is a mistake to assume that if a particular proposal has been rejected by an organization today, it will be rejected tomorrow. Different sets of people and concerns will be reflected each time a problem is considered or a proposal discussed. We noted earlier the ways in which the flow of participants leads to a flow of organizational concerns.[3] The specific combination of sentiments and people that is associated with a specific choice opportunity is partly fortuitous, and Fortune may be more considerate another day.

For the same reason, it is a mistake to assume that today's victory will be implemented automatically tomorrow. The distinction between decision making and decision implementation is usually a false one. Decisions are not "made" once and for all. Rather they happen as a result of a series of episodes involving different people in different settings, and they may be unmade or modified by subsequent episodes. The participant who spends much time celebrating his victory ordinarily can expect to find the victory short-lived. The loser who spends his time weeping rather than reintroducing his ideas will persistently have something to weep about. The loser who persists in a variety of contexts is frequently rewarded.

Rule 3: Exchange status for substance. As we have indicated, the specific substantive issues in a college, or similar organization,

[3] For a discussion of the same phenomenon in a business setting, see R. M. Cyert and J. G. March (1963).

typically have low salience for participants. A quite typical situation is one in which significant numbers of participants and groups of participants care less about the specific substantive outcome than they do about the implications of that outcome for their own sense of self-esteem and the social recognition of their importance. Such an ordering of things is neither surprising nor normatively unattractive. It would be a strange world indeed if the mostly minor issues of university governance, for example, became more important to most people than personal and group esteem.

A college president, too, is likely to become substantially concerned with the formal acknowledgment of office. Since it is awkward for him to establish definitively that he is substantively important, the president tends to join other participants in seeking symbolic confirmation of his significance.

The esteem trap is understandable but unfortunate. College presidents who can forgo at least some of the pleasures of self-importance in order to trade status for substance are in a strong position. Since leaders receive credit for many things over which they have little control and to which they contribute little, they should find it possible to accomplish some of the things they want by allowing others to savor the victories, enjoy the pleasures of involvement, and receive the profits of public importance.

Rule 4: Facilitate opposition participation. The high inertia of organizations and the heavy dependence of organizational events on processes outside of the control of the organization make organizational power ambiguous. Presidents sense their lack of control despite their position of authority, status, and concern. Most people who participate in university decision making sense a disappointment with the limited control their position provides.

Persons outside the formal ranks of authority tend to see authority as providing more control. Their aspirations for change tend to be substantially greater than the aspirations for change held by persons with formal authority. One obvious solution is to facilitate participation in decision making. Genuine authoritative participation will reduce the aspirations of oppositional leaders. In an organization characterized by high inertia and low salience it is unwise to allow beliefs about the feasibility of planned action to outrun reality. From this point of view, public accountability, participant observation, and other techniques for extending the range of legitimate participation in the decision-making processes of the organization are essential means of keeping the aspirations of occasional actors within bounds. Since most people most of the time do not participate much, their aspirations for what can be done have a tendency to drift away from reality. On the whole, the direct involvement of dissident groups in the decision-making process is a more effective depressant of exaggerated aspirations than is a lecture by the president.

Rule 5: Overload the system.   As we have suggested, the style of decision making changes when the load exceeds the capabilities of the system. Since we are talking about energy-poor organizations, accomplishing overload is not hard. In practical terms, this means having a large repertoire of projects for organizational action; it means making substantial claims on resources for the analysis of problems, discussion of issues, and political negotiation.

Within an organized anarchy it is a mistake to become absolutely committed to any one project. There are innumerable ways in which the processes we have described will confound the cleverest behavior with respect to any single proposal, however imaginative or subjectively important. What such processes cannot do is cope with large numbers of projects. Someone with the habit of producing many proposals, without absolute commitment to any one, may lose any one of them (and it is hard to predict a priori which one), but cannot be stopped on everything.

The tactic is not unlike the recommendation in some treatments of bargaining that one should introduce new dimensions of bargains in order to facilitate more favorable trades.[4] It is grounded in the observation that the press of proposals so loads the organization that (as we noted in Chapter 5) a large number of actions are taken without attending to problems. Where decisions are made through oversight or flight, considerable control over the course of decision making lies in the hands of two groups: the initiators of the proposals, who get their way in oversight, and the full-time administrator, who is left to make the decision in cases of flight. The college president with a program is in the enviable position of being both a proposal initiator and a full-time administrator. Overload is almost certainly helpful to his program. Other groups within a col-

---

[4] See, for example, Iklé (1964) and Walton and McKersie (1965).

lege or university are probably also advantaged by overload if they have a positive program for action, but their advantage is less certain. In particular, groups in opposition to the administration that are unable to participate full time (either directly or through representatives) may wish to be selective in the use of overload as a tactic.

Rule 6: Provide garbage cans. One of the complications in accomplishing something in a garbage can decision-making process is the tendency for any particular project to become intertwined with a variety of other issues simply because those issues exist at the time the project is before the organization. A proposal for curricular reform becomes an arena for a concern for social justice. A proposal for construction of a building becomes an arena for concerns about environmental quality. A proposal for bicycle paths becomes an arena for discussion of sexual inequality.

It is pointless to try to react to such problems by attempting to enforce rules of relevance. Such rules are, in any event, highly arbitrary. Even if they were not, it would still be difficult to persuade a person that his problem (however important) could not be discussed because it is not relevant to the current agenda. The appropriate tactical response is to provide garbage cans into which wide varieties of problems can be dumped. The more conspicuous the can, the more garbage it will attract away from other projects.

The prime procedure for making a garbage can attractive is to give it precedence and conspicuousness. On a grand scale, discussions of overall organizational objectives or overall organizational long-term plans are classic first-quality cans. They are general enough to accommodate anything. They are socially defined as being important. They attract enough different kinds of issues to reinforce their importance. An activist will push for discussions of grand plans (in part) in order to draw the garbage away from the concrete day-to-day arenas of his concrete objectives.

On a smaller scale, the first item on a meeting agenda is an obvious garbage can. It receives much of the status allocation concerns that are a part of meetings. It is possible that any item on an agenda will attract an assortment of things currently concerning individuals in the group; but the first item is more vulnerable than others. As a result, projects of serious substantive concern should normally be placed somewhat later, after the important matters of individual and group esteem have been settled, most of the individual performances have been completed, and most of the enthusiasm for abstract argument has waned.

The garbage can tactic has long-term effects that may be important. Although in the short run the major consequence is to remove problems from the arena of short-term concrete proposals, the separation of problem discussion from decision making means that general organizational attitudes develop outside the context of immediate decisions. The exercise of problems and the discussion of plans contribute to a building of the climate within which the organization will operate in the future. A president who uses the garbage can tactic should be aware of the ways in which currently irrelevant conversations produce future ideological constraints. The same tactic also provides a (partly misleading) device for the training and selection of future leaders of the organization. Those who perform well in garbage can debates are not necessarily good leaders, though they may frequently be identified as potential leaders. Finally, the tactic offers a practical buffer for the organization from the instabilities introduced by the entry and exit of problems that drift from one organization to another. In recent years universities have become an arena for an assortment of problems that might have found expression in other social institutions. Universities and colleges were available and accessible to people with the concerns. Although the resulting strain on university processes was considerable, the full impact was cushioned by the tendency of such problems to move to decision-irrelevant garbage cans, to be held there until they could move on to another arena in another instituion.

Rule 7: Manage unobtrusively.   If you put a man in a boat and tell him to plot a course, he can take one of three views of his task. He can float with the currents and winds, letting them take him wherever they wish; he can select a destination and try to use full power to go directly to it regardless of the current or winds; or he can select a destination and use his rudder and sails to let the currents and wind eventually take him where *he* wants to go. On the whole, we think conscious university leadership is properly seen in third light.

A central tactic in high-inertia systems is to use high-leverage minor actions to produce major effects—to let the system go where it wants to go with only the minor interventions that make it go where it should. From a tactical point of view, the main objection to central direction and control is that it requires an impossible amount of attention and energy. The kinds of organizations with which we have been concerned are unable to be driven where we want them to go without making considerable use of the "natural" organizational processes. The appropriate tactics of management are unobstrusive and indirect.

Unobtrusive management uses interventions of greater impact than visibility. Such actions generally have two key attributes: (1) They affect many parts of the system slightly rather than a few parts in a major way. The effect on any one part of the system is small enough so that either no one really notices or no one finds it sensible to organize significantly against the intervention. (2) Once activated, they stay activated without further organizational attention. Their deactivation requires positive organizational action.

Given all the enthusiasm for elaborating a variety of models of organizations that bemoan bureaucracy and the conventional managerial tools associated with bureaucratic life, it is somewhat surprising to realize that the major instruments of unobstrusive management are bureaucratic. Consider the simple act of committing the organization by signing a piece of paper. By the formal statutes of many organizations, some people within the organization are conceded authority to sign pieces of paper. College presidents tend, in our judgment, to be timid about exercising such authority. By signing a piece of paper the president is able to reverse the burden of organizing the decision-making processes in the system. Many people have commented on the difficulty of organizing the various groups and offices in a college or university in order to do something. What has been less frequently noted is that the same problems of organization face anyone who wants to overturn an action. For example, the official charter of an institution usually has some kind of regulation that permits a desired action, as well as some kind of regulation that might be interpreted as prohibiting it. The president who solicits general organizational approval for action is more likely to obtain it if the burdens of overcoming organizational inertia are on his opposition. He reverses the burden of organization by taking the action.

Major bureaucratic interventions lie in the ordinary systems of accounting and managerial controls. Such devices are often condemned in academic circles as both dreary and inhibiting. Their beauty lies in the way in which they extend throughout the system and in the high degree of arbitrariness they exhibit. For example, students of business have observed that many important aspects of business life are driven by accounting rules. What are costs? What are profits? How are costs and profits allocated among activities and subunits? Answers to such questions are far from arbitrary. But they have enough elements of arbitrariness that no reasonable business manager would ignore the potential contribution of accounting rules to profitability. The flow of investments, the utilization of labor, and the structure of organization all respond to the organization of accounts.

The same thing is true in a college or university, although the process works in a somewhat different way because the convenient single index of business accounting, profit, is denied the university executive. Universities and colleges have official facts (accounting facts) with respect to student activities, faculty activities, and space utilization. In recent years such accounting facts have increased in importance as colleges and universities struggled first with the baby boom and now with fiscal adversity. These official facts enter into reports and filter into decisions made throughout the system. As a typical simple example, consider the impact of changing the accounting for faculty teaching load from number of courses to student credit hours taught. Or, consider the impact of separating in accounting reports the teaching of language (number of students, cost of faculty) from the teaching of literature in that language at a typical American university. Or, consider the impact of making each major subunit in a university purchase services (e.g., duplication services, computer services, library services) at prices somewhat different from the current largely arbitrary prices. Or, consider the consequences of allowing transfer of funds from one major budget line to another within a subunit at various possible discount rates depending on the lines and the point in the budget year. Or, consider the effect of having students pay as part of their fees an amount determined by the department offering the instruction, with the amount thus paid returning to the department.

Rule 8: Interpret history. In an organization in which most issues have low salience, and information about events in the system is poorly maintained, definitions of what is happening and what has happened become important tactical instruments. If people in the organization cared more about what happened (or is happening), the constraints on the tactic would be great. Histories would be challenged and carefully monitored. If people in the organization accepted more openly the idea that much of the decision-making process is a status-certifying rather than a choice-making system, there would be less dependence on historical interpretation. The actual situation, however, provides a tactically optimal situation. On the one hand, the genuine interest in keeping a good record of what happened (in substantive rather than status terms) is minimal. On the other hand, the belief in the relevance of history, or the legitimacy of history as a basis for current action, is fairly strong.

Minutes should be written long enough after the event as to legitimize the reality of forgetfulness. They should be written in such a way as to lay the basis for subsequent independent action— in the name of the collective action. In general, participants in the organization should be assisted in their desire to have unambiguous actions taken today derived from the ambiguous decisions of yesterday with a minimum of pain to their images of organizational rationality and a minimum of claims on their time. The model of consistency is maintained by a creative resolution of uncertainty about the past.

Presidents and Tactics
As we observed at the outset, practical tactics, if they are genuine, will inevitably be viewed as somewhat cynical. We will, however, record our own sentiments that the cynicism lies in the eye of the beholder. Our sympathies and enthusiasm are mostly for the invisible members of an organized anarchy who make such tactics possible. We refer, of course, to the majority of participants in colleges and universities who have the good sense to see that what can be achieved through tactical manipulation of the university is only occasionally worth their time and effort. The validity of the tactics is a tribute to their reluctance to clutter the important elements of life with organizational matters. The tactics are available for anyone who wants to use them. Most of us most of the time have more interesting things to do.

But presidents, as full-time actors generally occupying the best job of their lives, are less likely to have more interesting things to do. In addition, these tactics, with their low visibility and their emphasis on the trading of credit and recognition for accomplishment, will not serve the interests of a president out to glorify himself or increase his chances to be one of the very few who move up to a second and "better" presidency. Instead, they provide an opportunity chiefly for those who have some conception of what might make their institution better, more interesting, more complex, or more educational, and are satisfied to end their tenures believing that they helped to steer their institutions slightly closer to those remote destinations.

THE TECHNOLOGY OF FOOLISHNESS The tactics for moving an organization when objectives are clear represent important parts of the repertoire of an organizational leader.[5] Standard prescriptions properly honor intention, choice, and action; and college presidents often have things they want to accomplish. Nevertheless, a college president may sometimes want to confront the realities of ambiguity more directly and reconsider the standard dicta of leadership. He may want to examine particularly the place of purpose in intelligent behavior and the role of foolishness in leadership.

Choice and Rationality The concept of choice as a focus for interpreting and guiding human behavior has rarely had an easy time in the realm of ideas. It is beset by theological disputations over free will, by the dilemmas of absurdism, by the doubts of psychological behaviorism, and by the claims of historical, economic, social, and demographic determinism. Nevertheless, the idea that humans make choices has proved robust enough to become a matter of faith in important segments of contemporary Western civilization. It is a faith that is professed by virtually all theories of social policy making.

The major tenents of this faith run something like this:

Human beings make choices. Choices are properly made by evaluating alternatives in terms of goals and on the basis of information currently available. The alternative that is most attractive in terms of the goals is chosen. By using the technology of choice, we can improve the quality of the search for alternatives, the quality of information, and the quality of the analysis used to evaluate alternatives. Although actual choice may fall short of this ideal in various ways, it is an attractive model of how choices should be made by individuals, organizations, and social systems.

[5] These ideas have been the basis for extended conversation with a number of friends. We want to acknowledge particularly the help of Lance Bennett, Patricia Nelson Bennett, Michael Butler, Søren Christensen, Michel Crozier, Claude Faucheux, James R. Glenn, Jr., Gudmund Hernes, Helga Hernes, Jean Carter Lave, Harold J. Leavitt, Henry M. Levin, Leslie Lincoln, André Massart, John Miller, Johan Olsen, Richard C. Snyder, Alexander Szalai, Eugene J. Webb, and Gail Whitacre.

These articles of faith have been built upon and have stimulated some scripture. It is the scripture of the theories of decision making. The scripture is partly a codification of received doctrine and partly a source for that doctrine. As a result, our cultural ideas of intelligence and our theories of choice display a substantial resemblance. In particular, they share three conspicuous interrelated ideas:

The first idea is the *preexistence of purpose*. We find it natural to base an interpretation of human-choice behavior on a presumption of human purpose. We have, in fact, invented one of the most elaborate terminologies in the professional literature: "values," "needs," "wants," "goods," "tastes," "preferences," "utility," "objectives," "goals," "aspirations," "drives." All of these reflect a strong tendency to believe that a useful interpretation of human behavior involves defining a set of objectives that (1) are prior attributes of the system, and (2) make the observed behavior in some sense intelligent vis-à-vis those objectives.

Whether we are talking about individuals or about organizations, purpose is an obvious presumption of the discussion. An organization is often defined in terms of its purpose. It is seen by some as the largest collectivity directed by a purpose. Action within an organization is justified or criticized in terms of purpose. Individuals explain their own behavior, as well as the behavior of others, in terms of a set of value premises that are presumed to be antecedent to the behavior. Normative theories of choice begin with an assumption of a preexistent preference ordering defined over the possible outcomes of a choice.

The second idea is the *necessity of consistency*. We have come to recognize consistency both as an important property of human behavior and as a prerequisite for normative models of choice. Dissonance theory, balance theory, theories of congruency in attitudes, statuses, and performances have all served to remind us of the possibilities for interpreting human behavior in terms of the consistency requirements of a limited-capacity, information-processing system.

At the same time, consistency is a cultural and theoretical virtue. Action should be consistent with belief. Actions taken by different parts of an organization should be consistent with each other. Individual and organizational activities are seen as connected with each other in terms of their consequences for some consistent set of purposes. In an organization, the structural manifestation of consistency is the hierarchy with its obligations of coordination and control. In the individual, the structural manifestation is a set of values that generates a consistent preference ordering.

The third idea is the *primacy of rationality*. By rationality we mean a procedure for deciding what is correct behavior by relating consequences systematically to objectives. By placing primary emphasis on rational techniques, we have implicitly rejected—or seriously impaired—two other procedures for choice: (1) the processes of intuition, through which people do things without fully understanding why; and (2) the processes of tradition and faith, through which people do things because that is the way they are done.

Both within the theory and within the culture we insist on the ethic of rationality. We justify individual and organizational action in terms of an analysis of means and ends. Impulse, intuition, faith, and tradition are outside that system and viewed as antithetical to it. Faith may be seen as a possible source of values. Intuition may be seen as a possible source of ideas about alternatives. But the analysis and justification of action lie within the context of reason.

These ideas are obviously deeply embedded in the culture. Their roots extend into ideas that have conditioned much of modern Western history and interpretations of that history. Their general acceptance is probably highly correlated with the permeation of rationalism and individualism into the style of thinking within the culture. The ideas are even more obviously embedded in modern theories of choice. It is fundamental to those theories that thinking should precede action; that action should serve a purpose; that purpose should be defined in terms of a consistent set of preexistent goals; and that choice should be based on a consistent theory of the relation between action and its consequences.

Every tool of management decision making that is currently a part of management science, operations research, or decision-making theory assumes the prior existence of a set of consistent goals. Almost the entire structure of microeconomic theory builds on the assumption that there exists a well-defined, stable, and consistent preference ordering. Most theories of individual or organizational choice accept the idea that goals exist and that (in some sense) an individual or organization acts on those goals, choosing from among some alternatives on the basis of available information. Discussions of educational policy with their emphasis on goal setting, evaluation, and accountability, are in this tradition.

From the perspective of all of man's history, the ideas of purpose, consistency, and rationality are relatively new. Much of the technology currently available to implement them is extremely new. Over the past few centuries, and conspicuously over the past few decades, we have substantially improved man's capability for acting purposively, consistently, and rationally. We have substantially increased his propensity to think of himself as doing so. It is an impressive victory, won — where it has been won — by a happy combination of timing, performance, ideology, and persistence. It is a battle yet to be concluded, or even engaged, in many cultures of the world; but within most of the Western world individuals and organizations see themselves as making choices.

The Problem of Goals

The tools of intelligence as they are fashioned in modern theories of choice are necessary to any reasonable behavior in contemporary society. It is inconceivable that we would fail to continue their development, refinement, and extension. As might be expected, however, a theory and ideology of choice built on the ideas outlined above is deficient in some obvious, elementary ways, most conspicuously in the treatment of human goals.

Goals are thrust upon the intelligent man. We ask that he act in the name of goals. We ask that he keep his goals consistent. We ask that his actions be oriented to his goals. We ask that a social system amalgamate individual goals into a collective goal. But we do not concern ourselves with the origin of goals. Theories of individual, organizational, and social choice assume actors with preexistent values.

Since it is obvious that goals change over time and that the character of those changes affects both the richness of personal and social development and the outcome of choice behavior, a theory of choice must somehow justify ignoring the phenomena. Although it is unreasonable to ask a theory of choice to solve all the problems of man and his development, it is reasonable to ask how such conspicuous elements as the fluidity and ambiguity of objectives can plausibly be ignored in a theory that is offered as a guide to human choice behavior.

There are three classic justifications. The first is that goal development and choice are independent processes, conceptually and behaviorally. The second is that the model of choice is never satisfied in fact and that deviations from the model accommodate the problems of introducing change. The third is that the idea of changing goals is so intractable in a normative theory of choice that nothing can be said about it. Since we are unpersuaded of the first and second justifications, our optimism with respect to the third is somewhat greater than that of most of our fellows.

The argument that goal development and choice are independent behaviorally seems clearly false. It seems to us obvious that a description that assumes that goals come first and action comes later is frequently radically wrong. Human choice behavior is at least as much a process for discovering goals as for acting on them. Although it is true enough that goals and decisions are "conceptually" distinct, that is simply a statement of the theory, not a defense of it. They are conceptually distinct if we choose to make them so.

The argument that the model is incomplete is more persuasive. There do appear to be some critical "holes" in the system of intelligence as described by standard theories of choice. Incomplete information, incomplete goal consistency, and a variety of external processes facilitate goal development. What is somewhat disconcerting about the argument, however, is that it makes the efficacy of the concepts of intelligent choice dependent on their inadequacy. As we become more competent in the techniques of the model and more committed to it, the "holes" become smaller. As the model becomes more accepted, our obligation to modify it increases.

The final argument seems to us sensible as a general principle, but misleading here. Why are we more reluctant to ask how human beings might find "good" goals than we are to ask how they might make "good" decisions? The second question appears to be a more technical problem. The first seems more pretentious. It claims to say something about alternative virtues. The appearance of pretense, however, stems directly from the prevailing theory of choice and the ideology associated with it.

In fact, the conscious introduction of goal discovery for consideration in theories of human choice is not unknown to modern man. For example, we have two kinds of theories of choice behavior in human beings. One is a theory of children. The other is a theory of adults. In the theory of children, we emphasize choices as leading to experiences that develop the child's scope, his complexity, his awareness of the world. As parents, teachers, or psychologists, we try to lead the child to do things that are inconsistent with his present goals because we know (or believe) that he can develop into an interesting person only by coming to appreciate aspects of experience that he initially rejects.

In the theory of adults, we emphasize choices as a consequence of our intentions. As adults, educational decision makers, or economists, we try to take actions that (within the limits of scarce resources) come as close as possible to achieving our goals. We try to find improved ways of making decisions consistent with our perceptions of what is valuable in the world.

The asymmetry in these models is conspicuous. Adults have constructed a model world in which adults know what is good for themselves, but children do not. It is hard to react positively to the conceit. The asymmetry has, in fact, stimulated a large number of ideologies and reforms designed to allow children the same moral prerogative granted to adults — the right to imagine that they know what they want. The efforts have cut deeply into traditional childrearing, traditional educational policies, traditional politics, and traditional consumer economics.

In our judgment, the asymmetry between models of choice for adults and for children is awkward; but the solution we have adopted is precisely wrong-headed. Instead of trying to adapt the model of adults to children, we might better adapt the model of children to adults. For many purposes, our model of children is better. Of course, children know what they want. Everyone does. The critical question is whether they are encouraged to develop more interesting "wants." Values change. People become more interesting as those values and the interconnections made among them change.

One of the most obvious things in the world turns out to be hard for us to accommodate in our theory of choice: A child of two will almost always have a less interesting set of values (indeed, a *worse* set of values) than a child of 12. The same is true of adults. Values develop through experience. Although one of the main natural arenas for the modification of human values is the arena of choice, our theories of adult and organizational decision making ignore the phenomenon entirely.

Introducing ambiguity and fluidity to the interpretation of individual, organizational, and societal goals obviously has implications for behavioral theories of decision making. We have tried to identify and respond to some of those difficulties in the preceding chapters. The main point here, however, is not to consider how we might describe the behavior of systems that are discovering goals as they act. Rather it is to examine how we might improve the quality of that behavior, how we might aid the development of interesting goals.

We know how to advise a society, an organization, or an individual if we are first given a consistent set of preferences. Under some conditions, we can suggest how to make decisions if the preferences are consistent only up to the point of specifying a series of independent constraints on the choice. But what about a normative theory of goal-finding behavior? What do we say when our client tells us that he is not sure his present set of values is the set of values in terms of which he wants to act?

It is a question familiar to many aspects of ordinary life. It is a question that friends, associates, students, college presidents, business managers, voters, and children ask at least as frequently as they ask how they should act within a set of consistent and stable values.

Within the context of normative theory of choice as it exists, the answer we give is: First determine the values, then act. The advice is frequently useful. Moreover, we have developed ways in which we can use conventional techniques for decision analysis to help discover value premises and to expose value inconsistencies. These techniques involve testing the decision implications of some successive approximations to a set of preferences. The object is to find a consistent set of preferences with implications that are acceptable to the person or organization making the decisions. Variations on such techniques are used routinely in operations research, as well as in personal counseling and analysis.

The utility of such techniques, however, apparently depends on the assumption that a primary problem is the amalgamation or excavation of preexistent values. The metaphors—"finding oneself," "goal clarification," "self-discovery," "social welfare function," "revealed preference"—are metaphors of search. If our value premises are to be "constructed" rather than "discovered," our standard procedures may be useful; but we have no a priori reason for assuming they will.

Perhaps we should explore a somewhat different approach to the normative question of how we ought to behave when our value premises are not yet (and never will be) fully determined. Suppose we treat action as a way of creating interesting goals at the same time as we treat goals as a way of justifying action. It is an intuitively plausible and simple idea, but one that is not immediately within the domain of standard normative theories of intelligent choice.

Interesting people and interesting organizations construct complicated theories of themselves. To do this, they need to supplement the technology of reason with a technology of foolishness. Individuals and organizations sometimes need ways of doing things for which they have no good reason. They need to act before they think.

Sensible Foolishness

To use intelligent choice as a planned occasion for discovering new goals, we require some idea of sensible foolishness. Which of the many foolish things that we might do now will lead to attractive value consequences? The question is almost inconceivable. Not only does it ask us to predict the value consequences of action, it asks us to evaluate them. In what terms can we talk about "good" changes in goals?

In effect, we are asked either to specify a set of supergoals in terms of which alternative goals are evaluated, or to choose among alternatives *now* in terms of the unknown set of values we will have at some future time (or the distribution over time of that unknown set of future values). The former alternative moves us back to the original situation of a fixed set of values — now called "supergoals" — and hardly seems an important step in the direction of inventing procedures for discovering new goals. The latter alternative seems fundamental enough, but it violates severely our sense of temporal order. To say that we make decisions now in terms of goals that will be knowable only later is nonsensical — as long as we accept the basic framework of the theory of choice and its presumptions of preexistent goals.

As we challenge the dogma of preexistent goals, we will be forced to reexamine some of our most precious prejudices: the strictures against imitation, coercion, and rationalization. Each of those honorable prohibitions depends on the view of man and human choice imposed on us by conventional theories of choice.

Imitation is not necessarily a sign of moral weakness. It is a prediction. It is a prediction that if we duplicate the behavior or attitudes of someone else, not only will we fare well in terms of current goals but the chances of our discovering attractive new goals for ourselves are relatively high. If imitation is to be normatively attractive, we need a better theory of who should be imitated.

Such a theory seems to be eminently feasible. For example, what are the conditions for effectiveness of a rule that one should imitate another person whose values are close to one's own? How do the chances of discovering interesting goals through imitation change as the number of people exhibiting the behavior to be imitated increases? In the case of the college president we might ask what the goal discovery consequences are of imitating the choices of those at institutions more prestigious than one's own, and whether there are other more desirable patterns of imitation.

Coercion is not necessarily an assault on individual autonomy. It can be a device for stimulating individuality. We recognize this when we talk about education or about parents and children. What has been difficult with coercion is the possibility for perversion, not its obvious capability for stimulating change. We need a theory of the circumstances under which entry into a coercive relationship produces behavior that leads to the discovery of interesting goals. We are all familiar with the tactic. College presidents use it in imposing deadlines, entering contracts, making commitments. What are the conditions for its effective use? In particular, what are the conditions for goal-fostering coercion in social systems?

Rationalization is not necessarily a way of evading morality. It can be a test for the feasibility of a goal change. When deciding among alternative actions for which we have no good reason, it may be sensible to develop some definition of how "near" to intelligence alternative "unintelligent" actions lie. Effective rationalization permits this kind of incremental approach to changes in values. To use it effectively, however, we require a better idea of the metrics that might be possible in measuring value distances. At the same time, rationalization is the major procedure for integrating newly discovered goals into an existing structure of values. It provides the organization of complexity without which complexity itself becomes indistinguishable from randomness.

The dangers in imitation, coercion, and rationalization are too familiar to elaborate. We should, indeed, be able to develop better techniques. Whatever those techniques may be, however, they will almost certainly undermine the superstructure of biases erected on purpose, consistency, and rationality. They will involve some way of thinking about action now as occurring in terms of a set of future values different from those that the actor currently holds.

Play and Reason A second requirement for a technology of foolishness is some strategy for suspending rational imperatives toward consistency.

Even if we know which of several foolish things we want to do, we still need a mechanism for allowing us to do it. How do we escape the logic of our reason?

Here we are closer to understanding what we need. It is playfulness. Playfulness is the deliberate, temporary relaxation of rules in order to explore the possibilities of alternative rules. When we are playful, we challenge the necessity of consistency. In effect, we announce—in advance—our rejection of the usual objections to behavior that does not fit the standard model of intelligence.

Playfulness allows experimentation at the same time that it acknowledges reason. It accepts an obligation that at some point either the playful behavior will be stopped or it will be integrated into the structure of intelligence in some way that makes sense. The suspension of the rules is temporary.

The idea of play may suggest three things that are, in our minds, quite erroneous in the present context. First, play may be seen as a kind of "holiday" for reason, a release of the emotional tensions of virtue. Although it is possible that play performs some such function, that is not the function with which we are concerned. Second, play may be seen as part of some mystical balance of spiritual principles: fire and water, hot and cold, weak and strong. The intention here is much narrower than a general mystique of balance. Third, play may be seen as an antithesis of intelligence, so that the emphasis on the importance of play becomes a support for simple self-indulgence. Our present intent is to propose play as an instrument of intelligence, not a substitute.

Playfulness is a natural outgrowth of our standard view of reason. A strict insistence on purpose, consistency, and rationality limits our ability to find new purposes. Play relaxes that insistence to allow us to act "unintelligently" or "irrationally" or "foolishly" to explore alternative ideas of purposes and alternative concepts of behavioral consistency. And it does this while maintaining our basic commitment to intelligence.

Although play and reason are in this way functional complements, they are often behavioral competitors. They are alternative styles and alternative orientations to the same situation. There is no guarantee that the styles will be equally well developed, that all individuals, organizations, or societies will be equally adept in both styles; or that all cultures will be sufficiently encouraging to both.

Our design problem is either to specify the best mix of styles or, failing that, to assure that most people and most organizations most of the time use an alternation of strategies rather than persevering in either one. It is a difficult problem. The optimization problem looks extremely complex on the face of it, and the learning situations that will produce alternation in behavior appear to be somewhat less common than those that produce perseverance.

Consider, for example, the difficulty of sustaining playfulness as a style within contemporary American society. Individuals who are good at consistent rationality are rewarded early and heavily. We define consistent rationality as intelligence, and the educational rewards of society are associated strongly with it. Social norms press in the same direction, particularly for men. "Changing one's mind" is viewed as feminine and undesirable. Politicians and other leaders will go to enormous lengths to avoid admitting an inconsistency. Many demands of modern organizational life reinforce the same rational abilities and preferences for a style of unchanging purposes.

The result is that many of the most influential and best-educated citizens have experienced a powerful overlearning with respect to rationality. They are exceptionally good at maintaining consistent pictures of themselves, of relating action to purposes. They are exceptionally poor at a playful attitude toward their own beliefs, toward the logic of consistency, or toward the way they see things as being connected in the world. The dictates of manliness, forcefulness, independence, and intelligence are intolerant of playful urges if they arise. The playful urges that arise are weak ones, scarcely discernible in the behavior of most businessmen, mayors, or college presidents.

The picture is probably overdrawn, but we believe that the implications are not. Reason and intelligence have had the unnecessary consequence of inhibiting the development of purpose into more complicated forms of consistency. To move away from that position, we need to find some ways of helping individuals and organizations to experiment with doing things for which they have no good reason, to be playful with their conceptions of themselves. We suggest five things as a small beginning:

First, we can treat *goals as hypotheses.* Conventional theories of decision making allow us to entertain doubts about almost everything except the thing about which we frequently have the greatest doubt—our objectives. Suppose we define the decision-making process as a time for the sequential testing of hypotheses about goals. If we can experiment with alternative goals, we stand some chance of discovering complicated and interesting combinations of good values that none of us previously imagined.

Second, we can treat *intuition as real*. We do not know what intuition is or even if it is any one thing. Perhaps it is simply an excuse for doing something we cannot justify in terms of present values or for refusing to follow the logic of our own beliefs. Perhaps it is an inexplicable way of consulting that part of our intelligence and knowledge of the world that is not organized in a way anticipated by standard theories of choice. In either case, intuition permits us to see some possible actions that are outside our present scheme for justifying behavior.

Third, we can treat *hypocrisy as a transition*. Hypocrisy is an inconsistency between expressed values and behavior. Negative attitudes about hypocrisy stem mainly from a general onus against inconsistency and from a sentiment against combining the pleasures of vice with the appearance of virtue. It seems to us that a bad man with good intentions may be a man experimenting with the possiblity of becoming good. Somehow it seems more sensible to encourage the experimentation than to insult it.

Fourth, we can treat *memory as an enemy*. The rules of consistency and rationality require a technology of memory. For most purposes, good memories make good choices. But the ability to forget or overlook is also useful. If you do not know what you did yesterday or what other people in the organization are doing today, you can act within the system of reason and still do things that are foolish.

Fifth, we can treat *experience as a theory*. Learning can be viewed as a series of conclusions based on concepts of action and consequences that we have invented. Experience can be changed retrospectively. By changing our interpretive concepts now, we modify what we learned earlier. Thus we expose the possibility of experimenting with alternative histories. The usual strictures against "self-deception" in experience need occasionally to be tempered with an awareness of the extent to which all experience is an interpretation subject to conscious revision. Personal histories and national histories need to be rewritten continously as a base for the retrospective learning of new self-conceptions.

If we knew more about the normative theory of acting before thinking, we could say more intelligent things about the functions of management and leadership when organizations or societies do not know what they are doing. Consider, for example, the following general implications.

First, we need to reexamine the functions of management decision making. One of the primary ways in which the goals of an organization are developed is by interpreting the decisions it makes, and one feature of good managerial decisions is that they lead to the development of more interesting value premises for the organization. As a result, decisions should not be seen as flowing directly or strictly from a preexistent set of objectives. College presidents who make decisions might well view that function somewhat less as a process of deduction or a process of political negotiation, and somewhat more as a process of gently upsetting preconceptions of what the organization is doing.

Second, we need a modified view of planning. Planning can often be more effective as an interpretation of past decisions than as a program for future ones. It can be used as a part of the efforts of the organization to develop a new consistent theory of itself that incorporates the mix of recent actions into a moderately comprehensive structure of goals. Procedures for interpreting the meaning of most past events are familiar to the memoirs of retired generals, prime ministers, business leaders, and movie stars. They suffer from the company they keep. In an organization that wants to continue to develop new objectives, a manager needs to be tolerant of the idea that he will discover the meaning of yesterday's action in the experiences and interpretations of today.

Third, we need to reconsider evaluation. As nearly as we can determine, there is nothing in a formal theory of evaluation that requires that criteria be specified in advance. In particular, the evaluation of social experiments need not be in terms of the degree to which they have fulfilled our prior expectations. Rather we can examine what they did in terms of what we now believe to be important. The prior specification of criteria and the prior specification of evaluational procedures that depend on such criteria are common presumptions in contemporary social policy making. They are presumptions that inhibit the serendipitous discovery of new criteria. Experience should be used explicitly as an occasion for evaluating our values as well as our actions.

Fourth, we need a reconsideration of social accountability. Individual preferences and social action need to be consistent in some way. But the process of pursuing consistency is one in which both the preferences and the actions change over time. Imagination in social policy formation involves systematically adapting to and influencing preference. It would be unfortunate if our theories of social action encouraged leaders to ignore their responsibilities for anticipating public preferences through action and for providing social experiences that modify individual expectations.

Fifth, we need to accept playfulness in social organizations. The design of organizations should attend to the problems of maintaining both playfulness and reason as aspects of intelligent choice. Since much of the literature on social design is concerned with strengthening the rationality of decision making, managers are likely to overlook the importance of play. This is partly a matter of making the individuals within an organization more playful by encouraging the attitudes and skills of inconsistency. It is also a matter of making organizational structure and organizational procedures more playful. Organizations can be playful even when the participants in them are not. The managerial devices for maintaining consistency can be varied. We encourage organizational play by insisting on some temporary relief from control, coordination, and communication.

Presidents and Foolishness   Contemporary theories of decision making and the technology of reason have considerably strengthened our capabilities for effective social action. The conversion of the simple ideas of choice into an extensive technology is a major achievement. It is, however, an achievement that has reinforced some biases in the underlying models of choice in individuals and groups. In particular, it has reinforced the uncritical acceptance of a static interpretation of human goals.

There is little magic in the world, and foolishness in people and organizations is one of the many things that fail to produce miracles. Under certain conditions, it is one of several ways in which some of the problems of our current theories of intelligence can be overcome. It may be a good way, for it preserves the virtues of consistency while stimulating change. If we had a good technology of foolishness, it might (in combination with the technology of reason) help in a small way to develop the unusual combinations of attitudes and behaviors that describe the interesting people, interesting organizations, and interesting societies of the world. The contribution of a college president may often be measured by his capability for sustaining that creative interaction of foolishness and rationality.

References

Adams, Jesse E., and Herman Lee Donovan: "The Administration and Organization in American Universities," *Peabody Journal of Education,* vol. 22, May 1945.

Allison, Graham T: *Essence of Decision: Explaining the Cuban Missile Crisis,* Little, Brown and Company, Boston, 1971.

Baldridge, J. Victor (ed.): *Academic Governance: Research on Institutional Politics and Decision Making,* McCutchan Publishing Corporation, Berkeley, 1971.

Baldridge, J. Victor: *Power and Conflict in the University,* John Wiley & Sons, Inc., New York, 1971.

Beard, John L.: "A Study of the Duties Performed by College Administrators," Ph.D. dissertation in education, University of Texas at Austin, June 1948.

Bolman, Frederick de W.: *How College Presidents Are Chosen,* American Council on Education, Washington, D.C., 1965.

Bryan, William Lowe: "The Share of Faculty in Administration and Government," in Guy P. Benton (ed.), *Transactions and Proceedings of the National Association of State Universities in the United States,* Free Press Printing Company, Burlington, Vt., 1914.

Carnegie, Dale: *How to Win Friends and Influence People,* Simon and Schuster, New York, 1936.

Cohen, Michael D., James G. March, and Johan P. Olsen: "A Garbage Can Model of Organizational Choice," *Administrative Science Quarterly,* vol. 17, no. 1, pp. 1–25, March 1972.

Cyert, Richard M., and James G. March: *A Behavioral Theory of the Firm,* Prentice-Hall, Inc., Englewood Cliffs, N.J., 1963.

Demerath, Nicholas J., Richard W. Stephens, and R. Robb Taylor: *Power, Presidents, and Professors,* Basic Books, Inc., Publishers, New York, 1967.

Donovan, Herman Lee: "The State University Presidency: 1955," in C. P. McCurdy, Jr. (ed.), *Transactions and Proceedings of the National Association of State Universities in the United States,* National Association of State Universities, Washington, D.C., 1955.

Faculty Efforts and Output Study, University of California, Berkeley, 1970.

Ferrari, Michael R.: *Profiles of American College Presidents,* Michigan State University Business School, East Lansing, 1970.

Foote, Caleb, Mayer, Henry, and Associates: *The Culture of the University —Governance and Education,* Jossey-Bass Inc., San Francisco, 1968.

Frey, Frederick W.: "Comment: On Issues and Nonissues in the Study of Power," *American Political Science Review,* vol. 65, pp. 1081–1101, 1971.

Green, Paul E., and Frank J. Carmone: *Multidimensional Scaling and Related Techniques in Marketing Analysis,* Allyn and Unwin, Boston, 1970.

Hayes, Denis A., and James G. March: "The Normative Problems of University Governance," Assembly on University Goals and Governance, Stanford University, 1970. (Mimeographed.)

Hemphill, John K., and Herbert J. Walberg: *An Empirical Study of the College and University Presidents in the State of New York,* Regents Advisory Committee on Educational Leadership, Albany, 1966.

Hodgkinson, Harold L., and Richard L. Meeth (eds.): *Power and Authority* (Transformation of Campus Governance . . . Conference Papers) Jossey-Bass, Inc., San Francisco, 1971.

Hodgkinson, Harold L.: *Institutions in Transition: A Profile of Change in Higher Education,* McGraw-Hill Book Company, New York, 1971.

Iklé, Fred C.: *How Nations Negotiate,* Harper & Row, Publishers, Incorporated, New York, 1964.

Ingraham, Mark H.: *The Mirror of Brass: The Compensation and Working Conditions of College and University Administrators,* University of Wisconsin Press, Madison, 1968.

"The Invitational Seminar on Restructuring College and University Organization and Governance," *The Journal of Higher Education,* vol. 42, no. 6, pp. 421–542, June 1971.

Kerr, Clark: "Governance and Functions," *Daedalus,* vol. 99, no. 1, pp. 108–121, Winter 1970.

Kerr, Clark:"Presidential Discontent," in David C. Nichols (ed.), *Perspectives on Campus Tensions,* papers prepared for the Special Committee on Campus Tensions, American Council on Education, Washington, D.C., September 1970.

Kerr, Clark: *The Uses of the University,* Harvard University Press, Cambridge, Mass., 1963.

Klahr, David: "A Monte Carlo Investigation of the Statistical Significance of Kruskal's Nonmetric Scaling Procedure," *Psychometrika,* vol. 34, pp. 319–330, 1969.

Knode, Jay C.: "Presidents of State Universities," *Scientific Monthly,* vol. 58, March 1944.

Kruse, S. A., and E. C. Beck: "Study of the Presidents of State Teachers Colleges and of State Universities," *Peabody Journal of Education,* pp. 358–361, May 1928.

Kruskal, J. B.: "Multidimensional Scaling by Optimizing Goodness of Fit to a Nonmetric Hypothesis," *Psychometrika,* vol. 29, pp. 1–28, March 1964.

Kruskal, J. B.: "Nonmetric Scaling: A Numerical Method." *Psychometrika,* vol. 29, pp. 115–129, June 1964.

Long, Norton A.: "The Local Community as an Ecology of Games," *American Journal of Sociology,* vol. 44, pp. 251–261, 1958.

McNeil, Kenneth, and James D. Thompson: "The Regeneration of Social Organizations," *American Sociological Review,* vol. 36, pp. 624–637, 1971.

McVey, Frank, and Raymond A. Hughes: *Problems of College and University Administration.* Iowa State College Press, Ames, 1952.

March, James G., and Herbert A. Simon: *Organizations,* John Wiley & Sons, Inc., New York, 1958.

March, James G. (ed.): *Handbook of Organizations,* Rand McNally & Company, Chicago, 1965.

March, James G.: "The Power of Power," in David Easton (ed.), *Varieties of Political Theory,* Prentice-Hall, Inc., Englewood Cliffs, N.J., 1966.

Mayhew, Lewis B.: *Arrogance on Campus,* Jossey-Bass, Inc., San Francisco, 1971.

Monson, C. H., Jr.: "Metaphors for the University," *Educational Record,* vol. 48, pp. 22–29, Winter 1967.

Perkins, James A.: *College and University Presidents: Recommendations and Report of a Survey,* New York State Regents Advisory Committee on Educational Leadership, Albany, 1967.

Peter, Laurence J.: *The Peter Principle,* William Morrow & Company, Inc, New York, 1969.

Rauh, Morton A.: *The Trusteeship of Colleges and Universities,* McGraw-Hill Book Company, New York, 1969.

Reedy, George E.: *The Twilight of the Presidency,* The World Publishing Company, New York, 1970.

Riesman, David: "Vicissitudes in the Career of the College President," Speech given at the dedication of the O. Meredith Wilson Memorial Library at the University of Minnesota, Minneapolis, May 13, 1969.

Selden, William K.: "How Long Is a College President?" *Liberal Education,* vol. 46, no. 1, pp. 5–15, March 1960.

Simon, Herbert A.: "The Job of a College President," *The Educational Record,* vol. 48, no. 1, pp. 68–78, Winter 1967.

Singletary, Otis A. (ed.): *American Universities and Colleges,* American Council on Education, Washington, D.C., 1968.

Stephens, Richard W.: "The Academic Administration: The Role of the University President." Ph.D. dissertation, University of North Carolina, Chapel Hill, 1956.

Walton, Richard E., and Robert B. McKersie (eds.): *Behavioral Theory of Labor Negotiations,* McGraw-Hill Book Company, New York, 1965.

Warren, Luther E.: "A Study of the Presidents of Four-Year Colleges in the U.S.," *Education,* vol. 58, pp. 427–438, March 1938.

Weiner, Stephen S.: "Educational Decisions in an Organized Anarchy," Ph.D. dissertation, Stanford University, Stanford, Calif., 1972.

White, Harrison C.: *Chains of Opportunity: System Models of Mobility in Organizations,* Harvard University Press, Cambridge, Mass., 1970.

Wolfinger, Raymond: "Nondecisions and the Study of Local Politics," *American Political Science Review,* vol. 65, pp. 1063–1080, 1971.

Wolfinger, Raymond: "Rejoiner to Frey's 'Comments'," *American Political Science Review,* vol. 65, pp. 1102–1104, 1971.

Appendix A:
The 42-College Sample

All the original data reported in this volume (with a slight exception in the case of the newspaper study discussed in Appendix C) are derived from a single sample of 42 schools drawn from the universe of American institutions of higher education that grant bachelor's degrees. For our purposes this universe consisted of 1,235 entries in the tenth edition of *American Universities and Colleges.*

Sample stratification

At the outset of the study, two attributes of educational organizations—size and wealth—seemed to us conspicuous as probable sources of variation in presidential attitudes and behavior and in perceptions of the presidency by others. As indicators for these two variables we chose the number of full-time students attending the school and its total income *per full-time student.* These statistics were available for 1,235 schools, all but a handful of the entries in *American Universities and Colleges.*

As Figures A-1 and A-2 indicate, most American colleges and universities are small and relatively poor. A simple random sample of the universe could very well not have included enough large schools or schools with plentiful resources to allow a satisfactory examination of the data collected for size and wealth effects. We therefore ensured the presence of such variation by drawing a stratified sample. On examining the distribution in Figure A-1, we distinguished three categories of size: 9,000 or more full-time students (large), from 1,500 to 8,999 full-time students (medium), and less than 1,500 full-time students (small). In addition, we used two categories of wealth, distinguishing schools in the upper 20 percent of the distribution of income per student from all others. Using these distinctions, we divided our universe into six parts, from each of which a random sample of seven schools was drawn.

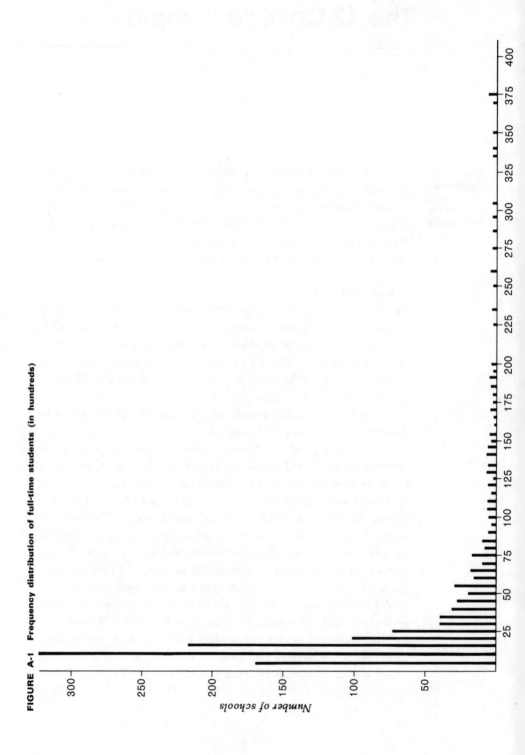

FIGURE A-1 **Frequency distribution of full-time students (in hundreds)**

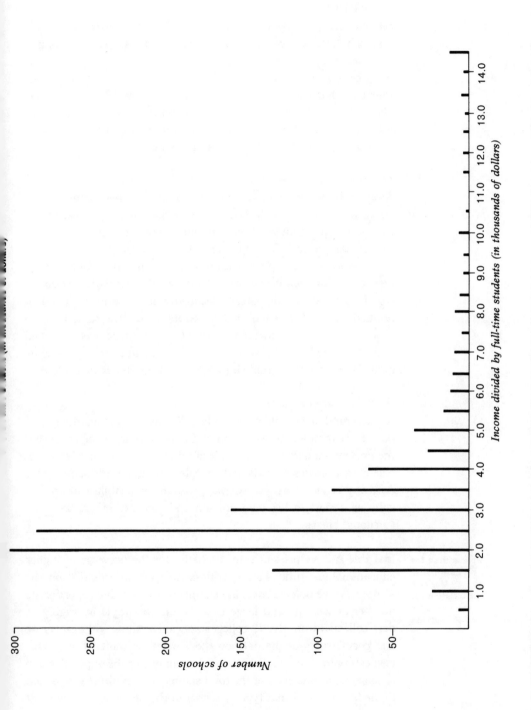

Sample size

Sample size was effectively determined by time constraints on the research, as it was our intention to visit each sample campus and interview the president, his major coworkers, and some students. A practical upper limit to the size of our sample was set by our determination that each of us would have time to make no more than about 20 such campus visits during the winter of 1969–70. Thus, 42 (7 per subsample) was the largest sample size consistent with both time availability and the sample stratification.

Drawing the samples

After each campus was assigned a unique number, sample campuses were selected with the aid of a random number table. Drawing continued without replacement until there were seven campuses in each sample cell. On September 9, 1970, a letter was mailed to the presidents of the 42 schools outlining the intentions of the study and requesting their cooperation. Of these, 36 eventually responded that they would participate, 5 declined, and 1 (former) president notified us that his school had closed its doors. The same random procedure was used to identify replacements, who were notified with the same letter on November 21. All six additional presidents agreed to cooperate, establishing our sample as shown in Table A-1.

Apparent sample bias

A small random sample necessarily will exhibit some unanticipated bias. For example, an inspection of the list of colleges suggests that the present sample is somewhat biased in the direction of overrepresenting women's schools and schools in Virginia. By using Table A-1, any reader may assess the possible applicability of the results we report to his own domain and consider other, less conspicuous, biases.

Procedures for Estimating Various Statistics for the Universe of Presidents

In Table A-2 we present some statistics for the universe of higher educational institutions along with comparable information on our sample. As we noted above, the sample contains a disproportionate number of wealthy and large schools, and a simple averaging of data collected from the 42 colleges and universities will exaggerate any peculiarities of the data on those overrepresented types. Our best estimate of any statistic should count each subsample of seven schools not as one-sixth of the total sample, but in direct proportion to the frequency of that type of school in the universe. To arrive at such a corrected estimate, weights have been applied to the sample data so that each subsample contributes in proportion to the first line of italicized percentages of Table A-2.

Student weights

Throughout the volume we are generally interested in establishing the attributes of an average president. At some points, however, it has been useful to examine instead the attributes of the president of a college attended by an average student. In these cases we have applied weights such that each subsample contributes in proportion to the second line of underscored percentages.

Variance of estimates

Because the use of weights in combination with a small sample size gives considerable importance to a relatively small number of cases, the variance of our estimates should be expected to be moderately high. We have tried to be appropriately cautious in interpretation. In particular, we have examined the unweighted data carefully and have not allowed important points in our argument to rest on estimates that have been altered dramatically by the application of weights to the data.

Regions For the purpose of studying geographic variations in the data, we defined four regions: East (E), South (S), Middle West (M), and Far West (W). The classification of our sample schools into these categories is indicated by the symbols, E, S, M, and W in Table A-1.

TABLE A-1
The 42-college sample

Size of school	Rich	Region
	Columbia University	E
	Cornell University	E
	Harvard University	E
Large	New York University	E
	University of California at Los Angeles	W
	University of Pittsburgh	E
	University of Washington	W
		(3.6)
	Johns Hopkins University	S
	Howard University	S
	North Carolina State University	S
Medium	Skidmore College	E
	University of Virginia	S
	Vassar College	E
	Virginia State College	S
		(6.3)
	Bowie State College	S
	California State College at San Bernardino	W
	Chapman College	W
Small	Connecticut College	E
	Grinnell College	M
	Presbyterian School of Christian Education	S
	Sweet Briar College	S
		(10.0)
TOTAL		(19.9)

NOTE: The figures in parentheses indicate the proportion of the universe (1,235 colleges listed in the tenth edition of *American Universities and Colleges*) that fall in each cell. Our sample is deliberately biased in the direction of the large and rich schools.

Poor	Region	Total
Long Island University	E	
Miami University	M	
San Diego State College	W	
San Francisco State College	W	
University of California at Santa Barbara	W	
University of Hawaii	W	
Wayne State University	M	
	(4.0)	(7.7)
Kearney State College	M	
Moorhead State College	M	
Niagara University	E	
Radford College	S	
Rhode Island College	E	
Russell Sage College	E	
Seattle Pacific College	W	
	(28.3)	(34.6)
California Lutheran College	W	
Cardinal Cushing College	E	
Findlay College	M	
Mary Baldwin College	S	
Mississippi College	S	
Morris Brown College	S	
William Carey College	S	
	(47.7)	(57.7)
	(80.0)	

TABLE A-2
Attributes of
universe and
sample of
American
colleges and
universities

Universe and sample	Large, rich	Large, poor	Medium, rich	Medium, poor	Small, rich
Universe:					
Number of schools	45	50	78	349	124
Percentage of total	3.6	4.0	6.3	28.3	10.0
Number of students (full-time)	866,233	694,521	333,441	1,253,481	97,270
Percentage of total	23.4	18.7	9.0	33.8	2.6
Mean number of students per school	19,520	13,890	4,275	3,592	787
Sample:					
Number of schools	7	7	7	7	7
Percentage of total	16.7	16.7	16.7	16.7	16.7
Number of students (full-time)	115,621	89,888	33,754	18,520	5,152
Percentage of total	43.0	33.4	12.5	6.9	1.9
Mean number of students per school	16,517	12,841	4,822	2,646	736

Small, poor	All rich	All poor	All large	All medium	All small	Total
589	247	988	95	427	713	1,235
47.7	20.0	80.0	7.7	34.6	57.7	100
463,898	1,296,944	2,411,900	1,560,754	1,586,922	561,168	3,708,844
12.5	35.0	65.0	42.1	42.8	15.1	100
787	5,230	2,441	16,429	3,716	787	3,003
7	21	21	14	14	14	42
16.7	50.0	50.0	33.3	33.3	33.3	100
6,243	154,527	114,651	205,509	52,274	11,395	269,178
2.3	57.4	42.6	76.4	19.4	4.2	100
892	7,352	5,460	14,679	3,732	814	6,409

Appendix B:
Role Similarity Study

Multidimensional Scaling Techniques

Multidimensional scaling may be useful whenever one wishes to investigate the internal structure of a set of items and has measurements (usually symmetric) relating every item to every other item in the set. It is often (though not exclusively) used in a fashion similar to factor analysis, but it requires much weaker assumptions about the data on which its output is based. In particular, a multidimensional scaling result depends only on the *order* of the measures between all the pairs of items (or to put it another way, on the order of the interpoint distances), but not on the relative magnitude of the measurements (distances).

If we have, for a set of n objects, data which allow us to order the resulting $n(n-1)/2$ pairs from the most to the least similar, then we can apply multidimensional scaling techniques to find that configuration of n points in a space of a given dimensionality which best represents the structure of similarities in the data. In 1964 W. H. Kruskal proposed a measure of this fidelity of a given configuration to data which he called stress. The stress number varies between one and zero with a configuration perfectly representing data relationships having a stress of zero. If any configuration's stress can be evaluated, then any two configurations can be compared. This makes it possible to search through the various possible configurations in a space of given dimensionality in order to find the one with lowest stress (i.e., with the best fit to the structure in the data). Kruskal also gave a method and a computer program for making such a search, and we have used version III of his procedures in the analysis of our data. Readers interested in a more complete introduction to multidimensional scaling might want to examine Kruskal's seminal articles (1964a, 1964b) and are also referred to Green and Carmone (1970) for a readable treatment of the subsequent profusion of refinements and applications of multidimensional scaling and related techniques.

245

Data Collection, Source Data Construction, and Pooling

At the close of almost all of our structured interviews we administered a similarity judgment task to our respondents that involved eight roles: labor management mediator, bookkeeper, business executive, mayor, clergyman, college president, military commander, and foreman. After a brief explanation, eight 3 x 5 cards were brought out, each bearing the name of one role. The mediator card was set to one side and the other seven were spread out before the respondent. He was then asked to pick the one role "most similar to a mediator." After he had done so, the chosen role card was removed. He was then asked to pick from the remaining six the role most similar to mediator. The card for that choice was removed and the request repeated for the remaining five roles, and so on. When all the cards had been picked up, their order was the order of the perceived similarities of the other seven roles to labor management mediator. Another set of eight cards was then brought out and bookkeeper was set aside to serve as the target for judgments of similarity to the remaining seven roles. The whole cycle was repeated a total of eight times so that each of the roles served as the target for judgments of similarity to the other seven. The respondents were encouraged to make their judgments quickly, and they usually completed the entire task in three to six minutes. Judgments of equal or tied similarity were not allowed.

Thus for each respondent we had a matrix like the one in Table B-1, which was obtained from a president of a large rich school. We need an ordering of the 28 distinct role pairs, an index of similarity that will enable us to determine, for a given respondent, the pair of roles seen as most similar, next most similar, and so on through the least similar pair. Two approaches to the construction of such an index are possible due to the fact that each role served two different functions during the task. On one occasion it was the target (or stimulus) and served to evoke an ordering of the seven other roles. On seven other occasions it served as one of the possible responses, as each of the other roles took its turn as stimulus. Thus, we might measure the similarity of two roles, say business executive and foreman, by comparing the orderings that each evoked. This approach evaluates the results along lines parallel to those used by the respondents who generated the data. We chose, instead, to approach the data at right angles to the respondents' view. Rather than comparing roles by examining what they evoked when serving as stimuli, we evaluated the similarity of a role pair by examining the covariation of the two items as responses. We said, in effect,

TABLE B-1 *Sample similarity judgments*

	Target roles (stimuli)							
Other roles (responses)	Labor management mediator	Book- keeper	Business executive	Mayor	Clergy- man	College president	Military commander	Foreman
Labor management mediator		7	5	3	1	2	5	6
Bookkeeper	7		7	7	7	7	7	7
Business executive	1	1		1	4	1	2	1
Mayor	2	4	2		5	4	4	3
Clergyman	4	3	4	5		3	6	4
College president	5	6	1	2	3		3	2
Military commander	6	2	3	4	6	6		5
Foreman	3	5	6	6	2	5	1	

that two roles were more similar when they tended to occur close together in the strings of responses evoked by all the stimuli. More specifically, we calculated for each respondent, for each role pair (e.g., the ith and jth roles) the statistic

$$\sum_{k=1,8} (r_{ik} - r_{jk})$$

where r_{ik} is the ranking of the ith role with respect to the kth stimulus and r_{ii} is defined as 0. In the example of Table B-1 this statistic for the pair business executive–foreman is 25. Thus, the procedure yielded 28 numbers for each respondent, the smallest number being associated with the most similar pair. We refer to these as the source data, and they give us the required ordering of the interpoint distances to which multidimensional scaling techniques could be applied.

Due to a variety of practical obstacles, we did not make a separate application of the Kruskal MDSCAL III program to each of 182 academic and 93 business school source data sets. Instead, we added together the source data half-matrices for groups of individuals in whom we had a priori interest and scaled the pooled result. The adding was done without weighting the individual cases by the universe frequency of the class from which they were drawn. The results, as we noted in Chapter 6, therefore reflect too heavily any peculiarities of the responses of those from larger or richer colleges and universities.

Stanford Sample Procedures

In collecting the similarity judgment data from our samples of businessmen at the Stanford University School of Business summer session, we used a slightly different collection technique. Rather than presenting each respondent with eight successive packages of cards, as we did in our interviews with academic personnel, we used eight separate mimeographed sheets. Each had the name of one of the target roles at the top along with instructions on ranking the other seven roles for similarity to the target. These were followed by a list of the other seven roles. Each role name stood next to a space where its ranking was to be written. Examination of the data gives us no reason to believe that the differences in presentation introduced any systematic biases into the results. All data sheets which contained any undecodable numbers, blanks, or ties were removed from the sample before scaling was done.

Authoritative, Mediative Subsamples

Theoretically, a preferable system for dividing the presidents into groups with "authoritative" and "mediative" views would have been to scale each respondent separately and then compare the interpoint distances of college president and military commander, foreman, clergyman, and mediator. However, we used a much lower-cost alternative for achieving the same end. For each president we took the interpoint distances for the four-point pairs given by the source data index discussed above. We found the median interpoint index value for each of the four-point pairs across the sample of presidential respondents. We then applied the following program. If a given president had rated the college presidency as having more than median similarity to military commander *and* less than median similarity to mediator, he was classified as "authoritative." If he rated the presidency as having more than median similarity to mediator *and* less than median similarity to military commander, he was classified "mediative." This procedure left 10 of 39 respondents unclassified, and a secondary criterion was applied in those cases. Those rating the presidency as having more than median similarity to foreman *and* less than median similarity to clergyman were classified as "authoritative." Those rating the presidency as having more than median similarity to clergyman *and* less than median similarity to foreman were classified "mediative." The application of this secondary criterion left only one president unclassified. He was excluded from further analyses involving this dimension.

We were able to check our distinction of authoritative and mediative views of the presidency by submitting the matrix of correlations of the subjects' raw responses to a Q-type factor analysis. This procedure also extracted what is apparently an "authoritativeness" dimension, which distributed the subjects in a fashion consistent with our categorization and which again appeared to be closely correlated with size.

Measures of Fidelity   As we noted in footnote 8 of Chapter 4, MDSCAL III produces for each configuration of points representing the relationship in the source data a measure of the fidelity of the former's representations of the latter. Table B-2 gives measures under Kruskal's revised stress formula number 2 for the two- and three-dimensional configurations best representing the relationships perceived among roles in the source data gathered from our seven groups of respondents. The rough standards based on experience for appraising these fits is that stress less than 0.10 is considered "good" and less than 0.05 "excellent." Moreover, in the five starred cases, computing was arbitrarily terminated at the first configuration with a stress less than or equal to 0.01. Continued computation and minor adjustment of the configuration might have produced even smaller stress values.

However, the conventional standard for appraising these results is based heavily on experience with configurations containing a larger number of points. For random source data stress values will be lower if the number of points is smaller. A study by David Klahr

TABLE B-2 *Stresses for two- and three-dimensional configurations representing similarity judgments for seven groups*

Configuration	Presidents	Academic officers	Business officers	Assistants to president	Secretaries	United States businessmen	Foreign businessmen
2 dimensions	0.057	0.022	0.283	0.038	0.107	0.028	0.096
3 dimensions	0.101*	0.010*	0.010*	0.006*	0.063	0.009*	0.014

(1969) indicates that in 100 random eight-point data sets, Kruskal's procedure yielded eight "excellent" stresses. Thus, it would appear that for each of the starred cases that are the backbone of our analysis in Chapter 4, the probability that the configurations are the result of analyzing pure noise is somewhat less than 0.08.

Appendix C:
Newspaper Study

The Sample and Data Collection

Our study of newspaper coverage was also based on a sample stratified into three categories of size and two of wealth, but there are slight differences in its composition from that of the final sample described in Appendix A. These arise from the fact that it was necessary to begin the newspaper study on the basis of our first stratified random drawing, before we were able to identify and replace those institutions unable to cooperate in our subsequent research.

For each campus we obtained the names and addresses of (1) the campus newspaper (if any); (2) the local newspaper published closest to the campus; and (3) the largest newspaper published in any city lying within 50 miles of the campus. Notice that it could, and for 22 schools did, happen that a single newspaper could satisfy both requirements (2) and (3). Since many schools did not have a campus newspaper and delivery from those which did was often spotty, we have not analyzed campus newspaper coverage of the presidency. Our collections of category (2) and (3) papers were fairly complete. In no case did we have newspapers for less than 23 of the 31 sample days. For an average paper we collected 28.3 of the 31 sample days.

Preliminary Abstracts

We owe a considerable debt of gratitude to Lance Bennett and Patti Nelson Bennett, who patiently read each of the 1,783 newspapers and clipped any article or picture mentioning the president or presidency of any of our sample schools. There were 164 such articles.

For each article they prepared an abstract that gave various statistics on the article and made a preliminary breakdown of that part of the article specifically involving the presidency. They provided a brief summary of the article's content with respect to six categories:

1   Was the president or presidency the direct subject of the article? If so, what was done or said?

2   If the president was a participant in some reported activity, what was it?

3   If the president made comments of some kind, what were they?

4   If the president appealed to any constituencies, which ones?

5   If he addressed himself to any particular audience, what was it?

6   What was the role of the president pictured in the reported activity or remarks?

Each of these summaries was typed onto a 3 x 5 card, as a preliminary to the preparation of codes to be used within these broad categories.

Deriving within Category Codes and Reliability

Codes were established for each category by sorting a complete set of the 3 x 5 cards for that category into clusters. The sorter then wrote out a brief description of the clusters and a record of the sort. The cards were shuffled and a second sorter went through them using the cluster descriptions. Disagreements (amounting to 12 percent of the cases) were settled by conferences of the two sorters.

TABLE C-1
Summary of the differences between the newspaper sample and the sample for all other studies*

Students	*Wealthy (20 percent)*	*Remaining (80 percent)*
9,000+	6 schools from final sample 1 other school	6 schools from final sample 1 other school
8,999—1,500	7 schools from final sample	6 schools from final sample 1 other school
1,499—	5 schools from final sample 1 other school 1 school defunct (no data collected)	6 schools from final sample 1 other school

*It should be noted that because one of the originally drawn schools had ceased to exist, our newspaper study effectively sampled the coverage of presidents of 41 colleges and universities.

Appendix D:
Time Allocation Study

The Sample and Data Collection The study of presidential time allocation was based on data gathered with the cooperation of presidential secretaries from 41 of the 42 colleges in our basic sample (see Appendix A). At the time of our interviews with the presidents, we solicited their cooperation and that of their secretaries. On April 6, 1970, we wrote to each of the secretaries, providing instructions and forms (see below).

The actual days chosen were selected randomly from six Tuesdays and six Fridays in the spring of 1970. The days selected were April 17 (Friday) and April 28 (Tuesday). On the day before each of the days selected, the secretaries were called and advised to begin recording the following morning.

Coding The 24-hour period was divided into half-hour periods. For each period on each day, each president's time was coded in terms of where he was, in what size group, and with whom. (The information on activity or general topic of discussion and the information on telephone calls were too erratically recorded to be used systematically.) The codings were in terms of the following categories:

Where:

Home	(0)
Own office or conference room	(1)
Other office on campus	(2)
Other on campus	(3)
Other in town	(4)
Out-of-town	(5)
In transit, local	(6)
In transit, long distance	(7)
Other	(8)
No information	(9)

Size group:

Alone	(0)
One person	(1)
Two people	(2)
Three or more people	(3)
No information	(9)

With whom: (coded separately the first and second named person)

No information	(00)
Alone	(01)
Family	(11)
Other social	(12)
Professional (noncollege)	(13)
Administrator/faculty from other college	(14)
Secretary	(21)
Assistant to president	(22)

Public relations	(23)
Other from president's office	(24)
Lawyer	(25)
Chancellor, *the* vice-president	(31)
Chief executive officer on campus	(32)
Academic vice-president, provost dean of college	(41)
Dean of school	(42)
Department chairman	(43)
Other academic administrator	(44)
Official in faculty government	(45)
Faculty	(46)
Prospective faculty	(47)
Vice-president, director of administration or development	(50)
Chief executive, business-finance	(51)
Lesser administrator, finance	(52)
Lesser administrator, business	(53)
Buildings and grounds, architect	(54)
Staff (other)	(55)
Registrar, director of admissions	(61)
Librarian, AVTV	(62)
Administrator, student affairs	(71)
Student officer, newspaper	(72)
Student (other)	(73)
Trustee, chairman	(81)
Trustee, other	(82)
Politician	(90)

Governmental official	(91)	Alumnus	(95)
Foundation official	(92)	Donor, outside fund raiser	(96)
Local citizen	(93)	Businessman, banker, insurance	(97)
Parent of student	(94)		

The coding was done independently by two coders and differences were reconciled. The differences were trivial.

The following letter was mailed to each secretary:

April 6, 1970

Name _____
Address _____
       _____
       _____

Dear _____:

As I indicated in my original letter to President _____ concerning our study of the American college presidency, we are interested in determining how each of the forty-two presidents in our panel spends two specific, randomly selected days this spring. I am grateful that you and the president have expressed your willingness to help us.

This study will permit us to understand better the way in which a college president allocates his time. While the days we choose will undoubtedly not be "typical," we expect the averages for our forty-two presidents to give us a good representation of typical calendars. For our results to be accurate, we need to know as exactly as possible what President _____'s schedule was for the two days. We are also providing a space for you to note your comments on features of the days which were unusual. We would appreciate any such comments you might make.

Essentially, we would like you to keep an accurate record of the president's time for two separate twenty-four-hour periods. There are two forms enclosed on which to record his activities for each day: (1) "President's Daily Schedule"— on which to record the president's face-to-face contacts and activities and (2) "President's Telephone Log"—on which to record his telephone contacts. We are interested in all of his activities during the working day; after working hours we are interested mainly in school-related activities, but we would appreciate your accounting for all of the twenty-four hour periods. With each form there is a page of instructions and a completed sample form. If you have any questions regarding these, please contact Mrs. Jackie Fry at (714) 833-5426 (collect). Mrs. Fry will be in touch with you the day before we want you to begin the record. We hope that in the meantime you will take a few minutes to look over the forms.

Once again, let me thank you for your help. We very much appreciate your cooperation.

Cordially,

James G. March

JGM/jf
Enclosures

The following forms were provided each secretary:

President's Daily Schedule

Instructions: On this form, please record the President's face-to-face contact and activities.

Column 1, "Time"—The time record begins and ends at midnight. We want an accounting of the full twenty-four-hour period. If the President is involved in personal business, simply write "personal" in Column 4, "Activity or General Topic of Discussion."

Column 2, "Where Was He?"—Self-explanatory.

Column 3, "With Whom?"—Identify the person by title rather than name (e.g., student; Art Department Chairman; President, Bank of America). If the President is with a group or organization, identify the group rather than individuals (e.g., Board of Directors, Math 134B class). If the President is spending the time alone, please so indicate. It will be necessary to make more than one entry per half hour when the President has several short contacts.

Column 4, "Activity or General Topic of Discussion"—Please indicate how the President is spending his time, whether he is alone or with others. If he is traveling, indicate in this column his destination.

PRESIDENT'S DAILY SCHEDULE

_____ Date   Log completed by:

_____ Institution

_____

Time	Where was he? (e.g., home, office, car, New York hotel)	With whom? (Identify by title rather than name, e.g., student; Art Department Chairman; President, Bank of America	Activity or general topic of discussion (e.g., staff meeting, travel to Chicago, discussion of program for disadvantaged students, personal)
Midnight			
1:00 A.M.			
2:00 A.M.			
3:00 A.M.			
4:00 A.M.			
5:00 A.M.			
6:00 A.M.			

Time	Where was he? (e.g., home, office, car, New York hotel)	With whom? (Identify by title rather than name, e.g., student; Art Department Chairman; President, Bank of America)	Activity or general topic of discussion (e.g., staff meeting, travel to Chicago, discussion of program for disadvantaged students, personal)
6:30 A.M.			
7:00 A.M.			
7:30 A.M.			
8:00 A.M.			
8:30 A.M.			
9:00 A.M.			
9:30 A.M.			
10:00 A.M.			
10:30 A.M.			
11:00 A.M.			
11:30 A.M.			
Noon			
12:30 P.M.			
1:00 P.M.			
1:30 P.M.			
2:00 P.M.			
2:30 P.M.			
3:00 P.M.			
3:30 P.M.			
4:00 P.M.			

Time	Where was he? (e.g., home, office, car, New York hotel)	With whom? (Identify by title rather than name, e.g., student; Art Department Chairman; President, Bank of America)	Activity or general topic of discussion (e.g., staff meeting, travel to Chicago, discussion of program for disadvantaged students, personal)
4:30 P.M.			
5:00 P.M.			
5:30 P.M.			
6:00 P.M.			
6:30 P.M.			
7:00 P.M.			
7:30 P.M.			
8:00 P.M.			
8:30 P.M.			
9:00 P.M.			
9:30 P.M.			
10:00 P.M.			
10:30 P.M.			
11:00 P.M.			
11:30 P.M.			

Comments:_____
_____
_____
_____
_____
_____
_____
_____
_____
_____
_____
_____
_____
_____
_____

President's Telephone Log

Instructions: On this form please record the President's telephone contacts. We are interested only in actual contacts between the President and others. In other words, do not list incoming or outgoing calls which the President does not personally handle.

One difficulty which may arise is a phone conversation with a person who occupies more than one role, for example a faculty member or student who is also a member of an important committee. In such a case, we would like to have both the name of the committee and some abbreviated indication of the individual's other role [e.g., University Senate Chairman (Hist. Prof.)].

PRESIDENT'S TELEPHONE LOG
(7:00 A.M. to 6:00 P.M.)

_____ Date   Log completed by:

_____ Institution   _____

Time of call	To whom did he speak? (Identify by title or position and organization rather than name)	Who initiated the call?		How long did they talk? (approximately)
		President	Contact	

Time of call	To whom did he speak? (Identify by title or position and organization' rather than name)	Who initiated the call?		How long did they talk? (approximately)
		President	Contact	

Comments: _____

_____

_____

_____

_____

_____

_____

_____

_____

_____

_____

Appendix E:
Presidential Time
Allocation 1970–1984

James R. Glenn, Jr.* and James G. March

In 1974 and again in 1979, Glenn replicated the Cohen and March study of time allocation by college presidents using the same sample of colleges and universities. Of the original 42-college sample, one institution had died. Detailed time records were obtained from 35 (85 percent) presidents in 1974 and from 31 (76 percent) in 1979. The procedures followed were the same as in the earlier study. We focus here only on the light the replications shed on the stability of the Cohen and March results, not on more general issues of executive time allocation. We ask whether there are changes in the allocation of time by college presidents over this period.

Because the sample sizes, both in the original study and in the replications, are small and stratified, the sampling error in estimates is relatively large and the chance of identifying a difference between 1970 and 1974 or 1979 that is, by itself, statistically significant is small. Even large apparent differences can be explained relatively easily as being due to sampling variation. As a result, we need to be cautious in identifying any particular apparent difference as reflecting a real shift. The strategy is to look for a set of consistent differences that seem collectively less likely to be explicable as sampling variation.

The overall impression to be drawn from looking at the data from 1970, 1974, and 1979, however, is not so much that there are many, possibly spurious, differences as that there is substantial stability in the pattern of time allocation across the three time points. At least with respect to the measured characteristics of their days, college presidents in 1974 and 1979 appear to have spent their time in ways not strikingly different from presidents in 1970; that is, with some exceptions to be noted shortly, presidents divided their time among locations, types of groups, and types of people in roughly the same way in all three studies. The differences noted by Cohen and March

* Professor of Management, San Francisco State University.

between time allocation in the morning and afternoon and between Tuesday and Friday remained about the same in the later studies. Most of the similarities and differences across types of institutions persisted. Some of those results are presented in Table E-1.

TABLE E-1
Percentage of time spent by presidents by location, group size, and category of persons, 1970, 1974, 1979

	1970	1974	1979
Location			
At home	16	9	7
Own office	35	49	37
Other on campus	12	16	17
In town	14	10	16
Out of town	22	17	22
Group Size			
Alone	25	28	29
One other person	35	35	19
Two or more people	40	37	51
Category of Persons			
Outsiders	32	32	38
Constituents	28	25	32
(Trustees)	(8)	(7)	(18)
(Students)	(9)	(6)	(6)
(Faculty)	(11)	(12)	(8)
Administration	40	43	30
(Pres. office)	(6)	(9)	(10)
(Acad. admin.)	(18)	(16)	(10)
(Nonacad. adm.)	(16)	(18)	(10)

* Estimates for location and group size are for the 8 a.m. to 6 p.m. weekday. Estimates for the category of persons exclude situations in which the president is alone or with family, but otherwise include the whole (24-hour) weekday.

There are a few consistent, small differences among the three studies. These differences suggest that the presidential role has shifted somewhat in the direction of becoming a bit more entrepreneurial and a bit less involved in the internal affairs of the college or university. The changes are not all consistent over the period, but there appears to be an increase in the attention given to trustees, outsiders, and persons in the president's own office. These increases have been at the expense of attention given to others within the university, specifically academic and nonacademic administrators, students, and faculty. Perhaps because of this change toward a more entrepreneurial role, presidents spend less time at home, more time away from their offices when they are on campus; they spend less time with one other person, more time in larger groups. The temporal variations in location are rather stable, except that the relatively frequent luncheons at home that were characteristic of a sizable fraction of presidents in 1970 seem to have become a casualty of the changing times, particularly (we assume) because of the increased involvement of spouses with activities away from the home.

Although this overall shift in attention has changed the aggregate allocation of time among the entrepreneurial, political, and administrative roles of the president, it has not changed the temporal shifts in relative emphasis. Cohen and March observed that there were both daily and weekly cycles in attention patterns in 1970. As the clock moved from morning to afternoon, presidents tended to move from administrative to entrepreneurial concerns; as afternoon became evening, presidential attention became more political. This pattern continued in both the 1974 and the 1979 data. Similarly, the new data support the Cohen and March observation that a president's attention is more directed to constituents and less to administrators on Friday than it is on Tuesday.

Most of the differences reported by Cohen and March among colleges and universities of different sizes appear to be sustained by the subsequent samples, but not all of them. Their major size effects — that presidents in larger schools are turned somewhat more "inward" and are more bureaucratic — seem consistent with most of the data. However, some of the specifics are less reliable than others. For example, Cohen and March observed that "presidents of 'rich' colleges are more likely to be out of town than are presidents of 'poor' colleges; presidents of poor colleges are more likely to be in town but not on campus than are presidents of rich colleges . . . presidents of small colleges are more likely to be found out of town than are presidents of large colleges." When we compare these observations with the 1974 and 1979 data, we have to conclude: either that the differences in the 1970 data reflect sampling variation or that there have been changes over this period; and the former seems a safer assumption.

The changes in presidential time allocation from 1970 to 1974 and 1979 are small enough and unreliable enough that extended speculation about them is probably unwarranted. We have tried to assess the extent to which the differences between 1970 and 1979 were due to changes in behavior of sitting presidents, and the extent to which they can be attributed to the replacement of some presidents with a new generation of administrators. Since dividing the sample into further strata on the basis of when a president came to the job makes the sample sizes very small, the conclusion must be suspect; but it appears that each cohort of new presidents either has a slightly different pattern of time allocation on taking office, or changes more quickly in response to new situations. As a result, those presidents who were in office before 1970 and were still in office in 1979 tended to allocate their time a bit more like the 1970 group than do presidents who took office later.

Cohen and March conclude that the allocation of time is regulated by the size of the school, a daily and weekly cycle, general expectations within the culture, role expectations of presidents, the ambiguity of the job, and the pleasures of presidents. The 1974 and 1979 replications of their study support that general conclusion. For the most part, very similar patterns of time allocation are observed. Where there are differences they seem to reflect incremental shifts in the role expectations, introduced into the job through gradual replacement of old presidents with (slightly different) new ones and through modest changes in the behavior of sitting presidents.

Appendix F:
Attrition Among College Presidents, 1970–1984

James R. Glenn, Jr.* and James G. March

On the basis of their examination of tenure among American college presidents from 1900 to 1970, Cohen and March proposed a career surface model for predicting college president tenure. This note explores the extent to which their career surface of attrition rates correctly predicts presidential departures within their sample in the 14 years since 1970. Since the career surface Cohen and March propose is based in part on empirical estimates of observed attrition rates over the 1900–1970 period, our data can also be seen as testing whether the tenure expectations of college presidents have changed.

We have identified all changes in presidents in the Cohen and March sample of colleges and universities up to December 31, 1984.[1] Of the 554 president-years that do not involve acting presidents during this period, 53 of them show a change in president. Thus, the crude departure rate for non-acting presidents is $53/554 = 0.096$. This compares with a comparable crude departure rate during the 1960s of 0.108. Historically, college president attrition has been most closely connected to college growth. Departure rates declined (and tenure lengthened) during the 1930s; departure rates increased (and tenure shortened) during the 1950s; since 1960 departure rates seem to be quite stable with a possible slight decline (increase in tenure). The rates in the 1970s are close to the historic norm. A decade-by-decade calculation of the crude departure rate (excluding acting presidents) during the twentieth century is plotted in Figure F-1.

Crude departure rates may, however, give a misleading picture. Since, as Table F-1 shows, the basic age, completed years of service, and age at entry characteristics of this sample exhibit modest changes

---

* Professor of Management, San Francisco State University.

[1] The sample is the Cohen and March random sample of American four-year colleges, stratified by size and income per student. One of the 42 colleges discontinued operation in 1971. As a result, the sample contains only 41 colleges.

FIGURE F-1
*Crude departure
rate for college
presidents, excluding
acting presidents,
1900 to 1984*

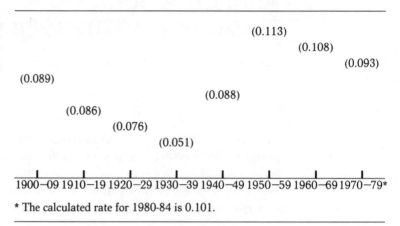

(0.113)

(0.108)

(0.093)

(0.089)

(0.088)

(0.086)

(0.076)

(0.051)

| | | | | | | | |
1900–09 1910–19 1920–29 1930–39 1940–49 1950–59 1960–69 1970–79*

* The calculated rate for 1980-84 is 0.101.

over time, an examination of tenure should control for the fact that actual departure rates from the presidency depend on both age and years of service. Cohen and March present a career surface model of attrition rate as a function of the age and years of service of a president. It is possible to use their estimates to find the expected number of presidential departures in the sample and to compare such predictions with the actual number of exits. Because such a comparison controls for possible extraneous variations in the distributions of age and completed years of service and allows for the identification of sources of prediction error, it is a relatively sensitive procedure for assessing changes. It also permits us to test the predictive power of the Cohen and March model.

Departures from the presidency occur in five ways that have different attrition rates:

TABLE F-1
*Comparison of college
presidents in office
1970 to 1984,
41-college sample,
by current age,
current completed
years of service,
and age at entry*

	1970–74	1975–79	1980–84
Age			
Mean	51.35	51.67	53.37
Range	38–66	39–70	36–73
Years of service			
Mean	6.47	6.58	7.92
Range	1–20	1–24	1–29
Age at entry			
Mean	45.87	46.10	46.41
Range	32–72	32–70	32–73

* Note that these are unweighted means. They are appropriate for comparing different times in this sample but not for estimating the comparable statistics in the universe. Weighted estimates would, however, be only slightly different.

Acting presidents Acting, or interim, presidents are distinctly temporary. In our sample of 575 president-years there are 21 occasions on which the chief executive in a college on December 31 was an acting president. According to Cohen and March, the historical attrition rate among acting presidents is 0.8.

Departure after age 65 After they reach the age of 65, college presidents depart rapidly by death and retirement. In our sample there are five occasions on which a non-acting president was more than 65 years of age on December 31. Cohen and March do not provide a precise attrition rate to reflect their assertion that departure is rapid; we have assumed an attrition rate of 0.9.

Death before age 65 Presidents sometimes die before they leave office or reach 65. For the 549 cases that do not involve either acting presidents or presidents over 65, we have assumed age-specific death rates equal to those of American professional and managerial groups of the appropriate sex.[2]

Departure by resignation after 15 years of service The Cohen and March career surfaces do not extend beyond 15 years of service. In our sample there are 41 presidential years in which a non-acting president who is 65 years of age or younger has served 16 years or more as of December 31. We have assumed an attrition rate of 0.20.[3]

Departure by resignation before age 66 and before 16 years of service Most presidents are neither over age 65 nor more than 15 years in office nor acting presidents. In our sample 508 (88 percent) of the president-years fall in this category. Cohen and March describe a career surface that models attrition rates among presidents in these cases. The surface specifies annual departure rates as functions of a president's age and years of service. The surface is a theoretical

[2]We have used the U.S. mortality rates for white males in 1969, deflated to 0.65 of the aggregate U.S. value. The deflator is based on several studies of differential mortality rates of executives. Since death in office is unlikely if preceded by an extended illness, we have further deflated the estimate by one-half. There is some difficulty posed by the fact that we have an estimate of death rates and resignation rates that are independent. Thus, there is some probability (according to the model) that a president would both die and resign in a given year. Since we are only interested in the event that occurs first, we have assumed that the chance that death occurs before a resignation, given that both would have occurred in the same year, is 0.5. These corrections are extremely small in any event.

[3] This rate is consistent with an extrapolation of the Cohen and March career surface but is not directly specified by them.

approximation to the observed departure rates in 42 colleges over the 1900–1970 period.

Using these estimates of the appropriate attrition rates, we can predict the number and type of presidential departures expected within our sample during the period from January 1, 1971 to December 31, 1984, given the age, years of service, and status (i.e., acting president or not) of the presidents in office. The results are shown in Table F-2.

Type of departure	N	Expected		Observed	
		Number	Rate	Number	Rate
Acting presidents	21	16.80	0.80	19	0.90
Over 65	5	4.50	0.90	4	0.80
Death before 65	549	1.96	0.00	1	0.00
After 15 years	41	8.20	0.20	8	0.20
Other resignation	508	43.44	0.09	42	0.08
Total	575*	74.90	0.13	74	0.13

* Presidents (other than acting presidents and presidents over 65) are treated as vulnerable both to death and to resignation in a given year. Thus, the total is $21+5+41+508=575$.

The estimates from the Cohen and March theoretical career surface yield a combined expectation of 74.90 departures from the presidencies in our sample, or an aggregate departure rate of 0.130. The difference between this and the observed 74 departures and the observed aggregate departure rate of 0.129 is negligible.[4] Just as the earlier study gave no support for hypotheses of decreases in presidential tenure during the 1960s, the present extension provides no support for hypotheses of decreases during the period from 1970 to 1984.

If we limit our attention to the cases directly predicted by the career surface, the predicted number of 43.44 is well within the sampling variation of the observed 42 departures. This small overestimation of the number of departures for presidents who are less than 66 years of age and who have served less than 16 years might be interpreted as some support for the Cohen and March prediction of a modest increase in presidential tenure expectations, but it seems more conservative to suggest that, on average, presidential attrition has continued to be substantially stable during the past 14 years. The theoretical parameters of the Cohen and March career

[4] These departure rates include departures by acting presidents, therefore are not comparable to those plotted in Figure F-1 and cited earlier.

surface of presidential departures predict the aggregate actuarial experience of this sample of college presidents very well during the 14 years since the completion of their study. Whether the same parameters would do as well on a different sample, or over a longer time period, is not established.

These results may, of course, mask some variation among types of colleges. Cohen and March noted that median tenure was somewhat different in different size schools and seemed to be linked to changes in size. From this, they speculated that there might be a slight increase in tenure (drop in attrition) associated with greater stability in college size. Since the major historic changes in college size have been in colleges and universities that are now large, the speculation can be treated as a guess that tenure among presidents for large colleges might show a slight upturn: thus, departure rates among presidents of larger schools would be less than those predicted from the career surface.

If we disaggregate the predictions made from the Cohen and March career surface and examine the errors in prediction by type of school, we find that the model does tend to overestimate attrition rates among larger schools and underestimate them among smaller schools. Similarly, the model overestimates departures of presidents in wealthier schools and underestimates them in poorer schools. Those results, for presidents who were less than 66 years of age and who had less than 16 years of experience, are shown in Table F-3.

The differences are small and based on relatively small numbers, thus subject to relatively large errors of estimation; but they are generally consistent with the idea that there may have been a small change in tenure expectations favoring presidents of larger and richer schools. Thus, they suggest some modest support for the Cohen and March speculation about a possible slight upturn in presidential tenure in schools with stable enrollment during the 1970s. At the same time, since small, poor schools represent a large fraction of the total population of colleges (though a much smaller fraction of the total population of college students), the data are also consistent with a speculation that the tenure of the average president (but not the average student's president) may have declined slightly.

It should be emphasized that these small differences in age- and tenure-specific departure rates, even if real, do not indicate any profound shift in the tenure expectations of college presidents. Judging from this long-term sample, average tenure expectations among college presidents have been relatively stable over extended periods in the United States. There was a lengthening of tenure, on average,

	Expected	*Observed*
By wealth of college (1970)		
Top 20% (income/student)	22.31	19
Bottom 80%	21.13	23
By size of college (1970)		
More than 9,000 students	15.72	12
1,500–8,999 students	15.68	15
Less than 1,500 students	12.04	15

from 1920 to 1940; there was a shortening of tenure, on average, from 1940 to 1960; there was a century-long gradual shortening of tenure in relatively large schools. Fluctuations in tenure during the past 25 years have been quite small. The aggregate attrition rate did not change appreciably during the campus riots of the 1960s, nor did it change appreciably during the financial troubles of the 1970s and early 1980s.

Appendix G: How We Talk and How We Act: Administrative Theory and Administrative Life

James G. March

I am not an administrator. I believe I am only the second person without experience as a college president to be invited to deliver the David D. Henry Lecture. I am a student of organizations and administration, and it is from that point of view that I talk. Nevertheless, I hope that some comments from the ivory tower may be marginally useful to the real world of administration. Students of organizations are secretaries to people who live in organizations. Much of our time is spent talking to people in administrative roles, recording their behavior, and trying to develop descriptions of organizational theory. As best we can, we try to make sense of what we see.

Making sense of organizational life is complicated by the fact that organizations exist on two levels. The first is the level of action where we cope with the environment we face; the second is the level of interpretation where we fit our history into an understanding of life. The level of action is dominated by experience and learned routines; the level of interpretation is dominated by intellect and the metaphors of theory. Ordinary administrative life is a delicate combination of the two levels. Managers act. They make decisions, establish rules, issue directives. At the same time, they interpret the events they see. They try to understand their own behavior, as well as that of others, in terms of theories that they (and others) accept. They try to present themselves in understandable, even favorable, terms. They try to improve the way they act by contemplating its relation to the

This paper was given as the David D. Henry Lecture on Administration at the University of Illinois, Urbana-Champaign, 25 September 1980. It is based, in part, on work done jointly with Michael Cohen, Martha Feldman, Daniel Levinthal, James C. March, and Johan P. Olsen, and supported by grants from the Spencer Foundation, the National Institute of Education, and the Hoover Institution. It was then included in: Thomas J. Sergiovanni and John E. Corbally, eds., *Leadership and Organizational Cultures.* (Urbana: University of Illinois Press, 1984).

way they talk, and they try to modify their talk by considering how they act.

The process has elegance, but it also has traps. The interweaving of experience and theory often makes it difficult for the student of administration to disentangle the events of organizational life from the theories about those events that participants have. The same interweaving complicates the ways in which administrators learn from their experience to improve their organizations. I want to explore some aspects of those complications today. My intentions are not grand. I want to talk about some parts of administrative theory and administrative life, about the implications of recent thinking on organizations, and particularly about the possibility that some of our administrative precepts — the way we talk — may sometimes be less sensible than our administrative behavior — the way we act.

Classical perspectives on administrative leadership are rich enough and varied enough to make any effort to describe them in broad terms ill informed. Nevertheless, there is a relatively standard portrayal of organizations and their leaders that is easily recognized and is implicit in most of our administrative theories. Without attempting to represent those theories in a comprehensive way, I want to focus on four assumptions of administrative thought that are important both to contemporary administrative action and the recent research on administrative life:

Assumption 1: The rigidity of organizations In the absence of decisive and imaginative action by administrative leaders, organizations resist change.

Assumption 2: The heterogeneity of managers Top managers vary substantially in their capabilities, and organizations that identify and reward distinctively able administrative leaders prosper.

Assumption 3: The clarity of objectives Intelligent administrative action presupposes clear goals, precise plans, and unambiguous criteria for evaluation.

Assumption 4: The instrumentality of action The justification for administrative action lies in the substantive outcomes it produces.

These assumptions permeate both our writings and our talk about organizations and administration. Although it is certainly possible to find counterexamples in the literature, they are part of generally received administrative doctrine. Moreover, they are not foolish. They reflect considerable good sense. One difficulty with them, however, is that they appear to capture only part of our experience. Most studies of administrative life present a somewhat different version of administrative roles. Although there is a tendency for some biographers of particular leaders to surround administrative life with grandeur, most studies and most reports from administrators present a different picture of what administrators do. Administrative life seems to be filled with minor things, short-time horizons, and seemingly pointless (and endless) commitments. The goals of an organization seem to be unclear and changing. Experience seems to be obscure. Life is filled with events of little apparent instrumental consequence. The ways in which administrative theory leads us to talk about administrative life seem to be partially inconsistent with the ways in which we have experienced and observed it.

Such an inconsistency is neither surprising nor, by itself, disturbing. Tensions between theory and experience are important sources of development for both. But in this case, I think our theories lead us astray in some important ways. In order to examine that thought, I want to note some observations about organizational life drawn from recent research. First, some observations about change; second, some observations about clarity; third, some observations about managers and managerial incentives; and fourth, some observations about instrumentality in administrative life. Taken together, these observations suggest some modest modifications in our assumptions of management.

Organizations and Change

Recent literature on organizations often details the ways that hopes for change are frustrated by organizational behavior. The contrariness of organizations in confronting sensible efforts to change them fills our stories and our research. What most of those experiences tell us, however, is not that organizations are rigid and inflexible. Rather, they picture organizations as impressively imaginative. Organizations change in response to their environments, including their managements, but they rarely change in a way that fulfills the intentional plan of a single group of actors. Sometimes organizations ignore clear policies; sometimes they pursue them more forcefully than was intended. Sometimes they protect policymakers from the follies of foolish policies; sometimes they do not. Sometimes they stand still when we want them to move. Sometimes they move when we want them to stand still.

Organizational tendencies to frustrate arbitrary administrative intention, however, should not be confused with rigidity. Organizations change frequently. They adopt new products, new procedures, new objectives, new postures, new styles, new personnel, new beliefs. Even in a short perspective, the changes are often large. Some of them are sensible; some are not. Bureaucratic organizations are not always efficient. They can be exceptionally obtuse. Change is ubiquitous in organizations; and most change is the result neither of extraordinary organizational processes or forces, nor of uncommon imagination, persistence, or skill. It is a result of relatively stable processes that relate organizations to their environments. Organizational histories are written in dramatic form, and the drama reflects something important about the orchestration and mythology of organizational life, but substantial change results easily from the fact that many of the actions by an organization follow standard rules that are conditional on the environment. If economic, political, or social contexts change rapidly, organizations will change rapidly and routinely.

In such a spirit, recent efforts to understand organizations as routine adaptive systems emphasize six basic perspectives for interpreting organizational action:

1. Action can be seen as the application of standard operating procedures or other rules to appropriate situations. The terms of reference are duties, obligations, and roles. The model is a model of evolutionary selection.

2. Action can be seen as problem solving. The terms of reference are alternatives, consequences, and preferences. The model is one of intended rational choice.

3. Action can be seen as stemming from past learning. The terms of reference are actions and experiences. The model is one of trial and error learning.

4. Action can be seen as resulting from conflict among individuals or groups. The terms of reference are interests, activation, and resources. The model is one of politics — bargaining and power.

5. Action can be seen as spreading from one organization to another. The terms of reference are exposure and susceptibility. The model is one of diffusion.

6. Action can be seen as stemming from the mix of intentions and competencies found in organizational actors. The terms of reference are attitudes, abilities, and turnover. The model is one of regeneration.

These standard processes of organizational action are understandable and mostly reliable. Much of the time they are adaptive. They facilitate organizational survival. Sometimes organizations decline, and sometimes they die. Sometimes the changes that are produced seem little connected either to the intentions of organizational actors or to the manifest problems facing an organization. A propensity to change does not assure survival, and the processes of change are complicated by a variety of confusions and surprises. Solutions sometimes discover problems rather than the other way around. Organizations imitate each other, but innovations and organizations change in the process. Environments are responded to, but they are also affected. The efforts of organizations to adapt are entangled with the simultaneous efforts of individuals and larger systems of organizations. In these ways, the same processes that sustain the dull day-to-day activities of an organization produce unusual events.

These six perspectives portray an organization as coping with the environment routinely, actively adapting to it, avoiding it, seeking to change it, comprehend it, and contain it. An organization is neither unconditionally rigid nor unconditionally malleable; it is a relatively complicated collection of interests and beliefs acting in response to conflicting and ambiguous signals received from the environment and from the organization, acting in a manner that often makes sense and usually is intelligent. Organizations evolve, solve problems, learn, bargain, imitate, and regenerate. Under a variety of circumstances, the processes are conservative. That is, they tend to maintain stable relations, sustain existing rules, and reduce differences among similar organizations. But the fundamental logic is not one of stability in behavior; it is one of adaptation. The processes are stable; the resulting actions are not.

Organizations change routinely and continually, and the effectiveness of an organization in responding to its environment, as well as much of the effectiveness of management, is linked to the effectiveness of routine processes. As a result, much of the job of an administrator involves the mundane work of making a bureaucracy work. It is filled with activities quite distant from those implied in a conception of administration as heroic leadership. It profits from ordinary competence and a recognition of the ways in which organizations change by modest modifications of routines rather than by massive mucking around. Studies of managerial time and behavior consistently show an implicit managerial recognition of the importance of these activities. The daily activities of a manager are rather distant from grand conceptions of organizational leadership. Administrators spend time talking to people about minor things, making trivial decisions, holding meetings with unimportant agendas, and responding to the little irritants of organizational life. Memoirs of administrators confirm the picture of a rewarding life made busy by large numbers of inconsequential things.

These observations describe administrative life as uncomfortably distant from the precepts of administrative theory and from hopes for personal significance. They have led to efforts to change the ways managers behave. Numerous training programs attempt to teach managers to bring their personal time allocation closer to the ideal. They provide procedures designed to increase the time for decision making, planning, thinking, and other things that appear more characteristic of theories of administration than of administrative jobs. These efforts may be mistakes. Making bureaucracy work involves effectiveness in executing a large number of little things. Making bureaucracies change involves attention to the minor routines by which things happen. Rules need to be understood in order to be interpreted or broken; simple breakdowns in the flow of supplies need to be minimized; telephones and letters need to be answered; accounts and records need to be maintained.

The importance of simple competence in the routines of organizational life is often overlooked when we sing the grand arias of management, but effective bureaucracies are rarely dramatic. They are administrative organizations that require elementary efficiency as a necessary condition for quality. Efficiency as a concept has been subject to considerable sensible criticism on the grounds that it is either meaningless or misleading if we treat it independent of the objectives being pursued. The point is well taken as a critique of the "cult of efficiency," but it is much too simple if we take it as an assertion that all, or even most, efforts in an administrative organization need a clear specification of global goals to be done well. An administrative organization combines large numbers of tasks into some kinds of meaningful combinations, but much of the effectiveness of the combination depends on the relatively automatic, local correction of local inefficiencies without continuous attention to the "big picture."

Much of what distinguishes a good bureaucracy from a bad one is how well it accomplishes the trivia of day-to-day relations with clients and day-to-day problems in maintaining and operating its technology. Accomplishing these trivia may involve considerable planning, complex coordination, and central direction, but it is more commonly linked to the effectiveness of large numbers of people doing minor things competently. As a result, it is probably true that the conspicuous differences around the world in the quality of bureaucratic performance are due primarily to variance in the competence of the ordinary clerk, bureaucrat, and lower manager, and to the effectiveness of routine procedures for dealing with problems at a local level. This appears to be true of armies, factories, postal services, hotels, and universities.

The classical administrator acts on the basis of knowledge about objectives. Goals are presumed to be clear — or it is presumed to be a responsibility of administration to make them clear. Administrative life often seems to be filled with ambiguous preferences and goals, and this becomes particularly conspicuous as one nears the top of an organization. Objectives are hard to specify in a way that provides precise guidance. That is not to say that they are completely unknown or that all parts are equally obscure. Administrative goals are often unclear; when we try to make them clear, they often seem unacceptable.

Goal ambiguity is particularly troubling to a conception of rational administrative action. As we normally conceive it, rational action involves two kinds of guesses: guesses about future consequences and guesses about future preferences for those consequences. We try to imagine the future outcomes that will result from our present actions, and we try to imagine how we will evaluate those outcomes when they occur. Neither guess is necessarily easy. Anticipating future consequences of present decisions is often subject to substantial error. Anticipating future preferences is often confusing. Theories of rational choice are primarily theories of these two guesses and how we deal with their complications. Theories of choice under uncertainty emphasize the complications of guessing future preferences.

In standard prescriptive theories of choice:

Preferences are relevant Prescriptive theories of choice require that action be taken in terms of preferences, that decisions be consistent with objectives in the light of information about the probable consequences of alternatives for valued outcomes.

Preferences are stable With few exceptions, prescriptive theories of choice require that tastes be stable. Current action is taken in terms of current preferences. The implicit assumption is that preferences will be unchanged when the outcomes of current actions are realized.

Preferences are consistent Prescriptive theories of choice allow mutually inconsistent preferences only insofar as they can be made irrelevant by the absence of scarcity or by the specification of trade-offs.

Preferences are precise Prescriptive theories of choice eliminate ambiguity about the extent to which a particular outcome will satisfy preferences, at least insofar as possible resolutions of ambiguity might affect the choice.

Preferences are exogenous Prescriptive theories of choice presume that preferences, by whatever process they may be created, are not themselves affected by the choices they control.

Each of these theoretical features of proper preferences seems inconsistent with some observations of administrative behavior. Administrators often ignore their own, fully conscious preferences in making decisions. They follow rules, traditions, hunches, and the advice and actions of others. Preferences often change over time in such a way that predicting future preferences is often difficult. Preferences are often inconsistent. Managers and others in organizations are often aware of the extent to which some of their preferences conflict with other of their preferences, yet they do nothing to resolve the conflict. Many preferences are stated in forms that lack precision. It is difficult to make them reliably operational in evaluating possible outcomes. While preferences are used to choose among actions, it is often also true that actions and experiences with their consequences affect preferences. Preferences are determined partly endogenously.

It is possible, of course, that such portrayals of administrative behavior are perverse. They may be perverse because they systematically misrepresent the actual behavior of administrators, or they may be perverse because the administrators they describe are, insofar as the description applies, stupid. It is also possible that the description is accurate and the behavior is intelligent, that the ambiguous way administrators sometimes deal with preferences is, in fact, sensible. If such a thing can be imagined, then perhaps we treat preferences inadequately in administrative theory.

The disparity between administrative objectives, as they appear in administrative theory, and administrative objectives, as we observe them in organizational life, has led to efforts to "improve" the way administrators act. These characteristically emphasize the importance of goal clarity and of tying actions clearly to prior objectives. Deviations from the goal precision anticipated by decision theory have been treated as errors to be corrected. The strategy has led to important advances in management, and it has had its successes. But it also has had failures. Stories of disasters attributable to the introduction of decision technology are clichés of recent administrative experience.

As a result, students of administrative theory have been led to ask whether it is possible that goal ambiguity is not always a defect to be eliminated from administration, whether perhaps it may sometimes reflect a form of intelligence that is obscured by our models of rationality. For example, there are good reasons for moderating an enthusiasm for precise performance measures in organizations. The introduction of precision into the evaluation of performance involves a trade-off between the gains in outcomes attributable to closer articulation between action and measured objectives and the losses attributable to misrepresentation of goals, reduced motivation for development of goals, and concentration of effort on irrelevant ways of beating the index. Whether we are considering a performance evaluation scheme for managers or a testing procedure for students, there is likely to be a difference between the *maximum* clarity of goals and the *optimum* clarity.

The complications of performance measures are, however, only an illustration of the general issue of goal ambiguity in administrative action. In order to examine the more general issue, we probably need to ask why an intelligent administrator might deliberately choose — or sensibly learn — to have ambiguous goals. In fact, rationalizing ambiguity is neither difficult nor novel, but it depends on perspectives somewhat more familiar to human understanding as it is found in literature, philosophy, and ordinary experience than as we see it in our theories of administration and choice. For example:

1. Many administrators engage in activities designed to manage their own preferences. These activities make little sense from the point of view of a conception of action that assumes administrators know what they want and will want, or a conception that assumes wants are morally equivalent. But ordinary human actors sense that they might come to want something they should not, or that they might make unwise or inappropriate choices under the influence of fleeting, but powerful, desires if they do not control the development of preferences or buffer action from preferences.

2. Many administrators are both proponents for preferences and observers of the process by which preferences are developed and acted upon. As observers of the process by which their beliefs have been formed and evoked, they recognize the good sense in perceptual and moral modesty.

3. Many administrators maintain a lack of coherence both within and among personal desires, social demands, and moral codes. Though they seek some consistency, they appear to see inconsistency as a normal, and necessary, aspect of the development and clarification of values.

4. Many administrators are conscious of the importance of preferences as beliefs independent of their immediate action consequences. They accept a degree of personal and social wisdom in ordinary hypocrisy.

5. Many administrators recognize the political nature of rational argument more clearly than the theory of choice does. They are unwilling to gamble that God made clever people uniquely virtuous. They protect themselves from cleverness by obscuring the nature of their preferences; they exploit cleverness by asking others to construct reasons for actions they wish to take.

If these characteristics of ambiguous preference processing by administrators make sense under rather general circumstances, our administrative theories based on ideas of clarity in objectives do not make as much sense as we sometimes attribute to them. Not only are they descriptively inadequate, they lead to attempts to clarify things that serve us better unclarified. Some of our standard dicta that managers should define and pursue clear objectives need to be qualified by a recognition that clarity is sometimes a mistake.

Organizations, Managerial Ambitions, and Managerial Incentives
    In most conceptions of administration, administrators are assumed to be ambitious for promotion, position, and success. Managerial incentive schemes are efforts to link such personal ambitions of managers with the goals of the organization so that the behavior of self-interested managers contributes to achieving organizational objectives. As you move toward the top of an organization, however, some things happen that confuse ambition. Promotions are filters through which successful managers pass. Assuming that all promotions are based on similar attributes, each successive filter further refines the pool, reducing variation among managers. On attributes the organization considers important, vice-presidents are likely to be significantly more homogeneous than first-level managers. In addition, as we move up the organization, objectives usually become more conflicting and more ambiguous. Exactly what is expected of a manager sometimes seems obscure and changing, and it becomes harder to attribute specific outcomes to specific managerial actions.

Thus, as we move up the organization, evaluation procedures become less and less reliable, and the population of managers becomes more and more homogeneous. The joint result is that the noise level in evaluation approaches the variance in the pool of managers. At the limit, one vice-president cannot be reliably distinguished from another; quality distinctions among top executives, however consistent with their records, are less likely to be justified than distinctions made at a lower level. Toward the top of an organization, it is difficult to know unambiguously that a particular manager makes a difference. Notice that this is not the same as suggesting that management is unimportant. Management may be extremely important even though managers are indistinguishable. It is hard to tell the difference between two different light bulbs also; but if you take all light bulbs away, it is difficult to read in the dark. What is hard to demonstrate is the extent to which high-performing managers (or light bulbs that endure for an exceptionally long time) are something more than one extreme end of a probability distribution of results generated by essentially equivalent individuals.

Because it has such properties, a mobility system in an organization is a hierarchy of partial lotteries in which the expected values of the lotteries increase as we move up the organization, but control over their outcomes declines. Of course, if the objective is to recruit ambitious and talented people into management, it may not matter whether potential managers are able to control outcomes precisely, as long as the expected values of the games are higher than other opportunities. Ambitious people will seek such careers even if they believe — which they may not — that the outcomes are chance. What is less clear is exactly what kind of managerial behavior will be stimulated by management lotteries.

At the heart of a managerial promotion and reward scheme is normally some measure of managerial performance. Managers are seen as improving organizational outcomes by trying to improve their own measured performance, but every index of performance is an invitation to cleverness. Long before reaching the top, an intelligent manager learns that some of the more effective ways of improving measured performance have little to do with improving product, service, or technology. A system of rewards linked to precise measures is not an incentive to perform well; it is an incentive to obtain a good score. At the same time, since managers are engaged in a lottery in which it is difficult to associate specific outcomes with specific managerial behavior, it becomes important to be able to say, "I did the things a good manager should do." We develop a language for describing good managers and bad ones, and individual managers are able to learn social norms of management. Not all managers behave in exactly the same way, but they all learn the language, expectations, and styles. They are socialized into managerial roles.

These analyses of the consequences of managerial incentives at the top seem inconsistent with the way we talk about leadership in organizations. In effect, we now have two contending theories of how things happen in organizations. The first is considerably influenced by stories of great figures — Catherine the Great, Bismarck, Alfred Sloan — and elaborated by the drama of success and failure of individuals in bureaucratic settings. It portrays administration in relatively heroic ways. Such portrayals lead us to attribute a large share of the variance in organizational outcomes to special properties of specific individual managers. They are comfortably reassuring in the major role they assign to administrative leadership, but they seem to describe a world rather far from administrative experience or research.

The second theory (filled with metaphors of loose coupling, organized anarchy, and garbage can decision processes) seems to describe administrative reality better, but it appears uncomfortably pessimistic about the significance of administrators. Indeed, it seems potentially pernicious even if correct. Consider two general types of errors a manager might make in assessing the importance of intentional actions in controlling organizational outcomes. A manager might come to believe in considerable personal control over outcomes when, in fact, that control does not exist. A "false positive" error. Such a belief would lead to (futile) attempts to control events, but it would not otherwise affect results. Alternatively, a manager might come to believe that significant personal control is not possible when, in fact, it is. A "false negative" error. Such a belief would lead to self-confirming withdrawal from efforts to be effective. Either type of error is possible, but the social costs of the first seem small, relative to the second. Given a choice, we would generally prefer to err on the side of making false positive errors in assessing human significance, rather than false negative errors.

Perhaps fortunately, organizational life assures a managerial bias toward belief in managerial importance. Top managers are not random managers; they are successful managers. They rise to the top on the basis of a series of successful experiences. We know that individuals often find it easy to believe that successes in their lives are attributable to their talents and choices, while failures are due more to bad luck or malevolence. Promotion to the top on the basis of successes at lower levels results in top-level executives believing in the possibility of substantial intentional control over organizational events. Even though their experiences might have led managers to such beliefs erroneously, managerial experience is likely to be subjectively very persuasive. In effect, the system of managerial mobility is designed to make managers much more resistant to false beliefs in impotence than to false beliefs in control. Administrative experience, as well as managerial self-esteem, will usually give managers a greater sense of personal importance and uniqueness than the second theory suggests.

In fact, there is a third theory, and it is probably closer to the truth than either of the others. In this third view, managers *do* affect the ways in which organizations function. But as a result of the process by which managers are selected, motivated, and trained, variations in managers do not reliably produce variations in organizational outcomes. In such a conception, administrators are vital as a class but not as individuals. Administration *is* important, and the many things that administrators do are essential to keeping the organization functioning; but if those vital things are only done when there is an unusually gifted individual at the top, the organization will not thrive. What makes an organization function well is the density of administrative competence, the kind of selection procedures that make all vice-presidents look alike from the point of view of their probable success, and the motivation that leads managers to push themselves to the limit.

Earlier, I used the analogy of a light bulb. I think it is a good analogy. If the manufacture of light bulbs is so unreliable that only a few actually work, you will not be able to do much reading. On the other hand, if light bulbs are reliable, you can read whenever you want to, but you won't much care which light bulb you use. One problem with some conventional administrative thought is that it encourages us to glorify an organization that finds the unique working light bulb in a large shipment of defective bulbs, rather than an organization that persistently produces a supply of nearly indistinguishable good bulbs. It is the latter organization that functions better.

Organizations, Rituals, and Symbols   Administrators and administrative decisions allocate scarce resources and are thereby of considerable social and individual importance, but decisions in organizations and the administration of them are important beyond their outcomes. They are also arenas for exercising social values, for displaying authority and position, and for exhibiting proper behavior and attitudes with respect to a central ideological construct of modern Western civilization — the concept of intelligent choice. Bureaucratic organizations are built on ideas of rationality, and rationality is built on ideas about the way decisions should be made. Indeed, it would be hard to find any institution in modern society more prototypically committed to systematic, rational action than a formal organization.

Thus, administrative action in an organization is a performance in which administrators try to behave in a normatively praiseworthy way. Making intelligent decisions is important, but the verification of intelligence in decision making is often difficult. As a result, it often becomes heavily procedural. For example, in the usual scenario for administrative performance, the gathering of information is not simply a basis for action; it is a representation of competence and a reaffirmation of personal virtue. Command of information and information sources enhances perceived competence and inspires confidence. The belief that more information characterizes better decisions and defensible decision processes engenders a conspicuous consumption of information. Information is flaunted but not used, collected but not considered.

Ideas about proper administrative behavior diffuse through a population of organizations and change over time. What makes a particular procedure appropriate for one manager is that it is being used in other successful organizations by other successful managers. What makes an administrative innovation new and promising is that it has been adopted by other organizations that are viewed as being intelligently innovative. Managerial procedures spread from successful organizations to unsuccessful ones, as the latter try to present themselves as equivalent to the former; the signal a particular procedure provides is gradually degraded by its adoption by organizations that are not "well managed" or "progressive," thus stimulating the invention of new procedures.

This competition among managers and organizations for legitimacy and standing is endless. As managers attempt to establish and maintain reputations through the symbols of good management, social values are sustained and elaborated. For symbols of administrative competence are, of course, symbols simultaneously of social efficacy. Belief in the appropriateness of administrative actions, the process by which they are taken, and the roles played by the various actors involved is a key part of a social structure. It is not only important to decision makers that they be viewed as legitimate; it is also useful to society that leaders be imagined to control organizational outcomes and to act in a way that can be reconciled with a sense of human control over human destiny.

Ritual acknowledgment of managerial importance and appropriateness is part of a social ceremony by which social life is made meaningful and acceptable under conditions that would otherwise be problematic. For example, managerial capabilities for controlling events are likely to be more immediately obvious to managers than to others in the organization. Since most of the managers with whom managers must deal are themselves successful managers, the problem is somewhat concealed from daily managerial experience. Many of the people whom we see in administration, particularly in a growing organization, are people who see themselves as successful; but there are others, less conspicuous, who do not derive the same prejudices from their own experience. So, we construct various myths of management. The same mobility process that encourages top managers in a belief in their own control over events tends to teach some others that managerial successes and the events associated with them are more due to luck or corruption.

The stories, myths, and rituals of management are not merely ways some people fool other people or a waste of time. They are fundamental to our lives. We embrace the mythologies and symbols of life and could not otherwise easily endure. Executive behavior and management procedures contribute to myths about management that become the reality of managerial life and reinforce a belief in a human destiny subject to intentional human control. They may not be essential to such a belief — it is reinforced in many subtle ways throughout society — but executive rituals and executive life are parts of that large mosaic of mutually supporting myths by which an instrumental society brings hope and frustration to individual lives. Since managerial rituals are important to our faith, and our faith is important to the functioning of organizations as well as to the broader social and political order, these symbolic activities of administration are central to its success.

Most administrators seem ambivalent about symbol management. On the one hand, they recognize that they spend considerable time trying to sustain beliefs in the intelligence, coherence, importance, and uniqueness of their organizations (and themselves). At the same time, however, they seem to view the activity as either somewhat illegitimate or as an imposition on more important things — such as decision making, directing, or coordinating. They treat the rituals of administration as necessary, but they talk about them as a waste of time.

Partly, of course, the ambivalence is itself socially dictated. In a society that emphasizes instrumentality as much as Western society does, leaders would be less acceptable if they were to acknowledge the ritual activities of their jobs as central. One of their key symbolic responsibilities is to maintain an ideology that denies the legitimacy of symbol maintenance. Thus, they tend to do it but to deny they do it, or to bemoan the fact that they must do it. It is a careful dance along a narrow beam, and there is the possibility of much grace in it. But the elegance of the dance probably depends on a fine modulation between talk and action, as well as some administrative consciousness of the meaning of the dance. In order to achieve that consciousness, we probably need to recognize the ambivalence and to encourage administrators to see how the activities in which they participate are an essential part of a larger social ritual by which they, as well as others in society, reaffirm purpose and order in a potentially disorderly world.

Many managers, of course, recognize the many elements of storytelling by which they present themselves. Successful managers are usually adept at managing their own reputations. They know how to manage symbols for that purpose. The self-serving character of managerial symbol manipulation is easily seen as unattractive, and few would want to legitimize the self-aggrandizement and self-delusion that are its corollaries. Nor would many observers welcome an unconditional enthusiasm for using symbols to sustain the existing social order against all counterclaims. Critics of the establishment cannot be expected to embrace symbolic performances that have as their main consequence the reinforcement of an unacceptable social system.

These reasonable concerns about symbol manipulation are reminders of its administrative importance. Life is not just choice. It is also poetry. We live by the interpretations we make, becoming better or worse through the meanings we impute to events and institutions. Our lives change when our beliefs change. Administrators manage the way the sentiments, expectations, commitments, and faiths of individuals concerned with the organization fit into a structure of social beliefs about organizational life. Administrative theory probably underestimates the significance of this belief structure for effective organizations. As a result, it probably underestimates the extent to which the management of symbols is a part of effective administration. If we want to identify one single way in which administrators can affect organizations, it is through their effect on the world views that surround organizational life; those effects are managed through attention to the ritual and symbolic characteristics of organizations and their administration. Whether we wish to sustain the system or change it, management is a way of making a symbolic statement.

Round Theories and Flat Experience

In general, these observations are not particularly surprising. In most ways, they are familiar to our experience. They are less familiar, however, to the way we talk about administration. I have tried to list four emphases of administrative theory that seem to be relatively distant from our observations and experience. First, the theoretical emphasis on change as produced by heroic leader action and the consequent emphasis on effectiveness (goal-oriented action) rather than efficiency (goal-free actions), on *leadership* rather than *management*. The theoretical rhetoric of change seems antithetical to routine, but I have argued that effective systems of routine behavior are the primary bases of organizational adaptation to an environment.

Second, the theoretical emphasis on problem-solving of a classical sort in which alternatives are assessed in terms of their consequences for prior goals that are stable, precise, and exogenous. I have argued that many situations in administration involve goals that are (and ought to be) ambiguous.

Third, the theoretical emphasis on explaining variations in organizational outcomes is due to variations in top leadership skills and commitment. I have argued that when an organizational system is working well, variations in outcomes will be due largely to variables unrelated to variations in attributes of top leaders. Where top leadership affects variation in outcomes, the system is probably not functioning well.

Fourth, the theoretical emphasis on administrative action as instrumental, is being justified by the way it produces substantive consequences for important outcomes. I have argued that much of administration is symbolic, a way of interpreting organizational life in a way that allows individuals in organizations to fit their experience to their visions of human existence. Administrative processes are sacred rituals at least as much as they are instrumental acts.

If informed opinion says the earth is round but we experience it flat, we are in danger of having to choose between our senses and our intellect. If we can, we want to discover behavior that is sensible but at the same time confirms our conventional probity — in the face of their apparent inconsistency. The usual procedure, of course, is to talk about a round world and use a flat map. In the case of the map and the earth, we are confident enough of the round theory to be willing to make a fairly precise rationalization of the map. In other cases, the issues are in greater doubt. If you experience planning as something you rarely do yet all the people you admire report that it is important, you might plausibly come to echo their comments without a clear understanding of why you talk about planning so much yet do it so little.

Like a person contemplating a naked emperor amidst courtiers exclaiming over the royal clothing, an administrator must simultaneously act intelligently and sustain a reputation for intelligence. Since theories of administration — and the talk that they generate — are part of the basis for reputation, their distance from ordinary administrative experience poses a problem. For most administrators, the difficulties are not likely to be seen as stemming from failures in administrative theory. What I have called "administrative theory" is not some set of esoteric axioms propagated by a few high priests of academe; rather, it is an elaboration of very general cultural beliefs about organizations, change, leadership, and administration. Most reasonable people accept them with as much confidence as they accept the notion that the earth is round, even while at the same time finding them inconsistent with important parts of organizational life.

The argument is not that administrative theory and administrative life should coincide. In general, they should not. The criterion for good normative theory is not its descriptive accuracy. It is not necessary that the theory be correct, consistent, or even meaningful in conventional terms. It is not necessary that the theory resolve all the difficult trade-offs that impinge on administrative life. In most human domains, we maintain the maxims of a good life by violating them judiciously without claims of virtue; we pursue goals we would not want to achieve in hopes thereby of becoming better than we are. For our theories of administration to be useful in administrative life, we require that *pursuing* (without necessarily fulfilling) the precepts of the theory improves organizations and administration. In such a spirit, administrators may struggle to follow the precepts of administrative thought, even though they are impossible, inconsistent, or unwise. Intelligent administrators might well do such a thing in full consciousness, not in hopes of fulfilling the precepts — for they would not want to do that — but in hopes of acting in a better way than they would without the struggle.

Much of standard administrative theory, including parts that have long been criticized by behavioral students of organizations, seems to me to meet such criteria. There are numerous elementary — but vital — rules of thumb that help improve the management of an organization when applied with intelligence, even though they seem either trivial or contradictory. For example, the dictum that managers should minimize the span of control *and* minimize the number of levels of the organization is obviously nonsensical as a statement of an optimization problem. It is, however, not foolish as a statement of contradictory complications in organizing. Many of the things that ancient texts on administration say seem to me similarly sensible — but not all of them. The fact that administrative theory, like a moral code, does not have to be prima facie sensible in order to be useful should not lead us to assume immediately that incomplete, inconsistent, or incorrect maxims are *necessarily* helpful.

Sometimes our assumptions are wrong, and the worlds we experience as flat actually are, if not entirely flat, not entirely round either. Administrators who feel that their experiences with the way organizations change, with ambiguity in objectives and experience, with management incentives and careers, and with symbolic action are consistent with the kinds of research observations I have noted may well want to question conventional administrative thought and welcome alternative formulations. If these research observations capture a part of organizational truth, some of the apparently strange things that an administrator does are probably more sensible than administrative theory recognizes, and the struggle to fulfill the expectations of administrative virtue may result in actions that are less intelligent than they would have been in the absence of administrative dogma. Sometimes our theories are misleading, and the way we talk confuses the way we act.

Index